Dostoevsky famously had his character Prin⟨⟩ will save the world' and in this book Parkison explores this idea from the perspective of dogmatic theology. This fascinating study considers biblical soteriological as the believer being drawn into union with Christ through faith as beholding irresistible beauty. In regeneration the Spirit enables a person to behold the beauty of the Trinity as mediated in Christ. Much of the work elaborates the metaphysical truths that render such a conception of salvation coherent, and the result is new insights into some very old truths concerning salvation. This is dogmatics in the service of the church at its finest.

CRAIG A. CARTER
Professor of Theology, Tyndale University, Toronto, Ontario

'Beauty is in the eye of the beholder,' is a belief that many of us admit but fail to recognize its shortcomings. Beauty is not a purely subjective opinion or feeling but rather lies first and foremost with the triune God. Samuel Parkison thoughtfully explores God's beauty in the doctrine of salvation. Only when the Spirit gives us eyes to behold the beauty of our triune God can we then truly know what is beautiful as we behold the glory of God's beatitude. Readers who want to plumb the nature of true beauty will do well to weigh carefully Dr Parkison's arguments.'

J. V. FESKO
Harriet Barbour Professor of Systematic and Historical Theology,
Reformed Theological Seminary, Jackson, Mississippi

Of the three transcendentals (truth, goodness, and beauty) theologians have given the least amount of attention to beauty. Parkison presents a systematic view of beauty, arguing beauty is an attribute of God the Trinity and revealed preeminently in the person of Christ. Parkison's work is a delight because of all the different subjects he broaches. Everything from philosophy, to history of interpretation, to exegesis is dealt with here. You will learn more than you planned on when you read this book.

PATRICK SCHREINER
Associate Professor of New Testament and Biblical Theology,
Midwestern Baptist Theological Seminary, Kansas City, Missouri

What does the beauty of God have to do with the Holy Spirit's work of regeneration in the beginning of the believer's life in Christ? That is precisely the question to which Parkison provides a compelling and robust systematic-theological answer. While theologically aligned with the Reformed tradition, this study of soteriology's aesthetic dimension integrates the insights of early church Fathers such as Gregory of Nyssa and Augustine, with Catholic figures such as Anselm, Aquinas, and Hans Urs von Balthasar, and classic Reformed theologians such as Martin Luther, John Owen, Jonathan Edwards, and Herman Bavinck. Grounding its argumentation in the triune Beauty, unveiled and dramatized in the person and work of Christ, *Irresistible Beauty* offers a thoroughgoing dogmatic treatment of the Protestant Reformed understanding of regeneration and faith. Doxology, not simply dogmatics, is the reader's reward.

JONATHAN KING
International Pastoral Training Director,
Family Discipleship Ministries

In our age of spectacle and special effects, preaching the glory of the crucified Christ may seem not only counter-cultural but counter-intuitive. Parkison rightly disagrees, and makes a compelling biblical case for retrieving the glorious beauty of the truth and goodness of the good news of Jesus Christ. *Irresistible Beauty* is an important argument for appreciating the aesthetic dimension of saving faith.

KEVIN J. VANHOOZER
Research Professor of Systematic Theology,
Trinity Evangelical Divinity School, Deerfield, Illinois

To love Christ is to embrace objective Beauty, for in Jesus the Trinitarian fullness is displayed, and in our affection every proper value finds its goal. *Irresistible Beauty* compels faith-filled worship of the living God as delight in and desire for true Beauty, manifest climactically in Christ's life, death, resurrection, and eternal reign. Through Jesus's glorious person and work, the reigning, all-glorious God saves and satisfies sinners who believe and progressively conforms us from one degree of beauty to another. This systematic study in theological aesthetics properly shows that true theology is doxology. I highly recommend it.

JASON S. DEROUCHIE
Research Professor of Old Testament and Biblical Theology,
Midwestern Baptist Theological Seminary, Kansas City, Missouri
Content Developer and Global Trainer, Hands to the Plow Ministries

R.E.D.S.
REFORMED,
EXEGETICAL
AND
DOCTRINAL
STUDIES

IRRESISTIBLE
BEAUTY

BEHOLDING TRIUNE GLORY
IN THE FACE OF JESUS CHRIST

SAMUEL G. PARKISON

SERIES EDITORS J.V. FESKO & MATTHEW BARRETT

MENTOR
Encouraging Christians to Think

Copyright © Samuel G. Parkison 2022

Paperback ISBN 978-1-5271-0914-8
Ebook ISBN 978-1-5271-0986-5

10 9 8 7 6 5 4 3 2 1

Published in 2022
in the
Mentor Imprint
by
Christian Focus Publications Ltd,
Geanies House, Fearn, Ross-shire,
IV20 1TW, Great Britain.

www.christianfocus.com

Cover design
by Pete Barnsley

Printed by
Bell & Bain, Glasgow

CONTENTS

For Shannon, and for Jonah, Henry, and Lewis, who are infinitely more important than anything I have ever done or will do.

Series Preface

Reformed, Exegetical and Doctrinal Studies (R.E.D.S.) presents new studies informed by rigorous exegetical attention to the biblical text, engagement with the history of doctrine, with a goal of refined dogmatic formulation.

R.E.D.S. covers a spectrum of doctrinal topics, addresses contemporary challenges in theological studies, and is driven by the Word of God, seeking to draw theological conclusions based upon the authority and teaching of Scripture itself.

Each volume also explores pastoral implications so that they contribute to the church's theological and practical understanding of God's Word. One of the virtues that sets R.E.D.S. apart is its ability to apply dogmatics to the Christian life. In doing so, these volumes are characterized by the rare combination of theological weightiness and warm, pastoral application, much in the tradition of John Calvin's *Institutes of the Christian Religion*.

These volumes do not merely repeat material accessible in other books but retrieve and remind the church of forgotten truths to enrich contemporary discussion.

MATTHEW BARRETT
J. V. FESKO

Acknowledgments

This work represents years of labor and one of the sweetest seasons of my life. Chief among my creditors of gratitude, of whom I am forever indebted, is my beloved wife, Shannon. This project is about divine Beauty, and it must be acknowledged that the single greatest expression of creaturely beauty in my life is my bride – a sunbeam to divine glory, a panoply of loveliness, a constant reminder of the Trinity's gratuitous creativity. She is a companion of whom there is no comparison. Alongside her, I must also mention my three sons, Jonah, Henry, and Lewis, two of whom were born while their dad was a PhD student, and none of whom have ever known their dad as less than a seminarian. My research has not been hindered by these future men; rather, it has been punctuated and transposed to a higher, richer key.

Emmaus Church also has my thanks. I am grateful to serve a body of believers who value theological contemplation, and do not bristle at, but rather celebrate, their pastors pursuing the life of the mind. In deciding on what to write about, I had two criteria. First, the topic had to offer enough staying power to keep me interested and passionate for several years. Second, the topic had to offer some benefit to my local church. By God's grace, I believe both expectations were upheld, and I hope and pray that the saints at Emmaus Church were truly served by their pastor's persistent contemplation of Christ's beauty.

On this note, I owe many thanks to the elders at Emmaus Church – my brothers in arms and fellow shepherds. I particularly must name

Joshua Hedger – who showed me tremendous grace in letting me take over our one office, and who freed me up with far more margin for research than most in my position would experience; serving Christ's flock alongside him is among the greatest privileges of my life; Ronni Kurtz – my fellow doctoral student, whose friendship and conversations have contributed more to my development as a pastor-theologian than I can put into words; virtually every page of this work contains thoughts that have been forged in the joyous furnace of our friendship; and Adam Sanders – who got into the trenches with me during the hardest summer of pastoral ministry I have experienced (which also happened to be the season in which this entire monograph was written); he is one of the most gifted wordsmiths I know, and a pastor *par excellence*.

Lastly, I must recognize with gratitude the mentorship I have received from various professors over the years. The central question this monograph addresses came to me in seed form in 2015, during a class taught by Owen Strachan on the life and ministry of Jonathan Edwards. His encouragement in that class – and in the subsequent classes he taught wherein I was given the freedom to explore these themes further – is a major factor in this work's existence at all. I also must acknowledge Jason DeRouchie, who came into my life toward the end of my research and gave me a living example of faithfulness and devotion to Christ and family while pursuing scholarship. Finally, Craig Carter and Matthew Barrett, my doctoral committee, deserve my thanks. Craig's insights and encouragement were instructive and formative, and his work was shaping me far before he came onboard for this project. Even up to and beyond my oral defense, Craig was hard at work to help me make this as potent a contribution as I could muster. His support in this work, and his affirmation of its thesis and mission, has been a surprising and cherished gift. Likewise, I cannot say enough about Matthew Barrett's influence on my life and ministry – he is by far the single greatest living theological force in my thinking, and his direct and indirect mentorship transcend what can be expressed in words.

There are, of course, many more names I can (and probably should) mention here. All I can say is that this book represents an embarrassment of God's kindness toward me in the form of friends and family. *I pray this work is glorifying to our Triune God and edifying to the Church of Christ. Amen.*

Foreword

The Reformed instinct to substantiate the soteriology of the Reformation for today is a worthy one. Even after five hundred years, the *ordo salutis* continues to be challenged by innovative attempts to reconfigure Reformation commitments. For that reason alone, our focus has often circulated around union with Christ, regeneration, conversion, justification, and perseverance.

However, a thorn festers in the flesh of Reformed theology: with such steadfast fixation on soteriology, Reformed theologians have on occasion neglected the metaphysical foundation of a classical theology proper and its Christology. In doing so, some corners of Reformed theology have not engaged the good and necessary consequences of that metaphysic for soteriology, operating as if one theological domain has little to do with the other. As a result, other traditions – Roman Catholicism in particular – have been quick to charge Reformed soteriology with departing from the participation metaphysic of classical Christianity. According to critics, forensic justification and imputed righteousness are grounded in a nominalism that betrays the realism of the Great Tradition and its emphasis on transformation. The lack of interest in theological aesthetics has only confirmed such suspicions in the minds of opponents.

Unfortunately, as long as Reformed theologians do not engage the intersection of theology proper and soteriology, Christology and conversion, these accusations remain unanswered and in the eyes of many still persuasive. For this reason, Sam Parkison's scholarship is a timely contribution. Rather than severing doctrines one doctrinal domain from another, Parkison asks Protestants to consider how the blessedness of the holy Trinity and the beauty of the incarnate Christ should inform a Reformed soteriology. Yet rather than leaving the participation metaphysic of classical theism to other traditions, Parkison challenges caricatures by claiming that Protestant soteriology is consistent with the *theologia* of classical theology. In fact, Parkison is so bold to ask whether the Reformed position may even be more consistent than other traditions. By doing so, Parkison joins the chorus of the Reformed scholastics who were eager to do the same.

Parkison is one of the bright young minds on the theological horizon. His scholarship exercises the theologian's imagination but with a persistent insistence on fidelity to Reformed orthodoxy. Parkison does not merely regurgitate what Reformed theologians believe but he probes the rationale behind such beliefs. He draws out the Reformed tradition's robust reasons for arriving at its soteriology *and* with an astute awareness of the classical Christology that must substantiate the Protestant cathedral of dogmatics. Not only is the reader pressed to stand face to face with the beauty of our Lord, but the reader is summoned to consider how such beauty nurtures a hearty faith, as the Heidelberg Catechism teaches us.

May this book – and the stimulating mind of Parkison himself – carry the reader higher up and higher in until we all see the glory of God in the face of Jesus Christ our Lord.

MATTHEW BARRETT
Associate Professor of Christian Theology,
Midwestern Baptist Theological Seminary

CHAPTER ONE

Introduction and Prolegomenon

While insolent and foolish people concoct a false notion of beauty,
reducing it to the level of their senses, beauty comes from heaven and
will lead any sane spirit to the place from which it came.

MICHELANGELO[1]

Introduction

What hath beauty to do with systematic theology? This is the question that concerns the present volume. For all of its symmetry and beauty, recent systematic theology treatments have largely neglected the locus of aesthetics. This is especially true for Protestants (Roman Catholic theologians largely have the corner on theological aesthetics).[2] With

---

1. Quoted in Dietrich von Hildebrand, *Beauty in the Light of the Redemption* (Steubenville, OH: Hildebrand Project, 2019), 14.

2. For example, Lee Barrett observes, 'Apart from their concern for the rhetorical properties of the word proclaimed (and sometimes sung), most Protestants have been notoriously deficient in developing a theologically informed Christian aesthetics. Most particularly, the aniconic and even iconoclastic tendencies in the Reformed and Anabaptist traditions have inhibited the exploration of the Christian significance of the concept of "beauty".' Lee Barrett, 'Von Balthasar and Protestant Aesthetics: A Mutually Corrective Conversation,' in *Theological Aesthetics After von Balthasar*, ed. O. V. Bychkov and James Fodor (Burlington, VT: Ashgate, 2008), 97. This point has also been hammered by Hans Urs von Balthasar, *The Glory of the Lord: A Theological Aesthetics*, ed. Joseph Fessio and John Kenneth Riches, trans. Erasmo Leiva-Merikakis, 2nd ed., 7 vols. (San Francisco, CA: Ignatius Press, 2009), 1:55. Charles Taylor, *A Secular Age* (Cambridge, MA: Harvard

this project we will therefore attempt to partially rectify a deficiency in systematic-theological literature in recent history. We emphasize *systematic-theological* literature because, of course, there is no dearth of literature on 'theological aesthetics', broadly speaking.[3] But even these volumes are, for the most part, primarily philosophical in nature. This does not mean that they neglect theological significance, only that they rarely relate their findings to the categories represented in systematic theology. Meanwhile, most systematic material remains silent on the topic of beauty (with a few notable exceptions). Seldom will one find a systematic work that includes sustained meditation on the beauty of God as a divine attribute, and the relationship between this attribute and His economic acts.[4]

In his recent work, *The Beauty of the Lord: Theology as Aesthetics*, Jonathan King recognizes this absence in systematic-theological literature and seeks to address the issue broadly. 'The core weakness of theological aesthetics throughout the history of its various developments,' writes King,

University Press, 2018), similarly holds the Protestant Reformation responsible, at least in part, for the disenchantment of modernity's malaise. Karl Barth raises a similar charge against the Reformers who, in his estimation, neglected beauty as a theological concept. Karl Barth, *Church Dogmatics, Vol. II/1: The Doctrine of God*, ed. G. W. Bromiley and T. F. Torrance, trans. T. H. L. Parker et al. (Edinburgh: T&T Clark, 1957), 608-77. However, this common accusation has been taken to task in recent years. See, for example, W. David O. Taylor, *The Theater of God's Glory: Calvin, Creation, and the Liturgical Arts* (Grand Rapids, MI: Eerdmans, 2017); Mark C. Mattes, *Martin Luther's Theology of Beauty: A Reappraisal* (Grand Rapids, MI: Baker Academic, 2017).

3. E.g., Bruno Forte, *The Portal of Beauty: Towards a Theology of Aesthetics*, trans. David Glenday and Paul McPartlan (Grand Rapids, MI: Eerdmans, 2008); Edward Farley, *Faith and Beauty: A Theological Aesthetic* (Burlington, VT: Ashgate, 2001); Thomas Brendan Sammon, *Called to Attraction: An Introduction to the Theology of Beauty* (Eugene, OR: Cascade, 2017); Brendan Thomas Sammon, *The God Who Is Beauty: Beauty As a Divine Name in Thomas Aquinas and Dionysius the Areopagite* (Eugene, Oregon: Pickwick, 2013); Richard Viladesau, *Theological Aesthetics: God in Imagination, Beauty, and Art* (New York: Oxford University Press, 2013); Alex García-Rivera, *The Community of the Beautiful: A Theological Aesthetics* (Collegeville, MN: Liturgical, 1999); Vicente Chong, *A Theological Aesthetics of Liberation: God, Art, and the Social Outcasts* (Eugene, OR: Pickwick, 2019); Nicholas Wolterstorff, *Art in Action: Toward a Christian Aesthetic* (Grand Rapids, MI: Eerdmans, 1980).

4. We are therefore distinguishing here between a systematic-theological approach to aesthetics and other theologies of aesthetics, which would include (1) natural theology of beauty, (2) theology of the arts, and (3) religious aesthetics. There will be important points of overlap between the areas of interest in this project and these theologies, but they remain distinct, nonetheless. For more on the distinction between these 'theologies of aesthetics', see Jonathan King, *The Beauty of the Lord: Theology as Aesthetics* (Bellingham, WA: Lexham, 2018), 2-7.

'has been the primary neglect of a specifically biblical- and systematic-theological treatment.'[5] His methodological commitments, therefore, do not contain any elements that are idiosyncratic for systematics – it is straightforwardly 'biblical- and systematic-theological'.[6] In many ways, the reader should treat this volume as a self-conscious continuation of King's evangelical retrieval project. He argues for the necessity of bringing the topic of beauty back into 'the work and pedagogy of systematic theology within a broadly evangelical perspective', and he does this by exploring and developing theological aesthetics with respect to the Trinity's economic work of creation, redemption, and consummation.[7] Whereas King is concerned with theological aesthetics more broadly, this work will drill down to address beauty's role more narrowly, specifically, in the Protestant Reformed conception of the *ordo salutis*. King's work looks at God's beauty through a telescope, mine under a microscope.

Central Thesis

In this work, I will consider soteriology's aesthetic dimension. Specifically, I wish to examine the relationship between regeneration and faith through the lens of divine beauty. Beauty, I will argue, is ultimately an attribute of God the Trinity, revealed wherever Triune glory is made manifest, which is preeminently so in the person and work of Christ. *When the Holy Spirit regenerates a sinner, He imparts the faculties necessary for such a person to behold the beauty of the Trinity mediated in Christ.* How does the Spirit impart these faculties? By virtue of His own indwelling presence. In regeneration the Spirit communicates – or, sovereignly brings the regenerate into participation with – the glorious *a se* beatitude of the Trinity, mediated through Christ. This He does by presenting Christ to the eyes of the regenerate's heart, and by enabling such hearty vision – which is far more than a mere intellectual act but also includes the affections – with His renovative presence. The *fiducia* component of saving faith therefore has an accompanying aesthetic aspect; it involves the existential recognition of Christ's infinite beauty.[8]

---

5. Ibid., 7.

6. Ibid., 1.

7. Ibid., 5.

8. This beholding of the 'glory of God in the face of Jesus Christ' (2 Cor. 4:6), which the Spirit enables in regeneration and illumination, and which begins with saving faith,

I say 'aspect' because there is obviously much more happening in the moment of conversion than aesthetic appreciation. If it were strictly this, the neglect of systematic-theological attention to aesthetics I am attempting to rectify with this project would constitute an essential misrepresentation of the *ordo salutis*, and that is not a claim I wish to make in the slightest. According to the Reformed tradition's conception of the *ordo salutis*, faith is the instrument whereby a sinner is legally declared righteous, and I heartily affirm such a conception. This project is not 'fixing' a notion of soteriology that is essentially broken; it is rather bringing more color to a notion that is sturdy and dependable already. Indeed, as I will show below, one of the features of beauty is its adorning characteristic – one cannot fixate on it in the abstract; it rather gives color to truth and goodness, which means one cannot see it directly apart from truth and goodness. This is true for the aesthetic dimensions of soteriology I will explore in this project as well: if one tries to reduce regeneration to the restoration of aesthetic-appreciating faculties alone, one will misrepresent the nature of the act.

It is also important to emphasize that salvation is described throughout Scripture in a variety of metaphors: 'receiving' (Rom. 3:25), 'eating and tasting' (John 6:51; 1 Pet. 2:3), 'trusting' (Heb. 2:13), 'building' (Luke 6:48), *entering* into 'access' (Rom. 5:2), etc. This work is concerned with exploring the mystery of salvation through the lens of faith as *beholding* (2 Cor. 3:18; 4:6). Within the metaphorical framework of faith as *beholding*, aesthetics can serve us as a helpful category.

A final caveat I must make, and will continue to make throughout this work, is that what I propose here should not be confused for other proposals that use similar language. The language of 'beauty' and 'affection' and 'love' are not broadly foreign to Christian discussions about salvation, but some such discussions have been less than biblical. For example, one way to square the topic of aesthetics with saving faith

---

largely characterizes the sanctifying process of the Christian life. In contemplating the beauty of Christ over a lifetime, one is sanctified – 'transformed from one degree of glory to another' (2 Cor. 3:18). The Christian life, from its infancy and beyond, is a doxological gaze – the glad-hearted acquiescence and contemplation of the Trinity's irresistible beauty, revealed in the Word made flesh (John 1:14). This ever-increasing apprehension of divine beauty will continue forever in the beatific vision. Thus, divine beauty is relevant for the entire *ordo salutis*. Unless otherwise indicated, Scripture quotations are from The Holy Bible, English Standard Version (ESV) (Wheaton, IL: Crossway, 2001).

is to conceptualize faith as incomplete until perfected by love. Justifying faith, in this conception, is faith that is fully formed through charity (or love), and that charity is motivated by an ever-increasing appreciation for divine beauty. This is the Roman Catholic conception of 'faith working through love',[9] and it is to be distinguished from my proposal. What I am describing as the aesthetic dimension of conversion, in terms of the relationship between regeneration and faith, is not a new work to complete or perfect faith. It is not a work at all. It is rather a way of describing the Protestant Reformed understanding of regeneration and saving faith with divine beauty in view – it is not faith *and* beholding (as if the beholding added to faith) but rather faith *as* beholding.

Methodologically, this volume will constitute the synthetic work of a generalist. It is not a work of exegesis, though it will stand firmly on exegetical findings. It is not a work of biblical theology, though it will be biblical-theological. It is not a work of historical theology, though it will engage in theological retrieval of the church's history. It is not a philosophical work, though, driven by a love for wisdom, it will be irreducibly philosophical. Rather, this is a systematic-theological work in the full sense of the term – informed and shaped by these disciplines and informing and shaping the pursuit of them.

Before we can begin to develop our thesis, however, we must address some matters of *prolegomena*. This introductory chapter will therefore (1) distinguish this project as principally *theological*, (2) establish the historical precedence for sustained theological meditation on divine beauty, and (3) offer a working definition for 'beauty' as it concerns this project.

'Theological Aesthetics' vs. 'Aesthetic Theology'

This point should be underlined and punctuated: the project at hand is concerned with *God's beauty* as it relates to soteriology. To say this is to flag my intention to keep theology theological; i.e., to keep God and God's actions as the central subject matter.[10] This approach's unique

---

9. As we will see in chapter 5, Jonathan Edwards uses the language of 'affections' in similar ways.

10. This language and spirit of keeping 'theology theological' comes from the late John Webster, who not only developed this idea cogently but demonstrated it powerfully in his own work. 'What Makes Theology Theological?,' in *God Without Measure: Working Papers in Christian Theology*, 2 vols. (New York: T&T Clark, 2018), 1:215.

character may be illustrated by the distinction Hans Urs von Balthasar helpfully makes between 'aesthetic theology' and 'theological aesthetics'.[11] The latter is concerned with letting contemplation of God's beauty set the agenda, while the former is concerned with letting 'this-worldly' beauty set the agenda. 'Theological aesthetics' harkens attention to God and resists the temptation to project 'worldly, limited' conceptions of beauty back up onto God.[12] 'Aesthetic theology,' on the other hand, commits the favorite dogmatic transgression of many a contemporary theologian to attempt to anthropize God,[13] such that the 'standard of beauty by which revelation and the Church are measured ... is ... a criterion and a measure of this-worldly, human, and cultural beauty, [which are] appropriate for the effects of Christianity but not valid for the essence of Christianity itself.'[14] As von Balthasar points out, aesthetic theology is fundamentally a failure to adequately distinguish between the Creator and the creature:

> [Aesthetic] theology ultimately failed because of a deep theological inadequacy, namely, that it did not sufficiently distinguish between creation and revelation, or to formulate it in the terms of our enquiry, we can say that Romantic theology foundered on a kind of aesthetic and religious monism.[15]

This project steadfastly resists the temptation to trifle in 'aesthetic theology' and instead engages in 'theological aesthetics'. This has ramifications for the structure of this project, as well as its ethos and telos. Structurally, the insistence on divine centrality means that our next chapter begins this project's argument with sustained contemplation of God's life *ad intra* before ever moving into considerations of God's *ad extra* involvement with creaturely affairs.[16] This safeguards the project from the tendency to tame the divine with palatable sentiments of earthly

---

11. See Balthasar, *The Glory of the Lord*, 77-114.

12. Ibid., 77.

13. For a critique of this kind of anthropizing, see James E. Dolezal, *All That Is in God: Evangelical Theology and the Challenge of Classical Christian Theism* (Grand Rapids, MI: Reformation Heritage, 2017).

14. Balthasar, *The Glory of the Lord*, 91-92.

15. Ibid., 102.

16. See Webster, 'Omnia ... Pertractantur in Sacra Doctrina Sub Ratione Dei: On the Matter of Christian Theology,' in *The Domain of the Word: Scripture and Theological Reason* (New York: T&T Clark, 2014), 3.

beauty. Relatedly, this keeps the project throughout from devolving into fanciful sophistry and irreverent play. This work is doxological – the only valid telos for any work of theology – which means the subject matter necessarily commands a humble reverence, with 'fear and awe, for our God is a consuming fire' (Heb. 12:28-29).[17] 'Theology is not itself,' remarks Fred Sanders, 'if it is not also praise. … Theology is faith seeking understanding because it is praise seeking underpinning.'[18]

Historical Precedence
Gregory of Nyssa (335–394)

We now turn our attention to the past in order to set precedents for this project's agenda to bring beauty back into the arena of dogmatic theology. One need not look far into the church's history to find theological reflections on divine beauty. It is true that the 'Fathers do not give systematic treatment to the beauty of God',[19] but this is not because the topic was peripheral; it was rather so ubiquitous that systematic treatment was not necessary.[20] This is particularly true for Gregory of Nyssa who believed – following the trajectory set out by Plato and Plotinus, who saw an intrinsic relationship between material beauty and the transcendent ideas they reflect[21] – 'human souls find

---

17. The creature who contemplates the Creator approaches his subject matter as a beggar. He stands not over his topic as a master, but under it as a servant. See, Webster, 'On the Matter of Christian Theology,' 10.

18. Fred Sanders, *The Triune God*, New Studies in Dogmatics (Grand Rapids, MI: Zondervan, 2016), 27-28.

19. Kin Yip Louie, *Beauty of the Triune God: The Theological Aesthetics of Jonathan Edwards* (Eugene, OR: Pickwick, 2013), 21.

20. 'There is no major controversy about divine beauty in the early church for the Fathers to reach maximal clarity' (ibid., 21).

21. See Hans Boersma, *Seeing God: The Beatific Vision in Christian Tradition* (Grand Rapids, MI: Eerdmans, 2018), chaps. 2–3; Natalie Carnes, *Beauty: A Theological Engagement with Gregory of Nyssa* (Eugene, OR: Cascade, 2014), chaps. 1–2. The fathers' influence from platonic and neoplatonic thought has often served as the occasion to dismiss much of their theological emphases as flies in their ointment. But, as Craig A. Carter (along with others) has recently pointed out, the idea that the church fathers stumbled into Platonism accidentally, or uncritically, is historically obtuse. Platonism was by no means the undisputed metaphysic of the day, which means early Christian appropriation of platonic concepts (as opposed to concepts from Atomism or Stoicism or Epicureanism, for example) was no mere historical accident. Further, the early Christians self-consciously rejected many platonic concepts as being inconsistent with Christianity.

their telos when in union with Christ they become ever purer, in an ever-increasing growth in the beatific vision.'[22] Gregory believed that the role of all earthly beauty was to direct the beholder Godward, to cherish and contemplate divine beauty above all else:

> Admiration even of the beauty of the heavens, and of the dazzling sunbeams, and, indeed, of any fair phenomenon, will then cease. The beauty noticed there will be but as the hand to lead us to the love of the supernal Beauty whose glory the heavens and the firmament declare, and whose secret the whole creation sings. The climbing soul, leaving all that she has grasped already as too narrow for her needs, will grasp the idea of that magnificence which is exalted far above the heavens.[23]

Following the sunbeam up to the sun is the journey Gregory envisions for the saint – his telos is beholding God's beauty. This, for Gregory, is the sum and substance of the Christian life, forever.[24] It is a satisfying act that is ever-longed for, where those 'in whom the divine yearning was deeply lodged ever [comes] to a point of rest in their desire … the soul that is joined to God is not satiated by her enjoyment of him, so too the more abundantly she is filled up with his beauty, the more vehemently her longings abound.'[25] The creature finds, in contemplating divine

---

This means that they were critical, strategic, and intentional with their use of Platonism. For more, see chapter 3 of Craig A. Carter, *Interpreting Scripture with the Great Tradition: Recovering the Genius of Premodern Exegesis* (Grand Rapids, MI: Baker Academic, 2018); Khaled Anatolios, *Retrieving Nicaea: The Development and Meaning of Trinitarian Doctrine* (Grand Rapids, MI: Baker Academic, 2018). Interestingly enough, the common dismissal of the fathers for their self-conscious appropriation of philosophical concepts of their contemporaries more often than not bespeaks an ignorance of one's own unconscious appropriation of Enlightenment metaphysics. See Carter, *Interpreting Scripture with the Great Tradition*, 63.

22. Boersma, *Seeing God*, 77.

23. Gregory of Nyssa, *On Virginity*, xi, 356. Unless otherwise specified, all future patristic sources are taken from Alexander Roberts and James Donaldson, editors, *Ante-Nicene Fathers: The Writings of the Fathers Down to A.D. 325*, 10 vols. (Grand Rapids, MI: Eerdmans, 1956), and Philip Schaff and Henry Wace, editors, *Nicene and Post-Nicene Fathers of the Christian Church*, Second Series, 14 vols. (Grand Rapids, MI: Eerdmans, 1956).

24. See Hans Boersma, 'Becoming Human in the Face of God: Gregory of Nyssa's Unending Search for the Beatific Vision,' *International Journal of Systematic Theology* 17, no. 2 (2015): 131-51.

25. Gregory, *Homilies on the Song of Songs*, trans. Richard A Norris (Atlanta: Society of Biblical Literature, 2012), cant. 31.10–32.8.

beauty, a satisfying yearning – he is not impoverished or dissatisfied when beholding God's beauty, but neither is he 'satiated'; he is contented in the presence of his beloved, but he has never had enough.[26]

An important feature of Gregory's conception of the Christian's contemplation of divine beauty is its Christological shape: the beloved, whose beauty transfixes and ravages the soul of the beholder, is Christ himself. 'For Gregory,' notes Hans Boersma, 'Christ is not only "beautiful" (πανεμορφη) but also "the very essence of the Beautiful"' (η ιδια ουσία του Ωραίου). On Nyssen's understanding, Christ is the very definition of beauty, which means that he always equates the vision of God's beauty with the vision of the beauty of Christ.'[27]

Augustine (354–430)

The impact that the great fifth-century bishop of Hippo left on the Christian Church can scarcely be exaggerated. Augustine's influence is felt in nearly every area of Christian theology, and aesthetics is no exception. This is because Augustine, more than any other theologian, was able to extract the wisdom of Platonism from its errors so as to develop for Christianity an entire outlook for everything.[28] 'Augustine had the instinct of a sailor,' writes Peter Kreeft: 'he negotiated the heavy seas of Platonism in the Christian boat without capsizing.'[29]

There is no appreciating Augustine on any particular theological emphasis without appreciating his overall metaphysic, which parted ways from the materialism of Epicurus, the dualism of Mani (i.e., Manichaeism), the nihilism of the hedonists, the impersonal 'Logos' of the stoics, and the creation despising of the Gnostics and Platonists. We should also emphasize that his metaphysic makes no peace with the

---

26. This characteristic longing was captured well by another original thinker much later in church history who, while not directly influenced by Gregory, made remarkably similar observations: C. S. Lewis. Lewis describes this satisfying longing as 'joy' in C. S. Lewis, *Surprised by Joy: The Shape of My Early Life* (Orlando, FL: Harvest, 1958).

27. Boersma, *Seeing God*, 88.

28. This point obviously contrasts with the lamentably common insistence that Augustine uncritically appropriated Platonism and with it, ruined Christianity. E.g., In Carol Harrison's seminal work, *Beauty and Revelation in the Thought of Saint Augustine* (New York: Oxford University Press, 1992), 36.

29. Peter Kreeft, *Socrates' Children: The 100 Greatest Philosophers*, 3 vols. (South Bend, IN: St. Augustine's Press, 2015), 2:29.

mechanistic reductionism of modernity. Instead of all these, Augustine gave Plato's 'ideas' their proper home in the mind of God – who created the cosmos *ex nihilo* for His good pleasure.

The upshot of this is that, for Augustine, the cosmos pulsates with life and meaning. Creation is good because it is formed in the good mind of the all-good God. The material universe is not good *despite* its physical form; its physical form is *itself* good. But its physical form does not exhaust its essence. The cosmos *means* more than it is. Hans Boersma calls this its 'sacramental ontology'.[30] Augustine's 'sacramental ontology' is illustrated well by one of Christianity's most widely recognized Christian Platonists (though he is seldom recognized *as such*), C. S. Lewis. He illustrates the point in a conversation between the Narnian star, Ramandu, and Eustace Scrubb in the fantasy classic *The Voyage of the Dawn Treader*:

> 'In our world,' said Eustace, 'a star is a huge ball of flaming gas.'
>
> 'Even in your world, my son, that is not what a star is but only what it is made of.'[31]

Augustine affirmed this kind of gratuitous cosmology, wherein the referent of any created thing is not the thing itself, but its God. Meaning, for Augustine, transgresses the boundaries of all creaturely subjects and finds its home in the ultimate Subject.[32] If this is true for his metaphysic in general, it is certainly true for his aesthetic in particular. Augustine writes,

> O God, Wisdom, in whom and by whom and through whom all those are wise who are wise. O God, True and Supreme Life, in whom and by whom and through whom all those things live which truly and perfectly live. O God, Happiness, in whom and by whom and through whom all those things are happy which are happy. O God, the Good and the Beautiful, in whom and by whom and through whom all those things are good and beautiful which are good and beautiful.[33]

---

30. See Hans Boersma, *Heavenly Participation: The Weaving of a Sacramental Tapestry* (Grand Rapids, MI: Eerdmans, 2011).

31. C. S. Lewis, *The Voyage of the Dwan Treader*, rev. ed. (New York,: HarperCollins, 1994), 115. Lewis goes on to make explicit that his Narnian cosmology is Platonic in *The Last Battle*, when earth and Narnia are shown to be expressions of the 'further up, further in' reality of Aslan's country. Lewis, *The Last Battle*, rev. ed. (New York: HarperCollins, 1994), 105.

32. Kreeft, *Socrates' Children*, 3:33.

33. Augustine, *Soliloquies: Augustine's Inner Dialogue* (Hyde Park, NY: New City Press, 2000), para. 2 and 3, pg. 344-45.

For Augustine, created beauty does not terminate on itself. It is a sign, itself pointing to the archetypal Beauty – God Himself. The beauty in the created order is reflective of the Beauty of the beautiful Trinity. Carol Harrison makes this point with some force:

> The implications of these ideas on Augustine's aesthetics cannot be overestimated: since beauty (*forma/formosus*) is thus inseparable from existence given by and oriented towards God, the whole of the Christian revelation ... all assumes an aspect of beauty which is at once immanent within the temporal, mutable realm, but which yet belongs to and originates in transcendent Divine Beauty.[34]

In a very real sense, Augustine's own search for God through hedonistic indulgence and Manichean dualism, recounted in his *Confessions*, is a search for ultimate truth and beauty. Before conversion, Augustine 'hungered and thirsted not even after' the created good he indulged in, but after God: 'Thee Thyself.'[35] The God whom Augustine panted after he identifies as 'Father, supremely good, Beauty of all things beautiful!'[36] The long delay in Augustine's desire satiated in Christ is, of course, what he laments in this memorable prayer:

> Too late did I love Thee, O [Beauty], so ancient, and yet so new! Too late did I love Thee! For behold, Thou wert within, and I without, and there did I seek Thee; I, unlovely, rushed heedlessly among the things of beauty Thou madest. Thou wert with me, but I was not with Thee. Those things kept me far from Thee, which, unless they were in Thee, were not. Thou calledst, and criedst aloud, and forcedst open my deafness. Thou didst gleam and shine, and chase away my blindness. Thou didst exhale odours, and I drew in my breath and do pant after Thee. I tasted, and do hunger and thirst. Thou didst touch me, and I burned for Thy peace.[37]

Before his conversion, Augustine was a sojourner in search of beauty, indulging in created goods and idolizing them for the beauty they reflected from God, as if they themselves were beauty's source. And while the search ultimately came up empty, setting aside his idolatrous

---

34. Harrison, *Beauty and Revelation*, 29.
35. Augustine, *Confessions*, book III, 6.10.
36. Ibid.
37. Ibid., book X, 27.38.

habits proved to be a sacrifice he was nearly unwilling to make.[38] After his conversion, however, the supremacy of God's beauty immediately dwarfed the lesser ones he had previously idolized, and he marvels at his prior indecision. 'And what at one time I feared to lose,' wrote Augustine,

> it was now a joy to me to put away. For Thou didst cast them away from me, Thou true and highest sweetness. Thou didst cast them away, and instead of them didst enter in Thyself – sweeter than all pleasure, though not to flesh and blood; brighter than all light, but more veiled than all mysteries; more exalted than all honor, but not to the exalted in their own conceits. Now was my soul free from the gnawing cares of seeking and getting, and of wallowing and exciting the itch of lust. And I babbled unto Thee my brightness, my richness, and my health, the Lord my God.[39]

Yet lest one think from a passage like this that Augustine, in the name of praising God above created things, develops a purely a-material view of beauty, which despises all lesser beauties, Augustine assures the reader that this is not the case. After conversion, all earthly delights fit into their proper place, as witnesses to the divine beauty his soul previously craved. Within the light of God's beauty, lesser beautiful things are beautified and rightly ordered. Even man-made works of art, 'shoes, vessels, and every kind of work, in pictures, too, and sundry images,' which are indulgently gaudy ('far beyond necessary and moderate use and holy signification') are not without reference to divine Beauty. Augustine insists that 'those beautiful patterns, which through the medium of men's souls are conveyed into their artistic hands, emanate from that Beauty which is above our souls, which my soul sigheth after day and night .... And though they see Him not, yet is He there.'[40] Any real beauty, he insists, is beautiful by virtue of its participation in Beauty.

Anselm of Canterbury (1033–1109) and Thomas Aquinas (1224–1274)

The medieval period of the church was not silent on the topic of beauty. Anselm of Canterbury and Thomas Aquinas explicitly argued that beauty was a divine attribute – an archetypal perfection in God and

---

38. This internal battle is viscerally described in Ibid., book VIII, chap. 11.
39. Augustine, *Confessions*, book IX, 1.1.
40. Ibid., Book X, 34.53.

reflected in ectypal fashion in creation (and revealed in redemption). 'Still You hide away, Lord, from my soul in Your light and blessedness,' writes Anselm,

> and so it still dwells in its darkness and misery. For it looks all about, and does not see Your beauty. It listens, and does not hear Your harmony. It smells, and does not sense Your fragrance. It tastes, and does not recognize Your savour. It feels, and does not sense Your softness. *For You have in Yourself, Lord, in Your own ineffable manner, those [qualities] You have given to the things created by You according to their own sensible manner.* But the senses of my soul, because of the ancient weakness of sin, have become dulled and obstructed.[41]

In this passage Anslem presupposes a relation between creaturely beauty as the ectype and divine beauty as the archetype. What he laments is his frailty and limitations, on account of sin, from being able to draw the connection effectively.

While Anselm's 'perfect being' theology is often criticized on the apologetic grounds of the ontological argument for God's existence,[42] one should not miss the doxological reasoning therein: Anselm can see plainly that there is truth, goodness, and beauty in creation, and if God is 'that than which none greater may be conceived',[43] then truth, goodness, and *beauty* are found in archetypical, infinite measure in the Godhead. This is fodder not only for chastising skepticism but also for worship – which is the inescapable flavor of the entirety of Anselm's writings. This is particularly the case for his *Proslogion*. Gavin Ortlund observes, for example, how 'Anselm's purpose in this book is not so much to establish the existence of God', as is so often assumed, but rather 'to arrive upon the sight and knowledge of God in an experience of joyful worship'.[44]

---

41. Anselm of Canterbury, *Proslogion*, chap. 17, 97, in *The Major Works*, ed. Brian Davies and G. R. Evans, Oxford World's Classics (New York: Oxford University Press, 1998), emphasis added. Also see, Gavin Ortlund, *Anslem's Pursuit of Joy: A Commentary on the Proslogion* (Washington, D.C.: The Catholic University of America Press, 2020), 160.

42. For a historical account of the argument's articulations, critiques, and rejoinders, see Graham Oppy, ed., *Ontological Arguments* (New York: Cambridge University Press, 2018); John Hick, *The Many-Faced Argument: Recent Studies on the Ontological Argument for the Existence of God* (Eugene, OR: Wipf and Stock, 2009).

43. Anselm *Proslogion*, chap. 2, 87-88.

44. Ortlund, *Anslem's Pursuit of Joy*, 95.

In similar fashion, Aquinas observes that the 'beauty of the creature is nothing else than the likeness of the divine beauty participated in things'.[45] Aquinas therefore operated within the Augustinian tradition, which posits that 'God is what he possesses in all the highest perfections. Each positive good on the creaturely plane of reality, beauty included, is carried to its highest perfection in God.'[46] This is why Aquinas stresses that

> the beautiful and beauty are distinguished with respect to participation and participants. Thus, we call something 'beautiful' because it participates in some way in beauty. Beauty, however, is a participation in the first cause, which makes all things beautiful. So that the beauty of creatures is simply a likeness of the divine beauty in which things participate.[47]

This quote is a good example of Aquinas' essentially *platonic* thought. Sebastian Morello calls attention to this feature of Aquinas in his recent work, *The World as God's Icon*. According to Morello, the common trope that Augustine was Plato's Christian heir while Aquinas was Aristotle's does not do adequate justice to Aquinas' metaphysic.[48] In this work, Morello labors to demonstrate how Aquinas is the great synthesizer, bringing the best of Plato (and particularly, Neoplatonism) and Aristotle together, helping the other with each's respective strength.

While 'Neoplatonism's weakness … was its unexplained, and therefore ambiguous, conception of individual substances,' Aristotle's weakness was primarily a missed opportunity: his doctrine of 'act and potency' was a tool powerful enough to apply metaphysically across the board, and not just for 'explaining the nature of change' (which is where Aristotle exclusively applies this topic). So, Aquinas brings Aristotle's doctrine of act and potency into the realm of a Neoplatonic metaphysic. In Morello's words, Aquinas, 'transformed the meaning of

---

45. Aquinas, *In Divinis Nominibus*, chap. 4, lect. 5, n. 337, quoted in King, *The Beauty of the Lord*, 34.

46. King, *The Beauty of the Lord*, 34.

47. Aquinas, *Commentary on the Sentences*, 1252, quoted in Umberto Eco, *The Aesthetics of Thomas Aquinas*, trans. Hugh Bredin (Cambridge, MA: Harvard University Press, 1988), 27.

48. Sebastian Morello, *The World as God's Icon: Creator and Creation in the Platonic Thought of Thomas Aquinas* (Brooklyn, NY: Anglico Press, 2020).

act and potency by situating them within the Neoplatonic participation-limitation framework.'[49] Morello goes on to summarize:

> Aquinas's entire ontology is a single participation structure, within which are substructures of participation accounting for the various relations within the matrix of contingent reality. In this ontology, whatever is the source must be by definition that which is the ultimate font of the perfection in question. The source cannot receive the perfection from something else; it must possess it by virtue of its own essence. The essence of the source must be identical and convertible with this perfection; if it were merely to *have* the perfection as part of its essence, it too would be a participant. In turn, it cannot merely *have* the perfection, it must *be* this perfection, and *be* it in purity and simplicity.[50]

This perfection in which everything participants is obviously God, and this is how it is possible for Aquinas to sound strikingly *Augustinian* in his description of beauty, like when he argues that beauty and goodness are metaphysically identical (even if they are conceptually different).[51] 'They differ logically,' says Aquinas,

> for goodness properly relates to the appetite (goodness being what all things desire); and therefore it has the aspect of an end (the appetite being a kind of movement towards a thing). On the other hand, beauty relates to the cognitive faculty; for beautiful things are those which please when seen.[52]

For Aquinas, then, as in the case for Augustine and the Neoplatonists, 'insofar as something is beautiful, it participates in a likeness of the beauty of the divine nature.'[53] Thus, for both Anselm and Aquinas, beauty was a worthy locus of contemplation for no lesser reason than that God was Beauty *par excellénce*, and God was *the* preeminent locus of contemplation. For them, to meditate on God was to meditate on the Beauty from whence came all other beauty.[54]

---

49. Ibid., 34-35.

50. Ibid., 46 (emphasis original).

51. Ibid., 108.

52. *Summa Theo.* I-II, 27, 1.

53. Morello, *The World as God's Icon*, 109.

54. This is an admittedly minimal engagement with Aquinas, but we shall engage him further in the following chapter.

Martin Luther (1483–1546)

Notwithstanding my earlier comments about the contemporary Protestant neglect of beauty, the problem does not go back to the Reformation, as is often assumed. While such an assumption has gone unchallenged for the past couple of hundred years, recent historical retrievals have thrown a wrench in the neat narrative that claims the Reformers came along as proto-Enlightenment thinkers and disenchanted the medieval conception of a transcendent and porous cosmos.[55] According to this narrative, the Reformers are largely to blame for the 'buffered identity' that suffocates within the 'immanent frame' wherein no meaningful theology of beauty can flourish.[56] A recent work that takes this narrative to task is Mark C. Mattes' *Martin Luther's Theology of Beauty: A Reappraisal*. One may be surprised to see Luther's name mentioned alongside the likes of Aquinas and Anselm on any philosophical topic, let alone aesthetics. We can forgive such a reaction, seeing as how Luther made it his habit to refer to philosophy as 'the Devil's whore'. Nevertheless, as Mattes points out, 'anyone who assumes that Luther believed that philosophy had no positive contribution to make to theology simply fails to deal with Luther's corpus.'[57]

Luther's theology of beauty, like his theology of *everything*, was centered on the crucifixion.[58] Luther's objection to metaphysics was never an objection to metaphysical categories or terms *per se*; he objected to 'metaphysics as seeking truth, beauty, and goodness outside and independently of the cross, which should test all things (*crux probat omnia*), as an expression of human love that is in opposition to God's love.'[59] Therefore, one has to conclude that beauty is not an insignificant concept in Luther's thinking – unless one regards the doctrine of justification as insignificant. In fact, not only can one not understand Luther's view of beauty apart from the doctrine of justification as God's imputed righteousness to believers, which also calls them from death

---

55. E.g., Taylor, *The Theater of God's Glory*.

56. This is the non-subtle suggestion of Charles Taylor in *A Secular Age*.

57. Mattes, *Martin Luther's Theology of Beauty*, 15.

58. An example of how his anthropology flows from the cross can be found in Marc Cortez, *Christological Anthropology in Historical Perspective: Ancient and Contemporary Approaches to Theological Anthropology* (Grand Rapids, MI: Zondervan, 2016), 83-110.

59. Ibid., 80.

to life, it would seem that one also cannot fully understand God's justification apart from beauty. God's beauty in its most proper form is revealed as mercy granted in Christ. To assume that the topic of beauty is insignificant to Luther is to go against Luther's own conviction that the question of beauty is crucial to human life with God: God loves sinners not because they are beautiful, they are beautiful because they are loved.[60]

John Owen (1616–1683)

It would be very easy to plagiarize John Owen in the development of this work's central thesis on the beauty of Christ in regeneration and faith, for he has said what I wish to say, only better. As is often the case when considering figures from the past, however, Owen's contribution to a theology of beauty is often missed on account of his differing terminology. Like Herman Bavinck (see below), Owen's theology of beauty is inextricably tied to his theology of glory, which is impossible to overemphasize in terms of weight and significance. Since Owen's corpus is so vast, and his insights on beauty and glory are so expansive, we will limit our discussion here (and our discussion in chapter 3) to the small scope of select sections from the first volume of Owen's collected works, *The Glory of Christ*. Here, much like the authors mentioned above, Owen identifies the goodness and beauty of the creation as a pointer to the goodness and beauty of the Creator: 'God made all things, in the beginning, good, exceeding good. The whole of his work was disposed into a perfect harmony, beauty, and order, suited unto the manifestation of his own glory which he designed therein.'[61]

Owen ties everything to the glory of God, and the creation's beauty in particular serves as a revelation of God and therefore a revelation of God's glory. This is certainly true of the general witness of creation, but it is preeminently true to the special revelation of Christ – who uniquely communicates and mediates the divine glory of God. In the person of Christ, says Owen,

> is there a blessed representation made unto us of all the holy properties
> of the nature of God – of his wisdom, his power, his goodness, grace,

---

60. Cortez, *Christological Anthropology*, 110.

61. John Owen, *The Works of John Owen*, ed. William H. Goold, 16 vols. (Edinburgh, UK: Banner of Truth Trust, 2000), 1:61.

and love, his righteousness, truth, and holiness, his mercy and patience. As this is affirmed concerning them all in general, or the glory of God in them, which is seen and known only in the face of Christ, so it were easy to manifest the same concerning every one of them in particular, by express testimonies of Scripture.[62]

In other words, since Christ is the supreme revelation of God's glory in general, and since God's glory in general may be specifically described with a litany of characteristics (i.e., wisdom, power, goodness, and we can safely add *beauty*, etc.), it can be demonstrated that Christ is the supreme revelation of each of those characteristics in particular. Obviously, much more can be said about this topic, but Owen will return to this work with some force in chapter 3, so for now we shall keep moving through our historical survey.

Jonathan Edwards (1703–1758)

As we continue down our jaunt through the history of Christian aesthetics, a nonnegotiable figure for our roll call must be the Northampton pastor Jonathan Edwards. It would be difficult to overstate how important beauty is as an interpretive key to understanding Edwards.[63] In their *The Theology of Jonathan Edwards*, Michael J. McClymond and Gerald R. McDermott write,

> Edwards regarded beauty as fundamental to his understanding of God, as the first of God's perfections, as key to the doctrine of the Trinity, as a defining aspect of the natural world, as basic to the phenomenon of conversion, as visible in the lives of saints, and as marking the difference between the regenerate and the unregenerate mind.[64]

It therefore comes as no surprise that Edwards' conception of God's intrinsic beauty is intimately related to everything he explores.[65] To

---

62. Owen, *The Works of John Owen*, 1:70.

63. See, Roland André Delattre, *Beauty and Sensibility in the Thought of Jonathan Edwards: An Essay in Aesthetics and Theological Ethics* (Eugene, OR: Wipf and Stock, 2006),1-2.

64. Michael James McClymond and Gerald R. McDermott, *The Theology of Jonathan Edwards* (New York: Oxford University Press, 2012), 93.

65. The fullest expression of Edwards' Trinitarianism can be found in his 'Discourse on the Trinity', in Jonathan Edwards, *Works of Jonathan Edwards Online*, vol. 21, *Writings on the Trinity, Grace, and Faith, 1740*, ed. Sang Hyun Lee (Jonathan Edwards Center at Yale University, 2008), but this aspect of Edwards' theology permeates the whole of his corpus.

speak of Edwards's Trinitarian idealism,[66] and to speak of his theory of beauty,[67] and to speak of his conception of the Trinity's *ad intra* excellency and perfection, are all to speak on the same subject.[68] 'In Edwards's theological aesthetic,' Jonathan King writes, 'the notion of consent to being has as its basis the social ontology of God's Being. His conception of beauty as involving "consent" and "agreement" thus provides the key philosophical link for identifying God's divine beauty with God's *Trinitarian* beauty.'[69]

Although Edwards' doctrine of the Trinity remains hotly debated,[70] one aspect of his Trinitarianism is indisputable: he roots his doctrine of beauty preeminently and supremely in the doctrine of the Trinity – particularly in person's consent to person within the 'society of the Trinity'.[71] Importantly, Edwards insists that the *ad intra* beauty of the Trinity must be definitional, and all other beauty is to be read

---

66. I.e., the concept that all created reality exists so intimately contingent on God's will that its ontology begins and ends in the divine, Triune 'Mind'. See Edwards, 'Of Being,' 'The Mind'; and Jeffery C. Waddington, 'The Mind,' in *The Jonathan Edwards Encyclopedia*, ed. Harry S. Stout (Grand Rapids, MI: Eerdmans, 2017), 380-82.

67. I.e., beauty consists of being consenting to being, ultimately in relation to God, who is metaphysically definitional for everything else. See Edwards, 'Of Being'; and McClymond and McDermott, *The Theology of Jonathan Edwards*, 93-101.

68. See McClymond and McDermott, *The Theology of Jonathan Edwards*, 193-206.

69. Jonathan King, 'Beauty,' in Harry S. Stout, ed., *The Jonathan Edwards Encyclopedia* (Grand Rapids, MI: Eerdmans, 2017), 63-64.

70. See Oliver Crisp, *Jonathan Edwards among the Theologians* (Grand Rapids, MI: Eerdmans, 2015); Oliver Crisp, *Jonathan Edwards on God and Creation* (New York: Oxford University Press, 2012); Amy Plantinga Pauw, '*The Supreme Harmony of All': The Trinitarian Theology of Jonathan Edwards* (Grand Rapids, MI: Eerdmans, 2002); Steven M. Studebaker and Robert W. Caldwell III, *The Trinitarian Theology of Jonathan Edwards: Text, Context, and Application* (Burlington, VT: Ashgate, 2012); Sang Hyun Lee, ed., *The Princeton Companion to Jonathan Edwards* (Princeton, NJ: Princeton University Press, 2020). Crisp summarizes and interacts with all of these works and more in *Jonathan Edwards Among the Theologians*, 36-59. Much of the debate surrounds the issue of whether Edwards' Trinitarianism primarily leaned toward the psychological (Augustinian) model of the Trinity, the social model, or some innovation that fits in neither category. Louie convincingly argues that Edwards uses both models in *Beauty of the Triune God*, 104-15.

71. See Edwards, 'Heaven,' in Jonathan Edwards, *Works of Jonathan Edwards Online*, vol. 13, *The 'Miscellanies': (Entry Nos. a–z, Aa–Zz, 1–500)*, ed. Harry S. Stout (Jonathan Edwards Center at Yale University, 2008), 327-28. In the next chapter we will show how *simplicity*, rather than *society*, is a more faithfully orthodox and conceptually fruitful foundation for Trinitarian theology.

as consequential. In other words, the Trinity is not beautiful because proportion and symmetry happen to be therein just like in every other beautiful thing (as if 'symmetry and proportion' are abstract standards for beauty to which the Trinity is subject); rather, symmetry and proportion are definitional for beauty because the Trinity – who *is* beauty *par excellence* – is symmetrical and proportionate. The eternal One-and-Three exists in harmonious, perichoretic relationship with one another,[72] and to the degree that creation resembles that relationship,[73] it is beautiful.

Herman Bavinck (1854–1921)

Although an explicit aesthetics did not occupy a major space in Herman Bavinck's theology,[74] his contribution to theological aesthetics is nevertheless significant.[75] Regardless of his minimal usage of explicit theological-aesthetic terminology, Bavinck's entire system may be described as an aesthetic theology, insofar as his theology centers on divine glory. This is certainly the case, though it is a fact understandably missed due to Bavinck's own intentional terminology shift:

> Just as the contemplation of God's creatures directs our attention upward and prompts us to speak of God's eternity and omnipresence, his righteousness and grace, so it also gives us a glimpse of God's glory. *What we have here, however, is analogy, not identity.* Speaking of creatures, we call them pretty, beautiful, or splendid; but for the beauty of God Scripture has a special word: glory. For that reason it is not advisable to speak – with the church father's scholastics, and Catholic theologians – of God's beauty.[76]

72. This is one of the central themes developed in Kyle C. Strobel, *Jonathan Edwards's Theology: A Reinterpretation* (Edinburgh: T&T Clark, 2014).

73. See Leithart, *Traces of the Trinity.*

74. The concept of beauty is named and tackled at length only a couple of times by Bavinck. This chapter will pull primarily from Bavinck's 1914 address for Almanak of the Vrije Universiteit entitled, 'Of Beauty and Aesthetics,' in Herman Bavinck, *Essays on Religion, Science, and Society*, ed. John Bolt, trans. Harry Boonstra and Gerrit Sheeres (Grand Rapids, MI: Baker Academic, 2013), and Bavinck, *Reformed Dogmatics*, 2:252-55.

75. Bavinck's aesthetic has been aptly summarized and analyzed by Robert S. Covolo, 'Herman Bavinck's Theological Aesthetic: A Synchronic and Diachronic Analysis,' *The Bavinck Review* 2 (2011): 43-58. Much of the discussion that follows is indebted to Covolo's article. See also, James Eglinton, 'Vox Theologiae: Boldness and Humility in Public Theological Speech,' *International Journal of Public Theology* 9 (2015): 5-28.

76. Bavinck, *Reformed Dogmatics*, 2:254, emphasis added.

Bavinck's reason for changing the terminology of God's 'beauty' to God's 'glory' comes from his own desire to enunciate the Creator-creature distinction in no uncertain terms. For Bavinck, earthly beauty differs from the divine beauty of God not only in degree but in nature ('analogy, not identity'). This means that all of Bavinck's discussions on God's glory can be understood in terms of divine beauty as long as the unique, archetypal nature of God's beauty is retained.

This makes divine beauty far more central to Bavinck's system than one might think based on the infrequency with which he uses the terminology. Glory, for Bavinck, was not merely one of many attributes of God; it was the perfection of all His attributes: 'The "glory of the Lord" is the splendor of brilliance that is inseparably associated with all of God's attributes and his self-revelation in nature and grace, the glorious form in which he everywhere appears to his creatures.'[77] Therefore, to the degree that Bavinck's theology is a theology of *God's glory* (and if God's glory is the perfection of all His attributes, then '*a theology of God's glory*' is tantamount to '*a theology of God*'), it is a theology of God's *beauty*.

Karl Barth (1886–1968)

Karl Barth, like Bavinck, associates beauty with the being and glory of God,[78] but he does not go so far as Bavinck as equating divine beauty with divine glory. Barth tends to conceptualize God's beauty in a more heuristic fashion: it is not an element of God's essence;[79] it is rather a function of His glory. 'If we can and must say that God is beautiful,' writes Barth, 'to say this is to say how He enlightens and convinces and persuades us. It is to describe not merely the naked fact of His revelation or its power, but the shape and form in which it is a fact and is power.'[80] This is an interesting space for Barth to navigate because

---

77. Ibid, 252.

78. Garrett Green observes that although 'Barth's primary concern is the attribute of divine glory, this consideration leads him to make some fascinating and controversial claims about beauty and the arts.' Garrett Green, *Imagining Theology: Encounters with God in Scripture, Interpretation, and Aesthetics* (Grand Rapids, MI: Baker Academic, 2020), 112.

79. 'Attention should also be given to the fact that we cannot include the concept of beauty with the main concepts of the doctrine of God, with the divine perfections which are the divine essence itself' (Barth, *CD II/1*, 652).

80. Barth, *CD II/1*, 650.

it both resembles a subjectivist view of beauty and it creates problems for the doctrine of divine simplicity.[81] It resembles a subjectivist view of beauty because, in this construction, beauty fulfills the pragmatic purpose to merely get the subject of the believer from unbelief to belief. It is not simply that this is one of the *effects* of divine beauty (something for which I will argue later in this work), but that this is the material *purpose* of divine beauty. Divine beauty, in this construction, has its justification and telos in what it accomplishes in the believer. This conception is also a problem for the doctrine of divine simplicity since it amounts to rendering divine beauty an accidental property. It is a pragmatic property that does not exist in the essence of God, but rather it exists in the purpose of God to draw men to Himself. The logical conclusion of Barth's construction is that, were it not for creatures who find the Creator beautiful for salvific purposes, the Creator would not be beautiful. Be that as it may, Barth makes a powerful point in that God reveals His beauty in the glory of His economic activity – the form of His glory is manifested in 'his self-revelation as the Lord, the Creator, Reconciler, and Redeemer.'[82]

Hans Urs von Balthasar (1905–1988)

That Barth could not seem to get past his allergy of secular philosophy in general, and Platonism in particular,[83] is why Hans Urs von Balthasar concludes that Barth 'has not succeeded in really shaping and transforming Protestant theology'.[84] For his own part, Balthasar followed a more traditional path on the question of beauty,[85] elevating beauty to the level of a transcendental property alongside the true and the good: 'May we not think of the beautiful as one of the transcendental

---

81. Of course, the more obvious problem that Barth faces with respect to harmonizing his views with the doctrine of divine simplicity is his dismissal of divine immutability. Dolezal makes this point cogently in James E. Dolezal, *God Without Parts: Divine Simplicity and the Metaphysics of God's Absoluteness* (Eugene, OR: Pickwick, 2011), 86-87.

82. King, *The Beauty of the Lord*, 38.

83. See James Kincade, 'Karl Barth and Philosophy," *The Journal of Religion* 40, no. 3 (1960): 161-69; Green, *Imagining Theology*, 111-21.

84. Balthasar, *The Glory of the Lord*, 1:55.

85. This is broadly true, even while he nevertheless innovates his theology proper on account of his Kenotic theology. The problems with von Balthasar's conception of the Son's 'self-emptying' will become apparent in chapter 3.

attributes of Being as such, and thereby ascribe to the beautiful the same range of application and the same inwardly analogous form that we ascribe to the one, the true, the good?'[86] Balthasar also resembles Aquinas and Anselm (and, we might add, Augustine and many others) when he notes a derivative relationship between divine and created beauty – they are analogous, but not univocal, which means the former defines the latter, and not the other way around.[87]

Apart from the obvious contribution Balthasar makes by way of theological retrieval of divine beauty,[88] he brings two other themes to the table that are of particular interest for this project. First, Balthasar's theological aesthetics was extremely practical and pastoral.[89] He felt down to his bones the disastrous effects that beauty's absence would cause. Beauty, for him, was not a luxury that one could dispense of with no damage to truth or goodness; it was rather a necessary safeguard for truth and goodness:

> In a world … which is perhaps not wholly without beauty but can no longer see it or reckon with it: in such a world the good also loses its attractiveness, the self-evidence of why it must be carried out. Man stands before the good and asks himself why *it* must be done and not rather its alternative, evil. For this, too, is a possibility, and even the more exciting one: Why not investigate Satan's depth? In a world that no longer has enough confidence in itself to affirm the beautiful, the proofs of the truth have lost their cogency. In other words, syllogisms may still dutifully clatter away like rotary presses or computers which infallibly spew out an exact number of answers by the minute. But the logic of these answers is itself a mechanism which no longer captivates anyone.[90]

Without beauty, then, 'Christianity withers away.'[91]

Second, Balthasar's vision of theological aesthetics was irreducibly Christological, since 'Jesus is the Word, the Image, the Expression

---

86. Ibid, 38.

87. Cf., Matthew Levering, *The Achievement of Hans Urs von Balthasar: An Introduction to His Trilogy* (Washington, D.C.: Catholic University of America Press, 2019), 46.

88. Carnes, for example, largely attributes the retrieval of scholarship on Gregory of Nyssa to the work of Balthasar, particularly his *Presence and Thought* (1942). See Carnes, *Beauty*.

89. Not, of course, in terms of accessibility, but in spirit.

90. Balthasar, *The Glory of the Lord*, 1:19.

91. Levering, *The Achievement of Hans Urs von Balthasar*, 46.

and the Exegesis of God.'[92] This is so crucial that Balthasar actually 'warns against the desire to see God more clearly than we see him in Christ.'[93] This is because, as Matthew Levering points out, 'In Christ, God has made himself definitely perceivable; there is no beatific vision unmediated by the humanity of Christ. God's perceivable form in Christ fulfills the entirety of God's revelation in history.'[94] The first of these two themes bears import on this project because it saturates it with urgency and significance (beauty *matters*). The second of these themes will resurface in chapter 3, which is a crucial component to the thesis described above.

This (all too) brief survey constitutes a mere sampling. In subsequent chapters, these figures will reemerge to speak into various topics, but this initial roll call is sufficient for establishing historical precedents for this project. Despite appearances (in light of contemporary systematics), the drive to consider the aesthetic dimensions of the Triune God and His saving works is no new thing; it is the ancient manner of theologizing.

Beauty Defined[95]

At this point 'beauty' cries out for a definition,[96] and this section offers one. However, the definition is not neat or univocal but rather descriptive

---

92. Balthasar, *The Glory of the Lord*, 1:29.

93. Levering, *The Achievement of Hans Urs von Balthasar*, 65.

94. Ibid, 65. However, as Boersma, *Seeing God*, 22-33, has pointed out, this excellent point by von Balthasar leads to the unnecessary conclusion that 'no beatific vision apart from Christ' amounts to 'no beatific vision'. Von Balthasar reaches this conclusion because he wrongly assumes that the 'beatific vision' is incompatible with the idea of Christ's role as epistemic mediator, as if the 'beatific vision' were somehow a Christless look at the essence of God. Boersma demonstrates that while the Christian tradition contains various conceptions of the 'beatific vision', the strongest ones never dispensed with Christ as the 'Exegesis of God'.

95. What follows is a conception of beauty that falls comfortably within the Augustinian tradition. Which is to say, the Christian tradition that critically pulls from Plato and, more explicitly, from Plotinus. For a helpful summary of this tradition, see Monroe C. Beardsley, *Aesthetics from Classical Greece to the Present: A Short History* (Tuscaloosa, AL: University of Alabama Press, 1998), 30-114.

96. This is an intrinsically difficult task, given beauty's transrational nature. Patrick Sherry, *Spirit and Beauty*, 2nd ed. (London: SCM, 2002), 43, gets at the difficulty well when he notes that in 'the case of beauty, two seemingly contradictory tendencies often jostle with each other: people want to explicate the criteria which govern their use of the concept, yet they also want to leave the nature of beauty something of a mystery. The former tendency is motivated by the desire to delineate the sorts of reasons which warrant

and indirect. This is because beauty is intrinsic *to the object it adorns,* and therefore is unintelligible in the abstract. 'Beauty, for its part,' writes Umberto Eco, 'acquires concreteness and a quality of necessity, an objectivity and dignity.'[97] This means that beauty is necessarily objective. It does not originate in the subject upon whom beauty presents itself, nor in the organ of perception, nor in the sensation of perceiving, nor even in the material substance of the object perceived as beautiful.[98] Beauty stands objectively outside of these surface-level categories and is the quality with which these categories interact. This view is therefore to be distinguished from a non-realist view of aesthetics,[99] which accompanies certain forms of Phenomenalism.[100] Such a clarification is necessary because even though the classical view of beauty posits objectivity, the 'apperception of the quality of beauty depends on the percipience of the mind (the mental faculty of perceiving), since it is the mind that renders relation of aesthetic properties as something perceived.'[101] Beauty is recognized subjectively, but this does not mean that beauty is itself subjective.[102] On the contrary, beauty presents itself to the perceiver as

---

an ascription of beauty, and to explain the logical relationship between such ascriptions and the reasons on which they are based.'

97. Eco, *The Aesthetics of Thomas Aquinas*, 22.

98. For example, the beauty of a painting is not found in the material form of the paint or canvas. It is something that transcends these material characteristics. Beauty is not *in* the paint or canvas – rather, the paint on canvas *is* beautiful.

99. Eco continues, 'This is why the question has been of interest not just to historical commentators but also in neo-Thomist apologetics, in which it is thought necessary to combat aesthetic subjectivism by reaffirming the objectivity of beauty.' Eco, *The Aesthetics of Thomas Aquinas*, 22.

100. I.e., the view that the aesthetic quality of an object exists strictly in the subjective experience of the subject. This is a non-transcendental view that remains incapable of distinguishing between the beauty of an object and the subject's recognition of beauty through experience. Such a view neatly harmonizes with the standard subjectivism that is presupposed in most popular conceptions of beauty, which is summarized nicely by David Hume: 'Beauty is no quality in things themselves: It exists merely in the mind which contemplates them; and each mind perceives a different beauty. One person may even perceive deformity, where another is sensible of beauty; and every individual ought to acquiesce in his own sentiment, without pretending to regulate those of others.' David Hume, 'Of the Standard of Taste,' in *Essays: Moral and Political* (London: George Routledge and Sons, 1894), 136.

101. King, *The Beauty of the Lord*, 9.

102. Dietrich von Hildebrand, makes this point powerfully in *Aesthetics: Volume I*, ed. John F Crosby, trans. Brian McNeil (Steubenville, OH: Hildebrand Project, 2016), 48-49.

an objective value, intrinsic to the object it adorns. Intrinsic to the object it adorns, but not exhausted (or even originated) thereby. Beauty *exceeds*.

Beauty, therefore, is real. It is as real and central to the very fabric of reality as truth and goodness, and everything that we recognize as beautiful is beautiful to the degree that it participates in transcendental Beauty. It is the evocative brilliance of the True and Good, calling forth the affectionate response of its perceiver. Beauty is more real than the beautiful expressions through which it is revealed. Indeed, since Beauty is a transcendental – along with Truth and Goodness – is an attribute of the Triune God, which makes it ultimate *reality.*

We take our stand on beauty, therefore, alongside the realists of the Christian Platonic tradition.[103] Over and against the nominalist (or, non-realist) outlook – which denies the reality of transcendent universals, and concludes rather that universals are mere artificial heuristics in the mind ('names') – we affirm the reality of transcendent universals.[104] The invisible Beauty of visibly beautiful objects is *more real* than their material expressions. It *exceeds* beyond the finite boundaries of its perceptible object. This we know, in part, because of the delightful discontentment the experience of beauty creates within the perceiver. The beholder of beauty aches for more of it.

Beauty cannot merely exist in the eye of the beholder, as if it originated there. It is not thrust upon the object's beholder at the beholder's request; rather, Beauty beckons from – and to – somewhere beyond the object. It is *in-and-beyond* the object the beholder beholds, drawing the beholder forcibly to the object and beyond it – further up and further in. The Beauty he beholds in the object is real, and undeniably so – the object of his adoration is beautiful because it in some way participates in this transcendent Beauty. Even if the perceiver attempts to convince himself

---

103. On this realist outlook, see Jordan Cooper, *In Defense of the True, the Good, and the Beautiful: On the Loss of Transcendence and the Decline of the West* (Ithaca, NY: Just and Sinner, 2021); Paul Tyson, *Returning to Reality: Christian Platonism for Our Times* (Eugene, OR: Cascade Books, 2014); Craig A. Carter, *Contemplating God with the Great Tradition: Recovering Trinitarian Classical Theism* (Grand Rapids, MI: 2021); and Louis Markos, *From Plato to Christ: How Platonic Thought Shaped the Christian Faith* (Downers Grove, IL: InterVarsity Press, 2021).

104. A great overview of nominalism is Tyson's section on Scotus and Ockham, the 'architects of modernity', in *Returning to Reality*, 64-77. See also, Cooper, *In Defense of the True, the Good, and the Beautiful*, 38-42.

of its artificial nature, the force of Beauty in the object perceived belies his make-believe: his soul calls his theory's bluff.

The alternative is to say that a statement about a beautiful object is not truly a statement about the object itself but rather merely about the person speaking.[105] If I stand at the edge of the Grand Canyon and comment on the compelling beauty of a setting sun, which paints the canyon in shades of orange and purple and pink, the non-realist view of beauty would have us believe that I had not actually said anything about the *canyon*. That was just *me* I was talking about; the beauty that pulled such observations out of me, was, in fact, nothing other than 'me'. But the notion that the subject's recognition of beauty in an object has nothing whatever to do with the object's intrinsic value is self-evidently absurd. Consider the notion when applied, for example, to the passion of young romantic love. The notion that a suiter's infatuation with his love interest has no correlation with her intrinsic beauty – since no such intrinsic beauty exists but is rather a 'fiction of desire' – would ordinarily be considered by him a laughable (if not, blasphemous) proposition.

This denial of nominalism does not contradict the notion, shared by most ancient philosophers, that a person can have better or worse tastes in beauty (i.e., that their perception of an object's intrinsic aesthetic value is not static but has the capacity to improve or deteriorate); it is only to say that when someone recognizes true beauty, they recognize a characteristic intrinsic to the object (or concept, or idea, etc.) they perceive. Indeed, the ability to have better or worse tastes regarding beauty implies beauty's objectivity. 'The beautiful is not a fiction of desire,' notes David Bentley Hart,

> nor is its nature exhausted by a phenomenology of pleasure; it can be recognized in spite of desire, or as that toward which desire must be cultivated. There is overwhelming givenness in the beautiful, and it is discovered in astonishment, in awareness of something fortuitous, adventitious, essentially indescribable; it is known only in the moment of response, from the position of one already addressed and able now only to reply.[106]

---

105. This is precisely the notion that C. S. Lewis attacks in *The Abolition of Man*, as represented by 'Gaius and Titius' in 'the Green Book'. C. S. Lewis, *The Abolition of Man* (San Francisco, CA: HarperCollins, 2001), 1-26.

106. David Bentley Hart, *The Beauty of the Infinite: The Aesthetics of Christian Truth* (Grand Rapids, MI: Eerdmans, 2005), 17.

There is something intuitive about what Hart says here. The recognition of beauty is not irrational, but it is certainly *pre-rational*. Beauty does not ask for permission when it thrusts itself upon a subject. It places demands on the perceiver that the perceiver can either obey or disobey, but he cannot be the originator or the obliterator of those demands. He may ignore them, but he cannot create or erase them.

The non-realist who truly experiences beauty must come to embrace a sort of cognitive dissonance, whereby he experiences beauty as compellingly legitimate while simultaneously denying the genuineness of the experience. Again, he may propositionally deny the realism of beauty self-consciously, but his soul – to the degree that *he truly experiences beauty* – debunks his nominalist myth. But this sort of cognitive dissonance cannot exist forever. Eventually, either the non-realist theory or the realist experience will win out. It is possible for a person to almost entirely cut himself off from experiencing real beauty when the non-realist theory is given greater prominence than the realist experience. The man who keeps telling himself that his adoration for his beloved is not owing to any objective beauty she embodies will eventually buy his own press and convince himself that there is no such thing as beauty at all, even in his beloved. Thus, his beloved will fail to be so called; she will receive no adoration because, he has convinced himself, no such adoration is ever fitting. It is the child's play of a fooled imagination. If beauty is not *real*, no one and nothing owes the affection we would render to the beautiful. This is what it means, in part, for man to *lose his chest*, as Lewis puts it, and the state of affairs is a sad one. Lewis predicts what will happen with this loss of transcendence in *The Abolition of Man*: 'In a sort of ghastly simplicity we remove the organ and demand the function. We make men without chests and expect of them virtue and enterprise. We laugh at honor and are shocked to find traitors in our midst. We castrate and bid the geldings be fruitful.'[107]

There is one other point in favor of the realist position that is worth mentioning. Not only is the non-realist position logically incoherent, intuitively unviable, and (as just shown) existentially bleak, it is also aesthetically repugnant. While we might not construct an entire argument from this fact alone, it is a least a clue: the theory of beauty

---

107. Lewis, *The Abolition of Man*, 26.

that is itself ugly – the one that sucks the cosmos of all its loveliness and texture and color and transcendent meaning, leaving the landscape of reality drab, boring, and tasteless – is not easy to defend. It is an unpleasant burden to have to passionately argue that passion is artificial (i.e., it does not correspond to transcendent *meaning*). The need to push the *theory* as far away from the *experience* as possible is a good indication that the theory is unworkable.[108]

Having established *that* beauty is objectively real and subjectively perceived, we must now turn to consider the *way* that beauty is perceived by the subject. This question has been the topic of much contemplation and debate over the centuries. How does beauty identify itself? How does the mind recognize it? Symmetry, harmony, functionality, disinterestedness, and the sublime have often been cited as essential features of beauty.[109] These are helpful, but ultimately an exhaustive list is futile, since beauty 'crosses boundaries'.[110] The obvious effort to grasp for words is reflective of beauty's ineffable quality. This can be aggravating for some and, indeed, a challenge for an academic project since the

---

108. For a brilliant extrapolation of this line of argument, see Ortlund, *Why God Makes Sense in a World That Doesn't*, 87-101.

109. King, *The Beauty of the Lord*, 9, offers a non-exhaustive list of examples, including proportion, unity, variety, symmetry, harmony, intricacy, delicacy, simplicity, and suggestiveness. Nicholas Wolterstorff's list includes fittingness, unity, internal richness, potency or activity, and intensity. See Wolterstorff, *Art in Action*, 156-74.

Von Hildebrand, *Aesthetics: Volume I*, 261-81, offers several antitheses and pseudo-antitheses of beauty in order to triangulate how beauty is perceived; these include ugliness, triviality, boringness, the prosaic, the sentimental and more. 'This beauty, wherever it appears, calls into being in our minds a whole spiritual world that is laden with a host of spiritual elements: the poetic as opposed to the prosaic, necessity as opposed to arbitrariness, inner abundance as opposed to every falsehood and affection, inner greatness as opposed to everything mediocre, breadth and depth as opposed to all that is insipid and trivial' (von Hildebrand, *Beauty in the Light of the Redemption*, 16-17).

In *Aesthetics from Classical Greece to the Present*, Beardley shows, however, that the need for finding objective characteristics for beauty began to disappear at around the eighteenth century, when the interest in beauty shifted from the transcendental to the anthropological. The need has all but evaporated for modern aestheticians and art critiques, who esteem 'beauty' as having little significance on their field. 'As it happens, beauty has fallen into considerable disfavor in modern philosophical discourse, having all but disappeared as a term in philosophical aesthetics' (Hart, *The Beauty of the Infinite*, 15). This has been lamented by Rookmaaker and Scruton in different ways. See Roger Scruton, *Beauty* (New York: Oxford University Press, 2009); H. R. Rookmaaker, *Modern Art and the Death of a Culture* (Wheaton, IL: Crossway, 1994).

110. See Hart, *The Beauty of the Infinite*, 20.

nature of such a work is precision. Yet a real tension must be held, for if talk of beauty loses this element of ineffableness, it will not have been explained but rather explained away.[111]

Any categories we use to characterize beauty, therefore, must be intentionally broad and unexhaustive. In her recent work *Beauty: A Theological Engagement with Gregory of Nyssa*, Natalie Carnes proposes such a way of characterizing beauty. Following her reading of Gregory, Carnes advocates for two central characteristics for beauty: 'fittingness' and 'gratuity'.[112] In contrast to 'functional', Carnes opts for 'fitting', (a category broad enough to include 'harmony' or 'symmetry') and in contrast to 'disinterest', she opts for 'gratuity'. This allows for a dynamism and dexterity when describing beauty: with 'fittingness and gratuity', one is able not only to make sense of some existential dimensions of recognizing beauty, one is also able to make sense of beauty's transcendency. Beauty is gratuitous in the sense that it points beyond itself and beyond sheer utility – it is better, more attractive, more delightful than it needs to be.[113] Dietrich von Hildebrand revels in this aspect of beauty with a flurry of rhetorical questions:

> Is God not lavish in His creation? Do we not meet this divine profusion in the realm of propagation? Is beauty in nature not the clearest proof of this divine profusion, since it is in no way practically indispensable in the economy of nature? Is creation itself, as such, not the fruit of this divine profusion? Is it not the pure emanation of the infinite love of God and in no way necessary?[114]

In this way, every creaturely beauty points beyond itself and ultimately runs into the infinitude of the Triune God.[115] 'If, for example, we

---

111. See Hart, in *The Beauty of the Infinite*, 16.

112. Carnes, *Beauty*, 45-59.

113. Carnes (and Gregory) share much, in this respect, with von Hildebrand's notion of 'beauty to the second power', which 'proclaims much higher realities. It kindles in us a yearning for the world of lofty immaterial realities. Basically, this is a longing for that which is "above us," *quae sursum sunt* ("the things above," Colossians 3:1); it draws us upward' (von Hildebrand, *Aesthetics: Volume I*, 209-10).

114. Von Hildebrand, *Beauty in the Light of the Redemption*, 10.

115. This is another reason Carnes is compelled to find an alternative to 'functionality' and 'disinterestedness': 'The shift to fittingness and gratuity is warranted not just by the way disinterestedness and functionality fail to account for the experience and judgment of beauty, but also because they fail as theological descriptions of a God who is Beauty' (Carnes, *Beauty*, 120).

view a lofty mountain range bathed in gleaming sunlight,' observes Hildebrand, 'it is not that which we see directly before us to which beauty is attached, but the thought of God's creative power is the real beauty.'[116] Any notion of 'beauty', therefore, that is divorced from God as the ultimate reference point is destined to cave in on itself.[117]

Again, I ultimately take beauty, then, to be a transcendental property (along with truth and goodness)[118] and therefore an attribute of the Triune God. 'In [God], beauty is not present in one part rather than in another, nor is it present under some aspect. Rather, God is beautiful simply and in all respects.'[119] As an attribute of God, beauty is inseparable from other divine attributes and is rightly recognized as the brilliance, the majesty, the splendor of truth and goodness. All this is why Jonathan King concludes that 'the beauty of God manifested economically (*pulchritudo Dei ad extra*) is expressed and perceivable as *a quality of* the glory of God inherent in his work of creation, redemption, and consummation. The display of God's glory is thus always beautiful, always fitting, always entails an aesthetic dimension to it.'[120] This point is rendered a necessity on account of the doctrine of divine simplicity (more on this doctrine in chapter 2). Earthly beauty therefore reflects *and participates in* divine beauty. 'It was you who made [the heavens and the earth],' wrote Augustine, 'for You are beautiful, and they are beautiful.'[121]

However, a tension may be anticipated here. I am trying to resist the temptation of projecting this-worldly conceptions of beauty back onto God and am therefore stressing the precedence of divine beauty. The Triune God is aesthetically definitional – the Trinity *is* beauty *par*

---

116. Von Hildebrand, *Beauty in the Light of the Redemption*, 17.

117. Appealing to beauty as an eternal abstraction will not do, since beauty is fundamentally descriptive; it does not have ontological independence but rather requires an object to describe. It is also futile to appeal to beauty as an ultimately subjective innovation of the human mind. To do so is to make man the absolute origin of a philosophical reality, but man, as an essentially contingent being, cannot ultimately originate anything.

118. One runs into a difficulty with even the mention of 'transcendentals', since the discussion is wrought with metaphysical difficulties. Transcendentals are properties that are distinct from being, yet inconceivable apart from being. This difficulty is summed up well by Eco, *The Aesthetics of Thomas Aquinas*, 21.

119. Ibid., 28.

120. King, *The Beauty of the Lord*, 51

121. Augustine, *Confessions*, book XI, 4.6.

excellénce and created beauty is beautiful to the degree that it reflects His glory. This claim is the photonegative of saying that the Trinity is beautiful because therein do we find characteristics that resemble this-worldly beauty. However, I am also saying that all beauty (even God's) is mediated to us through this-worldly means. Creatures can only receive God's revelation of Himself *as creatures*. How is it possible to resist the temptation of projecting immanent definitions of beauty back up onto God, if we finite creatures only experience beauty in a 'this-worldly' sense? Chapter 2 of this volume will, in large part, attempt to resolve this tension, but since the answer has immediate ramifications on theological methodology, we may begin to get at a solution with the help of Bavinck.

In his essay 'Of Beauty and Aesthetics', Bavinck argues that earthly beauty (be it natural beauty or the beauty found in art) is divine revelation – albeit general and secondary to special revelation. 'Both [natural and artistic forms of beauty] are revelations,' writes Bavinck, 'each in its own way, of *true beauty*, which is not sensory but spiritual – according to Plato [it is] found in the ideal, and according to Holy Scripture [it is] *found in God's splendor and displayed in all the works of his hands.*'[122] Created beauty is a revelation of *true beauty*, which is not sensory but is rather spiritual. For Bavinck, the 'true beauty' of which earthly beauty is a revelation is 'God's splendor'. It is God's Godness on display. We should not miss the significant epistemic implications in this claim. Bavinck consistently upholds Calvin's conviction that the Scriptures (i.e., special revelation) serve as spectacles through which all general revelation is to be viewed and understood.[123] If earthly beauty is general revelation of 'God's splendor', and if Bavinck (and Calvin) are correct in their belief that special revelation translates and interprets general revelation, then the special revelation of 'God's splendor' is *epistemologically* necessary for a *legitimate* understanding and interpretation of all earthly beauty. This is exactly where Bavinck goes with his argument: 'The acknowledgement of this spiritual beauty

---

122. Bavinck, 'Of Beauty and Aesthetics,' 250. Von Hildebrand, *Beauty in the Light of the Redemption*, 57, makes a similar point, making use of the same Platonic categories and parting ways with Platonism and joining the Christian tradition at the same conceptual fork in the road.

123. John Calvin, *Institutes of the Christian Religion*, (Peabody, MA: Hendrickson, 2008), Book I:14:1. See also Thiago Machado Silva, 'Scripture as Revelation in Herman Bavinck's Theology,' *Puritan Reformed Journal* 10, no. 1 (2018): 154-71.

is even the prerequisite for maintaining beauty in its supersensory reality and for doing justice to the truth that both natural and artistic beauty are independent revelations of beauty.'[124] In other words, without the 'prerequisite' understanding of beauty in an ultimate and spiritual sense (i.e., beauty as 'God's splendor'), natural and artistic beauty cannot be explained or justified in any ultimate sense.

This foundational understanding of Bavinck's belief about revelation in general, and beauty as revelation in particular, becomes important for informing his later claim that 'An aesthetics from below must precede an aesthetics from above.'[125] Taken in an unqualified sense, such a statement could seem to communicate that an aesthetics from below instructs an aesthetics from above (i.e., that earthly beauty must shape one's understanding of divine beauty). However, Bavinck means not to communicate the *epistemological* or *authoritative precedence* of a 'from below' aesthetics but rather its *experiential precedence*. Earthly beauty is experienced *first*. Indeed, the aesthetics that takes experiential precedence (i.e., an aesthetics 'from below'), according to Bavinck, actually functions to catapult human beings to an aesthetics that takes epistemological and authoritative precedence (i.e., an aesthetics 'from above' – 'God's splendor'). That is its purpose, its telos. Note:

> Even though philosophy and metaphysics have been greatly dishonored for a time, the unsatisfying results of empirical research have finally made it necessary to go from the sensory to the suprasensory and to find there a solution for the problems about the origin, essence, and purpose of things that arise in the human spirit. Aesthetics also rises immediately above the empirical if it wants to know what beauty is, why some things affect us aesthetically, and what the foundation of aesthetic appreciation is.[126]

In other words, the 'empirical' or experiential aesthetic 'from below' has a teleological purpose to direct one's attention to an aesthetic 'from above' (i.e., special revelation of 'God's splendor').[127]

---

124. Bavinck, 'Of Beauty and Aesthetics,' 250.

125. Ibid., 253.

126. Bavinck, 'Of Beauty and Aesthetics,' 253.

127. Bavinck describes this process by pointing to the 'longing deep in every human heart' stirred up by an aesthetics from below, the satisfaction of which is found in God's glory – an aesthetics from above.

If the final word on aesthetics rests not in the special revelation of 'God's splendor' (which, as we will see in chapter 3, finds its revelatory zenith in the redemptive work of Jesus Christ), it is incomplete – our contemplation of beauty begins 'from below', but it cannot stay there.[128] 'From below' beauty always inevitably points to the 'from above beauty', and it necessarily presents itself as ectypal – it refuses to be ultimate. From God's harmony, then, all earthly harmony extends. His beauty is the fountain, created beauty is the stream.

Conclusion

In this chapter I have raised the need for more theological-aesthetic work in the Reformed tradition from a distinctly systematic perspective. In the remaining pages of this volume I address this need in part by developing a theological-aesthetic *soteriology*. We began – with the help of Hans Urs von Balthasar – by distinguishing 'aesthetic theology' from 'theological aesthetics', noting how the former amounts to anthropocentric projection – a presumptive conflation of the Creator-creature distinction – while the latter amounts to keeping theology true to the word (i.e., *theological* theology). We then took a sampling of figures throughout the church's history who have made beauty a topic of theological contemplation (Gregory of Nyssa, Augustine of Hippo, Anselm of Canterbury, Thomas Aquinas, Martin Luther, John Owen, Jonathan Edwards, Herman Bavinck, Karl Barth, and Hans Urs von Balthasar), simply to allow them to lend their voice to justify this project. Their collective witness rings out: *the beauty of the divine should occupy most reverent theological contemplation.* I then sketched a definition of beauty, in which beauty is identified as a transcendental property, and thus as an attribute of God, manifested economically as an aspect of His glory revealed. We are now prepared to put some legs on the central thesis listed above, starting with where this chapter leaves off: the essence of God.

In the next chapter, I elaborate on the metaphysics of divine beauty, focusing centrally on God's Triune simplicity. We then take note of the biblical relationship between God's 'glory' and divine beauty.

---

128. Bavinck spends a considerable amount of space on this point that an 'empirical aesthetic' is insufficient for having the final word on aesthetics in 'Of Beauty and Aesthetics,' 250-51.

Chapter 2 concludes by developing the idea of revelation in general in order to further develop the idea of divine revelation of *beauty* in particular (specifically, we mark out the relationship between divine incomprehensibility and revelation, via divine accommodation).

In chapter 3 I continue to develop the idea of God's revelation of divine beauty and highlight its apex: the incarnation of Christ. Here I consider Christology and will examine how the revelation of the whole Christ (i.e., His person *and* work) relates to God's Triune beauty. The fourth chapter will serve as something of a caveated excursus – here I mark out regeneration and faith from a God's-eye view in order to distinguish what follows from similar-sounding, though crucially different, conceptions (specifically, Jonathan Edwards on one hand and Roman Catholicism on the other).

Chapter 5 constitutes the meat of this project's central thesis. In this chapter we consider divine beauty in relation to regeneration and saving faith. With the eyes of faith, restored and recreated by the Spirit of God, the believer beholds the beautiful glory of God in the face of Jesus Christ. And in chapter 6 we consider how the eyes of faith that began to behold the beauty of Christ at conversion continue to do so in sanctification and, finally, the beatific vision. We shall see, therefore, that Christ's ineffable, immutable beauty – the beauty of the Lord – anoints every step of the *ordo salutis*, adorning what is true and good in the sinner's transformation into sainthood with divine loveliness.

CHAPTER TWO

The Metaphysics of Divine Beauty

So they call him the beloved and the yearned-for since he is beautiful and good, and, again, they call him yearning and love because he is the power moving and lifting all things up to himself, for in the end what is he if not Beauty and Goodness, the One who of himself reveals himself, the good procession of his own transcendent unity?

PSEUDO-DIONYSIUS[1]

Introduction: Christian Theology vs. Metaphysics?

To begin a chapter in a work of systematic theology with 'the metaphysics of' is, in the estimation of some, to pick a fight. One of the more curious features of modern theology is its antipathy towards metaphysics. Indeed, Kevin Hector does anything but beat around the bush in positing this very idea, as is obvious from the title of his work, *Theology without Metaphysics: God, Language, and the Spirit of Recognition*.[2] This is nothing new for the broader philosophical and theological world, as

---

1. Pseudo-Dionysius, *The Classics of Western Spirituality, Pseudo-Dionysius, The Complete Works*, trans. Colm Luibheid, ed. Paul Rorem (London, SPCK, 1987), para. 113 and 114, pp. 82-3.

2. Kevin Hector, *Theology without Metaphysics: God, Language, and the Spirit of Recognition* (New York: Cambridge University Press, 2011). For a thorough and devastating response to this work, see John R. Betz, 'Theology without Metaphysics? A Reply to Kevin Hector,' *Modern Theology* 31, no. 3 (2015): 488-500.

many have pointed out.[3] It is not at all surprising to see the heroes of this present work, for example, contrasted with names like Kant, Hegel, Nietzsche, Barth, Heidegger, Derrida, Wittgenstein, Dorner, Moltmann, and Pannenburg.[4] The more surprising critics of metaphysics are those among the ranks of the Reformation's progeny. While the Reformers themselves were retrievers of the Great Tradition and her classical Trinitarian God, their heirs – evangelical scholarship – seem to think little of their inherited legacy. For example, T.F. Torrance contrasts what he calls a 'metaphysical conception' with what he portrays as the more biblical option, i.e., a 'powerful soteriological approach to the doctrine of God'.[5] John Feinberg suggests that deciding 'what to do about the classical conception of God that has been handed down through centuries of church history' is a pressing question. Rather than simply *worshiping* this God, Feinberg suggests that 'process theologians' and 'openness of God advocates' have challenged this inherited conception of God in such 'thought provoking ways' that 'a substantial overhaul and reconstruction' of the classical God 'seems more than appropriate'.[6]

This suspicion toward metaphysics is often attributed to a prioritization of the Scriptures over philosophy.[7] Hart helpfully depicts the position:

---

3. E.g., see Stanley J. Grenz and Roger E. Olson, *20th Century Theology: God and the World in a Transitional Age* (Downers Grove, IL: InterVarsity Press, 1997); Hart, *The Beauty of the Infinite*; David Bentley Hart, *The Experience of God: Being, Consciousness, Bliss* (New Haven, CT: Yale University Press, 2013); Kelly M. Kapic and Bruce L. McCormack, eds., *Mapping Modern Theology: A Thematic and Historical Introduction* (Grand Rapids, MI: Baker Academic, 2012); Kevin J. Vanhoozer, *Is There a Meaning in This Text? The Bible, the Reader, and the Morality of Literary Knowledge*, Landmarks in Christian Scholarship (Grand Rapids, MI: Zondervan, 2009); Dolezal, *All That Is in God*; Dolezal, *God without Parts*.

4. Betz is helpful in his lay of the land in 'After Heidegger and Marion: The Task of Christian Metaphysics Today,' *Modern Theology* 34, no. 4 (2015): 569-70. I agree with Charles Taylor's assessment that the common assumption that this development in theology was the unavoidable destiny of humanity's evolution is false. For Taylor's full argument, see Taylor, *A Secular Age*.

5. T. F. Torrance, *The Christian Doctrine of God: One Being Three Persons* (New York: T&T Clark, 2001), 248, quoted in Steven J. Duby, *God in Himself: Scripture, Metaphysics, and the Task of Christian Theology* (Downers Grove, IL: IVP Academic, 2019), 135.

6. John S. Feinberg, *No One Like Him: The Doctrine of God* (Wheaton, IL: Crossway, 2001), xxv-xxvi.

7. This is what Paul R. Hinlicky is after when he proposes a 'positive account of the divine attributes' over and against what he calls the 'metaphysical account' – he goes

Immutability, impassibility, timeless – surely, many argue, these relics of an obsolete metaphysics lingered on in Christian theology just as false belief and sinful inclinations linger on in a soul after baptism; and surely they always were fundamentally incompatible with the idea of a God of election and love, who proves himself God through fidelity to his own promises against the horizon of history, who became flesh for us (was this not a change, after all, in God?) and endured the passion of the cross out of pity for us .... This is why so much modern theology keenly desires a God who suffers, not simply with us and in our nature, but in his own nature as well; such a God, it is believed, is the living God of Scripture, not the cold abstraction of a God of the philosophers; only such a God would die for us.[8]

The dichotomy (i.e., the God of the Bible vs. the God of the philosophers) is easy to present when 'metaphysics' is discussed with 'an essentially univocal definition', as Betz points out, which can 'then serve the purpose of narrative caricature. Cast in theological terms, metaphysics can then be seen transgressing the temple precincts, storming into the sanctuary and audaciously attempting to lay hold of God in the Holy of Holies.'[9] Critics of metaphysics may prefer Scripture over philosophy, but Scripture itself does not seem to welcome this dichotomy.[10] As Betz points out elsewhere, 'an intelligible account of the Christian faith cannot do without *some kind* of metaphysics, inasmuch as it cannot fail to address the question and meaning of being.'[11] The doctrine of God's eternal transcendence was destined to make its way into the church's confession, irrespective of Greek philosophy, the moment Genesis 1:1 was written: 'In the beginning, God created the heavens and the earth.'

This sentence, located at the very beginning of God's Word, is a concise treatise that grounds all of metaphysics. 'In the beginning' – that is, in front of time itself – 'God' – ontologically existing independent of anything or anyone – 'created' – out of whatever co-existed with

---

on to note how his 'positive' biblical account 'declines the corresponding doctrine of analogy in favor of univocity'. Paul R. Hinlicky, *Divine Simplicity: Christ the Crisis of Metaphysics* (Grand Rapids, MI: Baker Academic, 2016), 16.

8. Hart, *The Beauty of the Infinite*, 159.

9. Betz, 'Theology Without Metaphysics?,' 495.

10. Even the closely related dichotomy of presumptuous and speculative 'natural theology' versus a biblical conception of 'special revelation' is false. Cf., Duby, *God in Himself*, 67.

11. Betz, 'After Heidegger and Marion,' 568.

Him, that which was *nothing* – 'the heavens and the earth' – that is, everything that exists besides Himself. These few words place God as the ontological center of the cosmos and as such make Him metaphysically definitional.[12] 'Creation thus is without foundations,' remarks David Bentley Hart; 'it attends God, possessing no essence apart from its character as a free and open utterance within the infinity of his self-utterance.'[13]

For 'the heavens and the earth' to be ontologically derivative upon God means we can only understand each fact therein, most fundamentally, in its relation to God.[14] No single fact of this universe has existential autonomy – all things are from and through and to the Trinity (Rom 11:36). 'We cannot raise ourselves higher and dominate the constitutive structure,' writes Henri Blocher, 'we cannot subsume it under an all-embracing notion of being. It involves a real duality, non-symmetrical: absolute independence on one side, total dependence on the other.'[15] God is definitional, which means that the Creator-creature distinction runs all the way through. It is expressed ontologically with the doctrine of *creatio ex nihilo*, and it also has an epistemological corollary (i.e., Creator-knowledge is 'archetypal' while creature-knowledge is 'ectypal')[16] and a linguistic corollary (i.e., Creator-language is 'univocal', and creature-language is 'analogical').

---

12. This is a particularly common point made by Cornelius Van Til. E.g., 'Every fact in the universe is what it is by virtue of the place that it has in the plan of God.' Cornelius Van Til, *The Defense of the Faith*, 3rd ed. (Phillipsburg, NJ: Presbyterian and Reformed, 1967), 204. His language of 'in the plan of God' might strike some as nominalist, especially when taken together with Van Til's seeming wholesale rejection of 'natural theology'. Though a careful reading of his essay 'Nature and Scripture' should put that accusation to rest, even if he comes down on Aquinas a bit too sharply. See Cornelius Van Til, 'Nature and Scripture,' in *The Infallible Word: A Symposium by the Members of the Faculty of Westminster Theological Seminary*, ed. Ned Bernard Stonehouse and Paul Woolley, 2nd ed. (Phillipsburg, NJ: Presbyterian and Reformed, 1967).

13. Hart, *The Beauty of the Infinite*, 252.

14. See Herman Bavinck, *Reformed Dogmatics Vol. 2: God and Creation*, ed. John Bolt, trans. John Vriend (Grand Rapids, MI: Baker Academic, 2003), 407.

15. Henri Blocher, 'Divine Immutability,' in *The Power and Weakness of God: Impassibility and Orthodoxy*, ed. Nigel M. de S. Cameron, Edinburgh Conference in Christian Dogmatics (Edinburgh: Rutherford House, 1990), 16.

16. On the distinction between God's archetypal knowledge and creaturely ectypal knowledge, see especially Franciscus Junius, *A Treatise on True Theology: With the Life of Franciscus Junius*, trans. David C. Noe (Grand Rapids, MI: Reformation Heritage, 2014), 107-20.

In this chapter we dwell at length on the Creator side of this Creator-creature divide so as to establish the theological foundation of transcendental beauty. We first define classical Trinitarian theism over against the social trinitarian models that have pervaded modern (specifically, evangelical) theology in recent years. We then illustrate divine simplicity with its corollary, divine immutability. God's life in Himself – that is, within this Triune, immutable simplicity – brims with *beatitude*. Thus, we see how God's *aseity* is the ground for creation and subsequently how God's *a se beatitude* is the foundation for creation's beauty. Finally, with revelation squarely in view, we relate beauty back to the divine essence by noting the biblical relationship between God's holiness, goodness, and beauty.

Tracing Classical Trinitarian Theism

One of the more stubbornly persistent narratives regarding the formation of Trinitarian theology in the early church trades in the 'East vs. West' paradigm.[17] At the risk of oversimplifying, we might summarize the narrative as positing that the East reasoned from the three divine persons to the one divine essence, whereas the West reasoned from the one divine essence to the three divine persons.[18] The net result of this narrative depicts Augustine as the quintessential Western father, fixated with Christianizing the inert, simple, and impersonal God of the philosophers, while the Cappadocians (Gregory of Nazianzus, Gregory

---

17. Lewis Ayers notes, 'The presence of these narratives may not seem to need demonstration, but it is important to note the wide range of theologians in whom they are present.' Lewis Ayres, *Nicaea and Its Legacy: An Approach to Fourth-Century Trinitarian Theology* (New York, NY: Oxford University Press, 2009), 384, n. 3. He then lists the following as example of works that propagate this narrative: Robert W Jenson, *Systematic Theology* (New York: Oxford University Press, 2001); Colin E. Gunton, *The Promise of Trinitarian Theology*, 2nd ed. (New York: T&T Clark, 2003); Jürgen Moltmann, *History and the Triune God: Contributions to Trinitarian Theology*, trans. John Bowden (New York: Crossroad, 1992); Wolfhart Pannenberg, *Systematic Theology*, trans. G. W. Bromiley, vol. 1 (Grand Rapids, MI: Eerdmans, 1991); Catherine Mowry La Cugna, *God for Us: The Trinity and Christian Life* (New York, NY: Harper Collins, 2006); William Placher, *A History of Christian Theology: An Introduction* (Philadelphia: Westminster, 1983); David Brown, *The Divine Trinity* (London: Duckworth, 1985).

18. This seems to be the general thrust of Cornelius Plantinga's essay, 'Social Trinity and Tritheism,' in *Trinity, Incarnation and Atonement: Philosophical and Theological Essays*, ed. R. J. Feenstra and Cornelius Plantinga (Notre Dame, IN: University of Indiana Press, 1984).

of Nyssa, and Basil of Caesarea) contrive of a divine community, legitimizing the current upsurge of social Trinitarians as their posterity.[19] Such a conceptualization can 'serve as quasi-confessional statements, indicating existing options, setting out a narrative that results in a range of possibilities for current use,'[20] which, at best, would seem to leave wide room for serious differences about how to conceptualize Trinitarian theology, all within the confines of Nicene orthodoxy. In reality, such narratives are a historical fiction. While the East and West would eventually find sharp disagreement regarding the *filioque*,[21] recent works from authors such as Khaled Anatolios and Lewis Ayres show that the Eastern and Western fathers built their Trinitarian theology on divine simplicity.[22]

This misunderstanding regarding the differences (and, importantly, the lack thereof) between the western fathers and the Cappadocians has provided conceptual justification for unhelpful articulations of Trinitarian theology. Anatolios notes some such articulations when he traces three trajectories in modern Trinitarian doctrine: the first 'concedes Kant's objection that trinitarian doctrine says nothing intelligible about God's intrinsic being'. This trajectory is plagued with an 'inner contradiction' of attempting 'the baffling balancing act of insisting both on the urgent meaning of trinitarian doctrine for Christian existence as revelatory of God's "being as communion" and yet cautioning that trinitarian doctrine does not really mean that God *is* Trinity.'[23] The second trajectory insists that Trinitarian doctrine 'asserts that the form of God's salvific self-communication to the world coincides with the form of divine being'.[24] Whereas the former trajectory renders Trinitarian doctrine unintelligible because of God's sheer transcendence,

---

19. E.g., John D. Zizioulas, *Being as Communion: Studies in Personhood and the Church* (Crestwood, NY: St. Vladimir's Seminary Press, 1985). See particularly his criticisms of Augustine.

20. Ayres, *Nicaea and Its Legacy*, 385.

21. See Robert Letham, *The Holy Trinity: In Scripture, History, Theology, and Worship*, rev. and exp. ed. (Phillipsburg, NJ: P&R Publishing, 2019), chaps. 10–11.

22. For example, Ayers, *Nicaea and Its Legacy*, 362-63. See also, Khaled Anatolios, *Retrieving Nicaea: The Development and Meaning of Trinitarian Doctrine* (Grand Rapids, MI: Baker Academic, 2018).

23. Anatolios, *Retrieving Nicaea*, 3.

24. Ibid., 4.

this one renders Trinitarian doctrine irreverent and pitiable because of sheer immanence.[25] The third trajectory Anatolios summarizes as 'the search for an appropriate creaturely analogy'.[26] This is apparent on the popular level in a far more conspicuous way than on the scholarly level.[27] In contrast to these trajectories, Anatolios contends rather that

> the development of fourth-century trinitarian orthodoxy indeed involve claims to objectively refer to the positive reality of the Triune God – yet not in the manner of a direct cognitive correspondence between propositions and their referents but rather by way of prescribing 'authoritative rules of discourse, attitude, and action' that ensures the success of the act of referring to the Triune God.[28]

Nicaea, in other words, was not strictly about defining the edges for who gets to be in or out of orthodoxy, but rather, on a far deeper level, it was concerned with theological methodology: laying out instructions for how to talk about the Trinity. If this is a fair assessment of fourth-century Trinitarian orthodoxy, it contradicts what we might add to Anatolios' list as a fourth trajectory: the trajectory to conceptualize Trinitarian theology along social lines.[29] This novel method for developing Trinitarian theology has its extreme proponents, but it also finds a home in evangelical circles.[30]

Both strands of Social Trinitarianism find their commonality in (a) refusing to begin with divine simplicity, (b) projecting human society back up onto the Godhead, (c) conceptualizing divine 'persons' as 'three centers

---

25. This, of course, has been cemented in Karl Rahner's 'rule': 'The "economic" Trinity is the "immanent" Trinity and the "immanent" Trinity is the "economic" Trinity.' Karl Rahner, *The Trinity*, 3rd ed. (Tunbridge Wells, Kent: Burns & Oates, 1986), 22.

26. Anatolios, *Retrieving Nicaea*, 4.

27. E.g., Michael Reeves, *Delighting in the Trinity: An Introduction to the Christian Faith* (Downers Grove, IL: IVP Academic, 2012), 10.

28. Anatolios, *Retrieving Nicaea*, 8.

29. See Jürgen Moltmann, *The Trinity and the Kingdom: The Doctrine of God* (Minneapolis: Fortress, 1993); Leonardo Boff, *Trinity and Society* (Eugene, OR: Wipf & Stock, 2005); Zizioulas, *Being as Communion*; La Cugna, *God for Us*.

30. Wayne A. Grudem, *Systematic Theology: An Introduction to Biblical Doctrine* (Grand Rapids, MI: Zondervan, 1994); Bruce A. Ware and John Starke, *One God in Three Persons: Unity of Essence, Distinction of Persons, Implications for Life* (Wheaton, IL: Crossway, 2015); Bruce A. Ware, *Father, Son, and Holy Spirit: Relationships, Roles, and Relevance* (Wheaton, IL: Crossway, 2005).

of consciousness and will', (d) defining persons in terms of relationships and roles, (e) the erasure of the distinction between God's life *ad intra* and work *ad extra*, and (f) finding within the Trinity a program for social theory (whether one is motivated to find egalitarian relationships of equality, or hierarchical relationships of authority and submission, both insist on the same essential move).[31] Most evangelicals who push their brand of Social Trinitarianism insist that they do so as Nicene-affirming theologians, but if Anatolios is correct in his assessment that fourth-century orthodoxy was concerned with prescribing a normative grammar and logic for conceptualizing trinitarian theology, then the attempt to stand within the Nicaean tradition while defining trinitarian theology along the lines of a divine society – agreement or unity of will – will not do.[32] For example, to attempt to define the relationship between the three Persons and one divine essence in terms of roles of authority and submission is to step away from the Nicaean tradition, which defines it very differently.[33] Pointedly, this means that, regardless of what creed one agrees to on paper, it is manifestly non-Nicene to assert that 'in God there are three distinct centers of self-consciousness, each with its proper intellect and will.'[34] Indeed, such an articulation sits comfortably beside Arius, Asterius, Eusebius, and Eunomius on the *primary* question that divided Nicaea from its opposers: *Is the Trinity defined in terms of unity of will or unity of being?*[35]

---

31. This list is taken from Matthew Barrett's recent work, *Simply Trinity: The Unmanipulated Father, Son, and Spirit* (Grand Rapids, MI: Baker, 2021). For a devastating critique of both these strands of social Trinitarianism, see chapters 2 and 7.

32. An influential way for evangelicals to do just this is to attempt to define Trinitarian theology proper by the roles and relationships among the persons in the divine economy in terms of authority and submission. This position is known as 'Eternal Functional Subordination' (EFS). See, Ware, *Father, Son, and Holy Spirit*; Ware and Starke, *One God in Three Persons*; Grudem, *Systematic Theology*. For an examination of Ware's Trinitarian methodology, see Scott Harrower, 'Bruce Ware's Trinitarian Methodology,' in *Trinity Without Hierarchy: Reclaiming Nicene Orthodoxy in Evangelical Theology*, Michael F. Bird and Scott Harrower (Grand Rapids, MI: Kregel, 2019).

33. Contra Michael J. Ovey, particularly in his essay 'True Sonship – Where Dignity and Submission Meet: A Fourth-Century Discussion,' in Ware and Starke, *One God in Three Persons*, 127-54.

34. J. P. Moreland and William Lane Craig, *Philosophical Foundations for a Christian Worldview* (Downers Grove, IL: IVP Academic), 583.

35. Anatolios, *Retrieving Nicaea*, 42-98. Note, I am not here saying that Moreland and Craig are Arians or Eunomians or adherents to any ancient heresy whatsoever, only

The classical Trinitarian answer to this question is uniform: the Father, Son, and Spirit share the same divine essence. The Trinity's unity is a unity of *being*. The simple, indivisible divine essence, one with its will and power, subsists eternally not in terms of distinct actions or roles but rather in terms of the personal properties of paternity (the Father is unbegotten), filiation (the Son is eternally begotten), and procession (the Spirit proceeds, or is spirated from, the Father and the Son).[36] I substantiate this claim with a brief sampling from Athanasius, Hilary, and the Cappadocians (Basil and the two Gregorys).

For Athanasius (c. 293–373), the simplicity of God is inextricably tied to one's conception of the Creator's relationship with creation. Thus, before he establishes God's *simplicity*, he establishes His *singularity*: on the Creator side of the Creator-creature divide sits one being,

> For we must not think there is more than one ruler and maker of Creation: but it belongs to correct and true religion to believe that its Artificer is one, while Creation herself clearly points to this. For the fact that there is one Universe only and not more is a conclusive proof that its Maker is one. For if there were a plurality of gods, there would necessarily be also more universes than one. For neither were it reasonable for more than one God to make a single universe, nor for the universe to be made by more than one, because of the absurdities which would result from this.[37]

Importantly, while Athanasius' pen is aimed here against pagan polytheism ('the gods of the poets are no gods … and … the God we worship and preach is the true One, Who is Lord of Creation and Maker of all existence'[38]), he uses the same rationale to debunk Arianism, which posits that the Son is a created sub-creator.[39] From this articulation of

---

that the above comment seems to agree with these heretics that the Trinity's unity is a unity, first and foremost, of will – three distinct wills and centers of self-consciousness in agreement. I am comfortable, however, with insisting that such an articulation, if consistently upheld, cannot avoid tritheism.

36. Shockingly, Feinberg, *No One Like Him: The Doctrine of God*, 492, not only denies the doctrines of eternal generation and eternal procession as necessary, he positively suggests that 'it seems wisest to *abandon* the doctrines of eternal generation and eternal procession' (emphasis added).

37. Athanasius, *Contra Gentes* §39.1.

38. Ibid., 40.1.

39. At best, this teaching renders creation the product of two creators; at worst, it denies that God Himself is the Creator. See Anatolios, *Retrieving Nicaea*, 116.

creation's origin in a single source, Athanasius immediately begins to implicate the Son in this work: 'Who then is this, save the Father of Christ, most holy and above all created existence, Who like an excellent pilot, by His own Wisdom and His own Word, our Lord and Savior Christ, steers and preserves and orders all things, and does as seems to Him best?'[40] Athanasius thus defends the divinity of the Son, in part, by pronouncing a 'complete break between the created and the uncreated' and then identifying Christ (and the Spirit) squarely on the uncreated 'side', where only one divine Being resides.

According to Athanasius, it is no contradiction to say that the creation is the work of one God and yet to attribute it to the work of the Father and the Son.[41] This is because, and only because, the Son shares the exact same essence as the Father, their relationship of paternity and filiation being eternal and intrinsic to the single divine essence.[42] Indeed, Athanasius will go on to defend the Son's divinity *on the grounds* of simplicity, since 'a primal Monad that produces an Image of itself amounts to a Trinity that comes into being through addition and is thus liable also to subtraction.'[43] 'Who will presume to say that the radiance is unlike and foreign to the sun?' reasons Athanasius,

> rather who, thus considering the radiance relatively to the sun, and the identity of the light, would not say with confidence, 'Truly the light and the radiance are one, and the one is manifested in the other, and the radiance is in the sun, so that whoso sees this, sees that also?' but such a oneness and natural property, what should it be named by those who believe and see aright but Offspring one in essence? and God's Offspring what should we fittingly and suitably consider, but Word, and Wisdom, and Power? Which it were a sin to say was foreign to the Father, or a crime even to imagine as other than with Him everlastingly.[44]

Note the differing hermeneutic between Athanasius and his opponents. Their conflict was not over some proof texts versus others. Rather, it was

---

40. Athanasius, *Contra Gentes* §40.2.

41. 'He being the Power of God and Wisdom of God causes the heaven to revolve, and has suspended the earth, by His own nod' (Athanasius, *Letters to Serapion on the Holy Spirit* 40.5).

42. See Athanasius, *Against the Arians*, 27.36.

43. Anatolios, *Retrieving Nicaea*, 108.

44. Athanasius, *De Decretis*, chap. 5.24.

a matter of what inferences one makes from certain passages in which the Son describes his relationship to the Father. The tendency for his opponents was to project the economic relationship into the Godhead,[45] but Athanasius reasoned *from* the divine economy *to* the divine essence with the aid of metaphysical categories. The net result for Athanasius is the conception of a genuine distinction between the Father and Son, but one that is eternally *rooted* in divine simplicity.

Hilary of Poitiers (315–368) reasoned in much the same way. J. Warren Smith observes that 'from the perspective of pro-Nicene bishops, such as Hilary of Poitiers, there is an absolute dividing line between creatures and the eternal, divine Creator. The Son must fall on one side or the other of that divide.'[46] 'God and God, true God and true God, true God the Father and true God the Son,' wrote Hilary, 'must be confessed as One true God, by unity of nature and not by confusion of persons.'[47] Such a statement well highlights Hilary's enigmatic way of speaking, but while some might be tempted to dismiss his phrasing as tautologic, he is making an important point about how we understand the Trinity. The Persons of the Trinity, according to Hilary, are mutually interpretative, such that to abstract one from another is to make one unconscionable: 'For it is only by the witness mutually borne that the Son can be known through the Father, and the Father through the Son.'[48] While our understanding of the distinct persons is clarified by one another, however, the understanding their mutual testifying yields is an essential unity of nature, since, 'the unity of light with light is a unity of nature, not unbroken continuation.'[49]

---

45. This is a mistake shared by proponents of EFS. Whereas fourth-century heretics projected the economy back up onto the Godhead in terms of temporality ('from the Father' = 'the Father existed and then created the Son'), EFS does the same in terms of relationships of authority and submission. 'Therefore, the different functions that we see the Father, Son, and Holy Spirit performing are simply outworkings of an eternal relationship between the three persons, one that has always existed and will exist for eternity' (Grudem, *Systematic Theology*, 250).

46. J. Warren Smith, 'The Fourth-Century Fathers,' in *The Oxford Handbook of the Trinity*, ed. Gilles Emery and Matthew Levering, Oxford Handbooks (New York: Oxford University Press, 2011), 119.

47. Hilary, *De Trinitate*, 11.8.

48. Ibid., 11.26.

49. Ibid., 11.12.

Perhaps unsurprisingly, in this case, as in the case of disputes over the same passages of Scripture, Hilary squared off with his opponents not with fundamentally different philosophical concepts but with different definitions for the same concepts. Whereas Hilary argued *for* a classical Trinitarianism with the doctrine of divine simplicity, his opponents attempted to use the same doctrine to argue against it. Speaking to his Arian interlocutor, Hilary acknowledges, 'You, in order to banish the birth and the Only-begotten from the faith of the Church, confront us with an unchangeable God, incapable, by His nature, of extension or development.'[50] He goes on to elaborate their charge:

> For you attribute, most godless of heretics, the birth of the Son to an act of creative will; you say that He is not born from God, but that He was created and came into existence by the choice of the Creator. And the unity of the Godhead, as you interpret it, will not allow Him to be God, for, since God remains One, the Son cannot retain His original nature in the state into which He has been born.[51]

How does Hilary respond? After a lengthy parenthetical prayer, where he asks for self-control and forgiveness for his 'excess of indignation',[52] he shows how the idea that divine simplicity contradicts a unity of essence assumes what it sets out to prove. Divine simplicity, the idea that the one divine being is not composed of parts, only poses a problem for Trinitarian theology if one assumes that the Persons of the Trinity differ in being (i.e., they are parts). But for Hilary, divine simplicity poses no threat to his Trinitarian theology, since he insists that the divine persons share not the same *kind* of nature but rather the *same identical* nature. Eternal generation, for Hilary, does not challenge the simplicity of the divine nature, because the divine nature is eternally characterized by it: 'For God is not born from God by the ordinary process of a human childbirth;' writes Hilary, 'this is no case of one being issuing from another by the exertion of natural forces. That birth is pure and perfect and stainless; indeed, we must call it rather a proceeding forth than a birth.'[53] He goes on to say,

---

50. Ibid., 11.17.

51. Ibid., 11.18.

52. Ibid., 11.19-21.

53. Ibid., 11.35.

For it is One from One; no partition, or withdrawing, or lessening, or efflux, or extension, or suffering of change, but the birth of living nature from living nature. It is God going forth from God, not a creature picked out to bear the name of God. His existence did not take its beginning out of nothing, but went forth from the Eternal; and this going forth is rightly entitled a birth [or generation], though it would be false to call it a beginning. For the proceeding forth of God from God is a thing entirely different from the coming into existence of a new substance.[54]

Not leaving any of these theological convictions behind, Ayres points how later on in the same work Hilary shifts his 'X from X' argument to a more mature and unambiguous articulation, which gives 'increased attention to the metaphysical relationships between natures, powers, and operations' and 'a dense account of the ways in which the Son does the same work as the Father and must therefore be considered as equal in nature.'[55] From beginning to end, in increasing degrees of precision, Hilary stresses how the mutually clarifying persons of the Godhead point invariably to an essential unity of nature.[56]

It is common to group Gregory of Nazianzen (329–390), Basil of Caesarea (330–379), and Gregory of Nyssa (335–394) together under the moniker of 'the Cappadocians'. Unless we are careful, this can inadvertently give the idea that their theology was monolithic.[57] What ties 'the Cappadocians' together is not a uniform expression of theology but rather a 'web of family and regional ties' and their 'shared significant involvement in the defense of some fundamental theological principles'.[58] What specifically justifies The Cappadocian grouping here is their shared involvement in defending pro-Nicene orthodoxy:[59] despite

---

54. Ibid., 11.35.

55. Ayres, *Nicaea and Its Legacy*, 182.

56. 'For Hilary, the more we understand the character of a perfect birth ... the more we understand the mysterious unity and distinction of [the Father and Son]' (ibid., 184).

57. We might say that unlike the Trinity, their unity was not *essential* but was rather *accidental*. Thus, Ayers, *Nicaea and Its Legacy*, 250, cautions, 'Nevertheless, we should not allow these similarities to hide from us their differences.'

58. Ibid., 250.

59. Ayres, ibid., 236, lists the three principles that identity a theology as fully 'pro-Nicene' as '1. A clear vision of the person and nature distinction, entailing the principle that whatever is predicated of the divine nature is predicated of the persons equally and understood to be one .... 2. Clear expression that the eternal generation of the Son

the fact that they conceptualized the doctrine with slight variations,[60] their pro-Nicene rebuttal to 'the Eunomians' was built upon divine simplicity. Basil, for example, notes how 'all conceptions and terms proper to God are held of equal honor one with another, though the fact that there is no discrepancy in the signification of the subject .... [W]hatever terms you use, the thing that is signified by them all is one.'[61] This point is routinely made in the works of the Cappadocians: the various qualities attributed to each divine person (i.e., 'goodness,' 'wisdom,' 'power,' etc.) are constituent not of the person per se but rather to the single, undivided nature. 'Since the divine nature is not composed of parts,' writes Basil, 'union of the persons is accomplished by partaking of the whole.'[62] Or consider this stark affirmation of divine simplicity in Gregory of Nazianzen's fifth theological oration:

> To us there is One God, for the Godhead is One, and all that proceedeth from Him is referred to One, though we believe in Three persons. For One is not more and another less God; nor is One before and another after; nor are They divided in will or parted in power; nor can you find here any of the qualities of divisible things; but the Godhead is, to speak concisely, undivided in separate Persons; and there is one mingling of Light, as it were of three suns joined to each other. When then we look at the Godhead, or the First Cause, or the Monarchia, that which we conceive is One; but when we look at the Persons in Whom the Godhead dwells, and at Those Who timelessly and with equal glory have their being from the First Cause – there are Three Whom we worship.[63]

One might be tempted to fault Nazianzen here for the misleading analogy of 'three suns', but this would be a failure to appreciate all that he says on the subject. The feebleness of human language is an ever-present limitation for Gregory, and he is more than aware that discussing the Trinity forces him to use analogies that seem to contradict

---

occurs within the unitary and incomprehensible divine being; 3. Clear expression of the doctrine that the persons work inseparably.'

60. E.g., see Andrew Radde-Gallwitz, *Basil of Caesarea, Gregory of Nyssa, and the Transformation of Divine Simplicity* (New York: Oxford University Press, 2009).

61. Basil, *Letters,* Trans. Roy J. Defferrari (Cambridge, MA: Harvard University Press, 1986), 59, as quoted in Roger E. Olson and Christopher A. Hall, *The Trinity* (Grand Rapids, MI: Eerdmans, 2002), 35.

62. Basil, *On the Holy Spirit*, 18.23.

63. Gregory of Nazianzen, *Orations*, 31.14.

one another on their face in order to approximate that which cannot be comprehensively described.[64] Regardless of the paradoxical language, the exclamation point with this metaphor of 'Light' and 'Sun' and 'suns' is placed squarely upon divine simplicity: 'But each of these Persons possesses Unity, not less with that which is United to it than with itself, by reason of the identity of the Essence and power. And this is the account of the Unity, so far as we have apprehended it.'[65]

Whereas Basil and Gregory of Nazianzen emphasized divine simplicity primarily in terms of their shared attributes, constituent with the divine nature, 'Nyssa ... demonstrates an account of the unity of divine nature and power that is considerably more developed than Basil's.'[66] For Nyssa, the divine Person's shared, undivided, and simple essence can be seen not only from their sharing in the names attributed to the divine nature but also by the inseparable operations of their divine action:

> If, then, we see that the operations which are wrought by the Father and the Son and the Holy Spirit differ one from the other, we shall conjecture from the different character of the operations that the natures which operate are also different. For it cannot be that things which differ in their very nature should agree in the form of their operation: fire does not chill, nor ice give warmth, but their operations are distinguished together with the difference between their natures. If, on the other hand, we understand the operation of the Father, the Son, and the Holy Spirit is one, differing or varying in nothing, the oneness of their nature must needs be inferred from the identity of their operation.[67]

Nyssa thus boldly invites his readers to consider the manifold work of the Trinity and draw the conclusion that the Persons' nature(s) differ if indeed their 'operations' differ in substance. He can do this because he is quite confident that a careful consideration of these 'operations' will conclude with an affirmation of their essential unity:

> The Father, the Son, and the Holy Spirit alike give sanctification, and life, and light, and comfort, and all similar graces. And let no one attribute the power of sanctification in an especial sense to the Spirit, when he hears the

---

64. E.g., Gregory of Nazianzen, *Orations*, 29.9.

65. Ibid., 31.16.

66. Ayres, *Nicaea and Its Legacy*, 250.

67. Gregory of Nyssa, *On the Holy Trinity*, 328.

Savior in the Gospel saying to the Father concerning His disciples, 'Father, sanctify them in Thy name.' So too all other gifts are wrought in those who are worthy alike by the Father, the Son, and the Holy Spirit: every grace and power, guidance, life, comfort, the change to immortality, the passage to liberty, and every other boon that exists, which descends to us.[68]

In contrast to a strong 'East vs. West' conception, then, the Cappadocians sound remarkably like the Western fathers – even, Augustine[69] – on the question of divine simplicity and the doctrine's role within Trinitarianism's defense of monotheism. Consider this summary of divine simplicity in Augustine:

> Wherefore nothing in Him is said in respect to accident, since nothing is accidental to Him, and yet all that is said is not said according to substance. For in created and changeable things, that which is not said according to substance, must, by necessary alternative, be said according to accident. For all things are accidents to them, which can be either lost or diminished, whether magnitudes or qualities; and so also is that which is said in relation to something, as friendships, relationships, services, likeness, equalities, and anything else of the kind; so also positions and conditions, places and times, acts and passions. But in God nothing is said to be according to accident, because in Him nothing is changeable; and yet everything that is said, is not said according to substance.[70]

Thus, while each of the fathers observed here certainly offered their own unique contributions, the tendency to centralize divine simplicity in their Trinitarian thought was uniform. If this much is true, the pedagogical strategy of constructing Trinitarian theology from the grounds of the divine Persons' relationships (as is the case for social Trinitarians, including the evangelical stripe of EFS/ERAS), as opposed to constructing Trinitarian theology from the grounds of the one undivided essence, is a historical aberration. J. V. Fesko summarizes the point nicely:

> Though social trinitarianism, which posits three separate centers of consciousness within the Trinity and has therefore opened itself to the criticism of tritheism, may be popular in our own day, in the bigger picture

---

68. Gregory of Nyssa, *On the Holy Trinity*, 362.

69. Augustine, *De Trinitate*, Book VI:4.6.

70. Augustine, *De Trinitate,* Book V:5.6.

of the church's nearly 2,000 years of reflection upon the doctrine it is a small and arguably insignificant trend.[71]

Excursus: Metaphysics and Hermeneutics

Antipathy towards metaphysics cannot but come with revisions of the Trinity. This is because the way one develops Trinitarian theology depends on the way one reads Scripture, and the way one reads Scripture depends on one's metaphysic. The fruit of Nicene Trinitarianism is the product of a particular kind of tree – a way of reading Scripture with roots deep in a particular kind of metaphysic.[72] Once those roots are cut, one ought not expect the same fruit.

Much of the blame (or credit, depending on one's position) for uprooting biblical hermeneutics from its natural, metaphysical soil goes to Johann P. Gabler (1753–1826). Gabler is often cited as the founding father of Old Testament (OT) theology, though this designation is a misnomer. For nearly two millennia Christians were doing theology with their whole Bibles, which included the OT. Further, the charge that Christian theology simply viewed the OT as fodder for systematic articulations until the nineteenth century, when Gabler and his ilk liberated the text from unruly dogmatic plunderers, is unfounded.[73]

71. J. V Fesko, *The Trinity and the Covenant of Redemption* (Ross-Shire, UK: Christian Focus, 2016), 175 n. 96.

72. What Craig Carter calls 'Christian Platonism', or what Hans Boersma calls 'Sacramental Ontology', or what Charles Taylor calls the 'enchanted world', or what G.K. Chesterton and C. S. Lewis might simply summarize as 'the medieval view', unsuitable for 'men without chests'. See Carter, *Interpreting Scripture with the Great Tradition*; Hans Boersma, *Scripture as Real Presence: Sacramental Exegesis in the Early Church* (Grand Rapids, MI: Baker Academic, 2017); Taylor, *A Secular Age*; C. S. Lewis, *The Abolition of Man* (San Francisco, CA: HarperCollins, 2001); G. K. Chesterton, *In Defense of Sanity: The Best Essays of G.K. Chesterton*, ed. Dale Ahlquist, Joseph Pearce, and Aidan Mackey (San Francisco: Ignatius, 2011).

73. Contra Robin Routledge, who claims the 'dogmatic view' of yesteryear 'saw the Bible as the repository of eternal, fixed, propositional truths.' Robin Routledge, *Old Testament Theology: A Thematic Approach* (Downers Grove, IL: IVP Academic, 2012), 39. One gets a similar impression from reading authors like Gerhard Hasel, who almost conceptualize the emergence of Old Testament theology – as a distinctive discipline – as the Old Testament's liberation from the shackles of dogmatics. See, Gerhard F. Hasel, *Old Testament Theology: Basic Issues in the Current Debate*, 4th ed. (Grand Rapids, MI: Eerdmans, 1991), 13. Even evangelical works more friendly to dogmatics, like Paul House's, seem to give a similar impression: 'Before this era the Old Testament's theological statements were systematized with New Testament statements to describe

Consider, for example, Irenaeus (A.D. 130–200), whose articulation of redemptive history is remarkably similar to contemporary biblical theologies.[74] The progressive nature of divine revelation was a functional concept long before the rise of the specialized discipline we now call 'biblical theology'. Gabler and those who followed him were, however, groundbreaking in their *approach* to Scripture and in particular to OT studies. It is true that until then no Christian attempted to understand the OT as disconnected from the Christ event. Gabler was unabashed in his attempt to read the OT in such a way as to untangle the enterprise from dogmatics.[75] The axiomatic ground zero for Gabler was Enlightenment rationalism – a prioritization of the self-authenticating authority of human reason, which brought with it a rejection of dogmatic authority from Scripture, the church, or anywhere else. The truly liberated reader of Scripture was not he who stood beneath it in humility but he who stood above it in judgment. Hasel illustrates this point well when he sums up Gabler's proposal with three methodological considerations:

> (1) Inspiration is to be left out of consideration .... (2) Biblical theology has the task of gathering carefully the concepts and ideas of the individual Bible writers .... (3) Biblical theology as a historical discipline is by definition obliged to 'distinguish between the several periods of the old and new religion.'[76]

This last point implies something important about Gabler's assumptions regarding the biblical authors. Since religion is by nature in flux, rather

---

Christian doctrine .... In Calvin and Aquinas the Old Testament contributes to a larger theological scheme but does not appear as a separate theological voice.' Paul R. House, *Old Testament Theology* (Grand Rapids, MI: IVP Academic, 2018), 13.

74. See Irenaeus, *Proof of the Apostolic Preaching*, trans. Joseph P. Smith (New York: Paulist, 1990). Another example of pre-Gabler biblical theology can be found in John Owen, *Biblical Theology*, 5th ed. (Morgan, PA: Soli Deo Gloria Publications, 2012).

75. Although such a move is itself the furthest thing from dogmatically neutral. 'Underlying Gabler's approach was a rationalistic view of the inspiration and reliability of Scripture' (House, *Old Testament Theology*, 16). He decries, for example, the readiness to mix completely diverse things, for instance the simplicity of what they call biblical theology with the subtlety of dogmatic theology; although it certainly seems to me that the one thing must be more sharply distinguished from the other than has been common practice up to now. See Johann P. Gabler, 'An Oration on the Proper Distinction Between Biblical and Dogmatic Theology and the Specific Objectives of Each,' in Ollenburger, *Old Testament Theology: Flowering and Future*, 501.

76. See Gerhard F. Hasel, *Old Testament Theology: Basic Issues in the Current Debate*, 4th ed. (Grand Rapids, MI: Eerdmans, 1991), 16-17.

than communicating divine speech the biblical record reflects the biblical authors' context in history. It is purely descriptive. For Gabler, it is ultimately up to the reader to determine if what the biblical authors say about God is true or not. There was coherence for Gabler in this respect: if, for example, one ought to read Paul's letters like any other letter, Paul must be treated as any other person, and his authority regarding the contents of his letters must be measured like anyone else's.

In this respect, Gabler has had no shortage of followers. From a historical perspective, there was no going back from this rationalist impulse.[77] So much of biblical theology's history to this point has been an effort to build off, and in many cases redeem, early works by men such as Gabler and Wellhausen.[78] However, one must ask the question, *why ought biblical theologians to attempt such a project?*[79] These men set the trajectory of a budding discipline in a direction that accords with philosophical presuppositions (i.e., the epistemology of rationalism, the metaphysics of Kant, and the history of Hegel) that does not abide orthodoxy. Might it be a fool's errand to rebuild the house of divine revelation on a foundation of rationalism? The fruit of this kind of effort is lamentable – as in the case of the embarrassing persistence of the belief that the Pentateuch was written six hundred years after the Prophets.[80] With Hegel in the basement, even edifices as lovely as Eichrodt's OT

---

77. Even those who move away from rationalism and toward empiricism or Kantian idealism maintain the spirit of rationalism in the sense that they are set to declare resolute epistemological independence from any authority akin to divine revelation. This is true, generally speaking, for Old Testament theology up to the mid-twentieth century (as can be seen below). Though there are notable exceptions, such as Gustav Oehler (1812–1872) and Johann Christian Konrad von Hofmann (1810–1877). See Ollenburger, *Old Testament Theology: Flowering and Future*, 9.

78. For a fantastic summary of the views and impact of Wellhausen, see Mark S. Gignilliat, *A Brief History of Old Testament Criticism: From Benedict Spinoza to Brevard Childs* (Grand Rapids, MI: Zondervan, 2012), 57-76.

79. In this respect I would share similar sentiments for the value of Gabler and Wellhausen in particular that Carter, *Interpreting Scripture with the Great Tradition*, 250, expresses toward the Enlightenment in general. Responding to D. A. Carson's essay, 'Theological Interpretation of Scripture: Yes, But ...,' in *Theological Commentary: Evangelical Perspectives*, ed. R. Michael Allen (New York: T&T Clark, 2011), Carter writes, 'Carson wonders if anybody has a kind word for the poor maligned Enlightenment. I am afraid I do not.'

80. A view originating merely from a Hegelian view of history, which insists that the theological formulations found in the Pentateuch are too sophisticated to be early. E.g., House, *Old Testament Theology*, 21.

theology cannot help but wobble. 'This tendency,' House rightly observes, 'left theologians trying to overcome the limitations Wellhausen's views represent while still embracing Wellhausen's presuppositions.'[81]

The splintering of Christian academic disciplines itself is the consequence of a philosophical stream (i.e., the anthropocentric rejection of biblical authority, which sprung up from the Enlightenment) that produces a particular view of biblical theology: that of Gabler's.[82] Specialization, for all its value, tends to foster a myopia in this setting that prevents practitioners from recognizing an important, though oft forgotten reality: the dividing walls of disciplines are not fixed laws of nature but are erected by philosophies. In this landscape, the default approach to the OT, for example, assumes that fairness to the discipline requires that consideration of other disciplines (e.g., NT studies, dogmatics) be relegated to the position of mere application.[83]

Because of this stalemate of dissenting philosophical trajectories, the current landscape of biblical theology is more radically diverse now than ever before. Sticking closely to the script of Gabler and others who wrote with Enlightened pens are figures like James Barr (1924–2006),[84] Ernst Käsemann (1906–1998),[85] and Udo Schnelle.[86]

---

81. Ibid.

82. For a case study on this 'splintering of Christian academic disciplines' via Enlightenment scholarship, see Michael C. Legaspi, *The Death of Scripture and the Rise of Biblical Studies* (New York: Oxford University Press, 2010).

83. E.g., Köstenberger and Patterson write, 'unlike systematic theology, which tends to be abstract and topical in nature, biblical theology aims to understand a given passage of Scripture in its original setting.' Andreas J. Köstenberger and Richard Duane Patterson, *Invitation to Biblical Interpretation: Exploring the Hermeneutical Triad of History, Literature, and Theology* (Grand Rapids: Kregel, 2011), 698. Cf., D. A. Carson, 'Systematic Theology and Biblical Theology,' in *New Dictionary of Biblical Theology*, ed. T. Desmond Alexander and Brian S. Rosner (Downers Grove, IL: InterVarsity Press, 2000), 103.

84. See James Barr, *The Concept of Biblical Theology: An Old Testament Perspective* (Minneapolis: Fortress, 1999); James Barr, *The Semantics of Biblical Language* (Eugene, OR: Wipf & Stock, 2004).

85. 'The one biblical theology, going from a single root and maintaining itself in unbroken continuity, is wish-fulfilment fantasy.' Ernst Käsemann, 'The Beginnings of Christian Theology,' in *Journal for Theology and the Church*, 6 (1969):17-46, 18, quoted in Matthew Barrett, *Canon, Covenant and Christology: Rethinking Jesus and the Scriptures of Israel* (Downers Grove, IL: IVP Academic, 2020), 13.

86. 'A 'biblical theology' is not possible because: (1) the Old Testament is *silent* about Jesus Christ, [and] (2) the resurrection from the dead *of one who was crucified* cannot be

Balancing between Enlightenment methodology and evangelical theology stand the likes of Walter C. Kaiser Jr.[87] and Robin Routledge.[88] And blazing a trail back to pre-modern convictions of the Bible's canonical context are figures like Brevard Childs (1923–2007),[89] John H. Sailhamer (1946–2017),[90] G. K. Beale,[91] and Peter Gentry and Stephen Wellum.[92] It is unsurprising that Barr was perhaps Childs's most vocal critic, with near mirror opposite convictions about methodology. Whereas Childs emphasized the Bible's final canonical form as the ideal context for biblical interpretation[93] – stressing a conceptual and organic unity – Barr thought that 'By and large there is no internal coherence' to Scripture.[94] Barr believed that attempting to synthesize biblical theology was a dubious enterprise, requiring imposition to join together what was naturally torn asunder.[95] Attempting a middle way between the two, Walter Kaiser represents the majority evangelical position.[96] Disagreeing with the conclusion

---

integrated into any ancient system of meaning formation.' Udo Schnelle, *Theologie des Neuen Testaments* (Göttingen: Vandenhoeck & Ruprecht, 2007), 52, quoted in Ibid.

87. See Walter C Kaiser, *The Uses of the Old Testament in the New* (Eugene, OR: Wipf and Stock, 2001); Walter C. Kaiser and Moisés Silva, *Introduction to Biblical Hermeneutics: The Search for Meaning*, rev. and exp. ed. (Grand Rapids, MI: Zondervan, 2007).

88. See Routledge, *Old Testament Theology*.

89. See Brevard S. Childs, *Old Testament Theology in a Canonical Context*, 2nd ed. (Philadelphia: Fortress, 1994); Brevard S. Childs, *Biblical Theology of the Old and New Testaments: Theological Reflection on the Christian Bible* (Minneapolis: Fortress, 1993).

90. See John H Sailhamer, *Introduction to Old Testament Theology: A Canonical Approach* (Grand Rapids, MI: Zondervan, 1995).

91. G. K. Beale, *A New Testament Biblical Theology: The Unfolding of the Old Testament in the New* (Grand Rapids, MI: Baker Academic, 2011).

92. Peter John Gentry and Stephen J. Wellum, *Kingdom through Covenant: A Biblical-Theological Understanding of the Covenant*, 2nd ed. (Wheaton, IL: Crossway, 2018).

93. See, for example, Childs, *Biblical Theology of the Old and New Testaments*, 8. However, we hasten to express exasperation over Childs' baffling infatuation with source criticism, as seen in Brevard S. Childs, *Myth and Reality in the Old Testament* (Eugene, OR: Wipf & Stock, 1962).

94. James Barr, 'Biblical Theology,' in *Interpreter's Dictionary of the Bible, Supplementary Volume*, ed. K. Crim and V. P. Furnish (New York,: Abingdon, 1976), 109.

95. See Barr, *The Concept of Biblical Theology*, 242.

96. E.g., Walter C. Kaiser, 'The Single Intent of Scripture,' in *The Right Doctrine from the Wrong Texts? Essays on the Use of the Old Testament in the New*, ed. G. K. Beale (Grand Rapids: Baker, 1994); Richard N. Longenecker, 'Negative Answer to the Question 'Who Is the Prophet Talking About?' Some Reflections on the New Testament's Use of the

of Barr but maintaining the method, Kaiser seems to bite the hand that feeds him – beginning with the theological presupposition of the Bible's unity while banishing theological presuppositions. It is unfortunate that Kaiser represents the dominant evangelical view. In the contest of the methodologies above, there is a clear victor for what *should* be considered the 'evangelical' option, as long as the contest is no matter of personal preference or historical happenstance but rather theological and philosophical consistency.

If history is strictly accidental, for example, then a discussion about 'biblical theology' is destined for a dead end.[97] Matthew Barrett is exactly right when he states that 'biblical theology is a fool's errand if the biblical scholar rids himself or herself of a commitment to the canon's intrinsic, conceptual unity.'[98] Reading the canon as an organic whole is an impossibility with a naturalist reading of history.[99] A view of history that attributes disinterested events occurring in sequence to no superintending cause is at odds with a view of history that attributes all events to divine providence.[100] Further, there is no way to be at odds with a providential view of history and functionally

---

Old" in Beale, *The Right Doctrine from the Wrong Texts?*; Longenecker, *Biblical Exegesis in the Apostolic Period*, 2nd ed. (Grand Rapids, MI: Eerdmans, 1999); Routledge, *Old Testament Theology*. Routledge, *Old Testament Theology*, 43, deals with typology in a similar 'don't try this at home" spirit as Longenecker: 'It has been widely assumed, however, that the NT generally follows contemporary interpretative approaches, which were valid within a particular context, but which do not provide us with a normative method.' This is what Carter, *Interpreting Scripture with the Great Tradition*, calls 'methodological naturalism'.

97. An example of this view of history can be seen in Robert L. Webb, 'The Historical Enterprise and Historical Jesus Research,' in *Key Events in the Life of the Historical Jesus: A Collaborative Exploration of Context and Coherence*, ed. Darrell L. Bock and Robert L. Webb (Grand Rapids, MI: Eerdmans, 2010).

98. Barrett, *Canon, Covenant and Christology*, 25.

99. With such a reading of history, the canon 'must be the result of contingent (and to some extent, arbitrary) human processes." Michael J. Kruger, *The Question of Canon: Challenging the Status Quo in the New Testament Debate* (Downers Grove, IL: InterVarsity Press, 2013), 38.

100. See John Webster, 'Providence' in *Reformed Catholicity: The Promise of Retrieval for Theology and Biblical Interpretation*, ed. R. Michael Allen and Scott R. Swain (Grand Rapids, MI: Baker Academic, 2015), 148-64; John Webster, 'Providence' in *Mapping Modern Theology: A Thematic and Historical Introduction*, ed Kelly M. Kapic and Bruce L. McCormack (Grand Rapids, MI: Baker Academic, 2012), 203-26; Herman Bavinck, *Reformed Dogmatics Vol. 2*, 374-88.

remain on good terms with the Christian theistic metaphysic.[101] The God who is not governing the cosmos and writing the story of human history is not the Christian God of Scripture. Craig Carter is right to observe, 'Inspiration is made up of both miracle and providence. In his miraculous acts, God introduces novelty into history in the form of special revelation.'[102] This much may be affirmed by many an evangelical scholar. The problem with the present discussion, however, is the possibility for such scholars to inadvertently smuggle 'naturalistic metaphysics into interpretation under the guise of "historical method".'[103] V. Philips Long describes such scholars as 'typified by an incongruency between the methods they employ and the model of reality they embrace.'[104] Unfortunately, the balancing act of personally embracing one vision of reality and methodologically assuming another can only exist for so long before the scales tip in one direction or another – 'history as accident' cannot harmonize with Christian theism any more than 'history as providence' can harmonize with metaphysical naturalism. Thus,

> Theistic and, more specifically, Christian thinkers should make certain that the historical method they employ is robust enough to take into account a full set of Christian background beliefs, including for instance belief in God as history's 'master semiotician,' belief in the Bible as revelatory of the divine character and divine activity, and so forth.[105]

Such a conception of history would categorize all events as revelation – either general or special – which does not eliminate the possibility, usefulness, or even necessity of historical background study but rather

---

101. Not only is the secular view of human history incompatible with the Christian worldview, it does historical injustice to the Bible's human authors themselves. The moment one is restrained to consider only the Bible's human authors' intentions, one faces the reality of considering the intention of a human author who sees himself within the larger context of God's progressive revelation. Nothing about the human author's historical context is *a-theological*, so an *a-theological* consideration of the human author's historical context is self-defeating.

102. Carter, *Interpreting Scripture with the Great Tradition*, 42.

103. Ibid., 13.

104. V. Philips Long, '"Competing Histories, Competing Theologies?" Reflections on the Unity and Diversity of the Old Testament('s Readers),' in *The Enduring Authority of the Christian Scriptures*, ed. D. A. Carson (Grand Rapids, MI: Eerdmans, 2016), 381-82.

105. Long, 'Competing Histories,' 377.

situates it all theologically.[106] Such a theologically minded philosophy of history alone makes the evangelical doctrine of inspiration even possible – a nonnegotiable for the whole concept of biblical theology.

This theologically minded philosophy of history, as a subset of a thick, theological metaphysic, was the ecosystem of the Nicene fathers. It was this ecosystem that produced classical Trinitarianism, and as such, classical Trinitarianism cannot rightly survive elsewhere.

And this point brings out this excursus' relevance on the thesis of this book. The contemplation of Beauty we are concerned with here arises from a particular way of reading the Scriptures – and, indeed, of reading *reality* – that jives well with one kind of metaphysic (the realist, enchanted, pre-modern one), and bristles against another (the non-realist, disenchanted, modern one). We may even go so far as to say that the metaphysical outlook behind the modern hermeneutic critiqued above is *incompatible* with (or is at least *inhospitable* to) this book's thesis. But the metaphysic that allows for the kind of pre-modern exegesis that produces Nicene trinitarian dogma is a foundation sturdy enough to build our thesis on. In the spirit of self-conscious retrieval, then, finding our bearings comfortably within the Nicene tradition, we now consider the metaphysics of divine beauty within the context of Triune *simplicity*.

Triune Simplicity[107]

The erosion of the doctrine of divine simplicity in the minds of theologians is nothing new. In 1932 Louis Berkhof observed that 'in recent works on theology the simplicity of God is seldom mentioned. Many theologians positively deny it, either because it is regarded as a purely metaphysical abstraction, or because, in their estimation, it conflicts with the doctrine of the Trinity.'[108] Even further back, writing in 1897, Bavinck similarly notes how 'the attribute of God's simplicity almost totally disappeared from modern theology. Its significance is no longer understood, and sometimes it is vigorously opposed, ... especially

---

106. Two excellent examples of what this looks like in action are Daniel Strange, *Their Rock Is Not Like Our Rock: A Theology of Religions* (Grand Rapids, MI: Zondervan, 2014); and Jeffrey Jay Niehaus, *Ancient Near Eastern Themes in Biblical Theology* (Grand Rapids, MI: Kregel, 2008).

107. This section is largely indebted to Dolezal, *God without Parts*, chap. 1.

108. Louis Berkhof, *Systematic Theology* (Edinburgh: Banner of Truth Trust, 1998), 62.

on the following two grounds: it is a metaphysical abstraction and inconsistent with the doctrine of the Trinity.'[109]

Unfortunately, little has changed. Ronald Nash objected to the doctrine on the grounds that humans 'could never have knowledge of any absolutely simple essence'.[110] By 'knowledge', Nash means *univocal* knowledge, and he is, of course, correct. What is incorrect is the consequent conclusion that *no* knowledge – even analogical knowledge granted via accommodation – is therefore possible for humans. Thus, Nash concludes that the metaphysical abstraction of ontological simplicity falters against the realism of biblical revelation, and 'Christian theologians have no good reason to affirm the doctrine of divine simplicity'.[111] This sentiment is shared by John Feinberg, who dismisses the notion that God has only essential properties (with no accidental ones) as a self-evident absurdity,[112] and J. P. Moreland and William Lane Craig, who boldly assert that the doctrine of divine simplicity is a 'radical doctrine that enjoys no biblical support and even is at odds with the biblical conception of God'.[113]

When evangelical detractors of the classical doctrine of divine simplicity voice their objection, they do so in the name of being 'biblical'.[114] The doctrine, they insist, is not biblically prescribed. Of course, the veracity of such a statement depends entirely on what 'biblical' means in this instance. Though never adequately argued for, the assumed definition turns out to be a form of crude biblicism – on its face, God's activity throughout Scripture does not seem to reveal a God who is pure act, identical with His attributes, so the doctrine must be rejected. Historically, this has never been a problem for affirmers of the doctrine (which either means that contemporary revisionists who

---

109. Herman Bavinck, *Reformed Dogmatics Vol. 2: God and Creation*, ed. John Bolt, trans. John Vriend (Grand Rapids, MI: Baker Academic, 2003), 114.

110. Ronald H. Nash, *The Concept of God* (Grand Rapids, MI: Zondervan, 1983), 85.

111. Ibid., 95.

112. Feinberg, *No One Like Him*, 330-35.

113. Moreland and Craig, *Philosophical Foundations for a Christian Worldview*, 524.

114. This is axiomatically assumed by Nash, *The Concept of God*, 95, when he insists the doctrine of divine simplicity 'leads to the odd suggestion that the biblical teaching that God is characterized by a variety of distinct properties is wrong.' This is stated even more explicitly by Hinlicky, *Divine Simplicity*, 19, who insists that 'this stance is in impossible contradiction to the witness of Scripture'.

have abandoned the doctrine in recent history are the first truly 'biblical' theologians in the Church's history, or that their functional definition of what constitutes as 'biblical' is insufficient).

This is because, as composite and finite beings who are incapable of comprehending ontological simplicity or infinity, we would expect for creatures to receive no other kind of revelation than the accommodated kind, which reveals the simple God in (what we perceive as) one distinct attribute at a time.[115] This incapability is not owing to any accidental deficiency, as if comprehension of simplicity could somehow be acquired if only the creature gained some special perspective. If the simple God is to reveal Himself to composite creatures at all, it must be by virtue of accommodation. The fact that Scripture reveals God in this way is not a hindrance to the doctrine of divine simplicity; it is an essential feature thereof.

This means the doctrine of divine simplicity's status as a 'biblical' doctrine is not determined by asking if it appears to contradict God's economic activity[116] but rather by asking (1) if the doctrine is a necessary implication of other biblical doctrines, and (2) if its denial harms other biblical doctrines. That both questions must be answered in the affirmative follows from Scripture's depiction of God's independence.

As out of fashion as it is to appeal to the *Tetragrammaton* for affirming God's aseity, the metaphysical implications from Exodus 3:14-15 are difficult to deny.[117] Yahweh sends Moses to the Israelites as the herald of 'I Am', and this designation carries a self-authenticating authority. Who is this God for whom Moses speaks? The one who *is* – the one who needs nothing or no one to validate His authority since it necessarily follows from the plentitude of His being. 'In the context,' writes Dolezal, 'God is reassuring Moses and Israel of His all-sufficiency to accomplish the great work of their redemption from Egypt. He grounds this perfect covenantal sufficiency on the perfect sufficiency of His own being, denoted by His name.'[118] Subject to none, all things depend on God (Rom 11:36). He is the 'Mighty One, God the LORD' (Ps 50:1), and His absolute independence He positively declares: 'For every beast of the

---

115. See Bavinck, *Reformed Dogmatics Vol. 2*.128.

116. Strictly speaking, it does not, so long as the distinction between His life in Himself and His actions in creation is maintained.

117. See Michael Allen, 'Exodus 3,' in Allen, *Theological Commentary*, 25-40.

118. Dolezal, *All That Is in God*, 46.

forest is mine, the cattle on a thousand hills I know all the birds of the hills, and all that moves in the field is mine. If I were hungry, I would not tell you, for the world and its fullness are mine' (Ps. 50:10-12).

At first it may not appear as though losing the doctrine of divine simplicity is of any consequence to the doctrine of divine aseity. But if God is composed of parts on any level, His essence is necessarily indebted to something other than *Himself*, and He is no longer independent.[119] This point is often lost in translation. One can dismiss the charge that denying simplicity denies God's independence if one understands the charge to be saying something about the physical – but it is not just His composition of body parts that would make God indebted to not-God; it is rather the composition of *anything*. If God is composed of substance and accidents, for example, one could affirm that apart from accidental attributes, He still exists, but not that He exists as the fullest and most well-rounded version of Himself. His accidental properties, which are non-identical with Him, would make Him more Himself than He would otherwise be. Or, as another example, if God is composed of *act* and *potentiality*, one could affirm that apart from the actualization of a potentiality, God still exists, but not that He exists as the most active version of Himself – some state of affairs outside of God's own existence is needed for Him to realize His fullest actuality.[120]

What of the tricky business of the Trinity, then? In truth, the charge that the doctrine of divine simplicity contradicts the doctrine of the Trinity manages to distort both simplicity *and* Trinitarianism. As we saw from the fathers cited above, the distinction between essence and person was intended from the very beginning to harmonize Scripture's teaching of the three distinct persons with its teaching of divine simplicity.[121] Without divine simplicity, there is no Nicene Trinitarianism to name. This, again, is lost in translation when the word 'person' is read with modern undertones.

If one affirms that God is one in 'essence' and three in 'persons', and 'persons' are read as 'distinct centers of will and consciousness', then it

---

119. See Bavinck, *Reformed Dogmatics Volume 2*, 176.

120. Francis Turretin, *Institutes of Elenctic Ttheology*, 3 vols. ed. James T Dennison, trans. George Musgrave Giger (Philippsburg, NJ: P&R, 1997), 1:III.vii.

121. See, e.g., Peter Liethart's essay, 'No Son, No Father: Athanasius and the Mutuality of Divine Personhood,' in Bird and Harrower, *Trinity Without Hierarchy*, 109-21.

would appear that composition in God is necessary – at the very least, at the level of these persons (i.e., God is composed of His three persons). But if 'persons' are understood rather as 'hypostases ... which are modes distinguishing indeed the persons from each other',[122] then the notion of *essential composition of 'persons'* is rendered nonsensical. The three persons, while their economic activity reveals and reflects their *eternal* relations of origin, are distinguished only by how they 'modify' and 'characterize' the one undivided essence (i.e., the Father is characterized by His unbegotten-ness and His eternally generating the Son, the Son by His eternal generation, and the Father's and Son's eternal spiration of the Spirit, who eternally proceeds from the Father and Spirit). In other words, the one undivided, simple essence of God is characterized by eternally unbegotten, generating, procession.[123] There is no essence apart from the Father begetting the Son, and the Father and Son spirating the Spirit. Eternal generation and procession *is* the eternal act of the divine essence. Bavinck summarizes well:

> Now, the divine being is not composed of three persons, nor is each person composed of the being and personal attributes of that person, but the one uncompounded (simple) being exists in three persons. Every person or personal attribute is not distinguishable in respect of essence but only in respect of reason.[124]

That this undivided, simple essence is what the persons share (and not what they collaboratively constitute) is a necessary inference from Trinitarian grammar of Scripture. 'Radiance' (Heb 1:3), 'Image' (Col. 1:15), 'Wisdom,' and 'Word' (Prov. 8, cf., John 1:1-18) all signify a common constituency.[125] Introducing composition between the divine Light and His 'radiance', for example, is not possible. They may be distinguished in a sense, but they constitute the single essential reality. As Webster puts it,

---

122. Turretin, *Institutes*, 1:III.vii.8.

123. See Webster, 'Trinity and Creation,' in *God Without Measure*, 87-88.

124. Bavinck, *Reformed Dogmatics Volume 2*, 177.

125. See, Barrett, *Simply Trinity*, chap. 6; also, Matthew Y. Emmerson, 'The Role of Proverbs 8: Eternal Generation and Hermeneutics Ancient and Modern,' Mark S. Gignilliat 'Eternal Generation and the Old Testament: Micah 5:2 as a Test Case,' D. A. Carson, 'John 5:26: *Crux Interpretum* for Eternal Generation,' and R. Kendall Soulen, '*Generatio, Processio Verbi, Donum Nominis:* Mapping the Vocabulary of Eternal Generation,' in *Retrieving Eternal Generation*, ed. Fred Sanders and Scott R. Swain (Grand Rapids, MI: Zondervan, 2017), 132-46.

'"begetting" must not be construed in terms of any ontological hiatus between begetter and begotten.'[126]

Aseity, Immutability, and Creation

If the divine essence is simple, then divine beauty is not a novelty introduced by God's artistry in creation. The beauty revealed in the created world correspondingly reflects God's essential beauty, which is a feature of His eternal beatitude. We may accentuate this point by highlighting the relationship between creation, God's immutability, and His aseity.

At first glance, the reality of creation itself seems to pose a problem for the doctrine of divine simplicity. How is one supposed to deny that God is composed of *act* and *potency* when the presence of a temporal creation seems to imply that God lacked the *actuality* of being 'Creator' until after He realized such potential in the act of *creatio ex nihilo*? Did God not change at one point from being a *potential* Creator to being an *actual* Creator? Does creation not flatly contradict divine simplicity's corollary doctrine, divine immutability? Insofar as we take the doctrine of divine immutability and the doctrine of *creatio ex nihilo* to be *biblical*, the answer must be 'no.'

That immutability has biblical precedence is clear from passages like Numbers 23:19; Malachi 3:6; James 1:17; and Hebrews 6:18, where God stakes His covenant promises upon His unchangeableness. Of course, no shortage of counterexamples exist that speak of God 'repenting' and 'regretting' and acting and reacting and moving toward His creatures in covenant. Critics of immutability do not hesitate to marshal such counterexamples against it.[127] Indeed, evangelical attempts to reformulate divine immutability are motivated by these very counterexamples.[128] However, historically, advocates for divine

---

126. Webster, 'Eternal Generation,' in *God Without Measure*, 33.

127. E.g., Bruce A. Ware, 'An Evangelical Reformulation of the Doctrine of the Immutability of God," *Journal of the Evangelical Theological Society*, 29 (1986): 431-46; Donald Macleod, *Shared Life: The Trinity and the Fellowship of God's People* (Ross-Shire: Christian Focus, 1994); Moreland and Craig, *Philosophical Foundations*; and John S. Feinberg, *No One Like Him*.

128. Ware, 'An Evangelical Reformulation." Cf., Bruce A. Ware, 'A Modified Calvinist Doctrine of God," in *Perspectives on the Doctrine of God: Four Views*, ed. Bruce A. Ware (Nashville, TN: B&H Academic, 2008), 91. Isaac A. Dorner makes this same point in

immutability have felt no need to ignore or minimize the reality of passages that seem to presuppose a certain kind of mutability in God. Thus, Herman Bavinck, the same theologian who can go so far as to say, 'If God were not immutable, he would not be God,'[129] can in the same breath grant, 'At first blush this immutability seems to have little support in Scripture.'[130]

How is the apparent biblical contradiction resolved? Bruce Ware, in a reformulation of the doctrine, proposes such a resolution is available in the distinction between God's ontological and ethical immutability on the one side and His relational mutability on the other.[131] This, however, is problematic, as James Dolezal points out, since 'it is incoherent to say that God is ontologically immutable while denying that He is absolutely immutable …. [E]very state of being, whether essential or nonessential [i.e., metaphysical or relational], is an ontological state.'[132] Instead, contra Ware's proposal, the classical response to the apparent contradiction is to 'regard these as yet further instances of the Bible's anthropomorphic (or anthropopathic) language, revealing something true about God … progressively under a modality (viz., change) that is improper to His plenitude of being.'[133] The so-called mutability passages do not intend to communicate any kind of metaphysical mutability on God's part (be it 'relational' or otherwise) but are rather highlighting certain immutable attributes with mutable language; such language accommodates human understanding. God uses mutable language to describe Himself to His creatures because mutable language is the only language they have.

In truth, every theological position must appeal to Scripture's analogical nature of language at some point or another. Objecting that the classical position gives short shrift to Scripture when appealing to such a concept in the face of passages that speak of God as if He were mutable is unwarranted. If one can call God's 'nostrils' anthropomorphic,

---

his important work, *Divine Immutability: A Critical Reconsideration*, trans. Robert R. Williams and Claude Welch (Minneapolis: Fortress, 1994), 180.

129. Bavinck, *Reformed Dogmatics Volume 2*, 154.

130. Ibid., 153.

131. Ware, 'An Evangelical Reformulation.'

132. Dolezal, *All That Is in God*, 26.

133. Ibid., 20.

why can one not call His 'repentance' anthropopathic?[134] The ontological Creator-creature distinction and its epistemological corollary (i.e., the archetypal-ectypal distinction of Creator-knowledge and creature-knowledge) necessitates a linguistic corollary: a distinction between univocal and analogical language (i.e., Creator-language is univocal, and creature-language is analogical). In a real sense, all our language about God is analogical, since God alone can speak of God (and to God) in an absolutely univocal sense. This means all His self-disclosure is accommodated and mediated through analogical speech. The burden of proof thus lies with the mutabilists to prove why passages describing God changing (even if only 'relationally', which, as Dolezal has shown, is an artificial qualifier) should have theological privilege for defining the doctrine of God over those that speak of God's inability to change. Indeed, the latter, by virtue of their remoteness to any creaturely experience, imply something closer to a self-disclosure of God's essence than the former.

In addition to enjoying biblical precedence, the doctrine of divine immutability is also logical. How could God change if not to His advantage or disadvantage? If God could stand to be advantaged or disadvantaged, He would not be the Bible's God (Ps. 50:12). This logic's snugness, however, is not intuitive in light of God's activity *ad extra*, which brings us back to the problem creation seems to pose on divine immutability, and subsequently on divine simplicity.

If God is unchangeable, how can He act in time? The traditional response to this quandary is found in the concepts of God's eternity and His 'divine ideas'.[135] These concepts relate thusly: 'divine ideas belong to God's simultaneously whole presencing (*totum esse praesens*) by which he is perfectly, intelligently, and creatively present to all things.'[136] Thus, as Bavinck explains, 'God is as immutable in his knowing, willing,

---

134. Paul Helm is instructive on this point: 'The Impossibility of Divine Passibility,' in *The Power and Weakness of God*, ed. Nigel M. de S. Cameron (Edinburgh: Rutherford House, 1990), 128-29, emphasis added.

135. This concept of 'divine ideas' is developed by Aquinas in *Summa Theologiae* Ia.14. Steven Duby also helpfully develops this point in 'Divine Immutability, Divine Action and the God-World Relation,' *International Journal of Systematic Theology* 19, no. 2 (2017): 144-62.

136. Matthew Levering, *Engaging the Doctrine of Creation: Cosmos, Creatures, and the Wise and Good Creator* (Grand Rapids, MI: Baker Academic, 2017), 55-56.

and decreeing as he is in his being …. Neither creation, nor revelation, nor incarnation (affects, etc.) brought about any change in God. No new plan ever arose in God.'[137] God's will, from eternity past, was to be Creator of, and economic Actor within, the cosmos. Though the analogical nature of language once again calls attention to itself: 'from' and 'past' and 'was' are unbecoming timebound words we now use to describe the timeboundlessness of God's eternity. Eternity, for creatures, is ultimately incomprehensible. Highlighted here is the 'difference between the Creator and the creature', which 'hinges on the contrast between being and becoming. All that is creaturely is in process of becoming.'[138]

Creatures do not have any experience of genuine interaction absent 'becoming'. For creatures, to interact is to become. Were an interaction not to yield a sense of change, we would consider such an interaction impotent, or such a creature deficient (or lifeless). Demanding that God change for His interaction with creation to be genuine, however, is an illogical projection; creaturely experience does not bind the Creator. Indeed the Creator-creature distinction seems to demand that, in any transaction between creature and Creator, the creature alone changes. God's inability to change in such an interaction is not owing to any deficiency in Him (relational or otherwise) but rather to a superabundance of sufficiency. 'God is unchangeable not because he is inert or static like a rock,' Thomas Weinandy points out, 'but for just the opposite reason. He is so dynamic, so active that no change can make him more active. He is act pure and simple.'[139]

If this much is true, then creation must be understood as existing *within* the context of God's *a se*, overflowing generosity. Much of this chapter has constituted a prolonged reflection of the Trinity because 'concepts developed in articulating the Christian doctrine of God, including the concept of aseity, are fitting insofar as they correspond

---

137. Bavinck, *Reformed Dogmatics Volume 2*, 154.

138. Ibid.156

139. Thomas G. Weinandy, *Does God Change? The Word's Becoming in the Incarnation* (Still River, MA: St. Bede's Publications, 1985), 79. Cf. Dolezal, *God Without Parts*, 86, 'In addition to ensuring that God is absolutely immutable in his being and essence, the DDS also makes certain that the doctrine of divine immutability is not misunderstood as teaching that God is somehow cold, inert, and lifeless.'

to the particular being of the Triune God in his self-moved self-presentation.'[140] A doctrine of aseity that is not uniquely Christian is a deficient doctrine of aseity. Once the doctrine is understood in Trinitarian terms, the concept extends beyond mere independence, if by independence one means unconditioned or undetermined by something else. It is not only that the Christian God needs nothing; rather, He needs nothing because in His Triune fullness – as Father, Son, and Holy Spirit – He constitutes the infinite plenitude of life and being. 'Aseity is not only the quality of being (in contrast to contingent reality) underived; it is the eternal lively plentitude of the Father who begets, the Son who is begotten, and the Spirit who proceeds from both.'[141]

As a temporal and contingent reality, creation owes its existence to the eternal Trinity. As such, creation is not a temporal product that somehow exists outside of the Trinity's infinitude. To suggest that creation intimates an additional or accidental characteristic of God (i.e., the 'accidental' name of 'Creator') is to get the relationship entirely backward; to do so is to attribute existential autonomy to creation. But creation, while 'not nothing', is what it is, and participates in the 'good of being' by nothing other than 'divine gift'.[142] 'What does creation out of nothing indicate about the relation of God and creatures?' asks Webster, 'Creation is an operation of generosity on the part of one who in his inner-trinitarian life is wholly realized, satisfied and at rest.'[143]

This signifies an asymmetrical participation of creation with the Triune God's eternal beatitude. Its asymmetrical form is crucial to emphasize, since what the creature experiences is not the *a se* state of the divine essence but rather, by virtue of the Trinity's generosity, a creaturely corollary. The Triune God does not participate in creation, as if He owed any aspect of Himself to creation, but He nevertheless grants that creation might participate in His beatitude.[144] 'All things that are dwell in the glory of God,' says Hart,

---

140. Webster, 'Life in and of Himself,' 14.

141. Ibid. 20.

142. Webster, '"Love is Also a Lover of Life": *Creatio Ex Nihilo* and Creaturely Goodness' in *God Without Measure*, 106.

143. Ibid., 107.

144. For a marvelous elaboration on Scripture's teaching on 'participation', see Duby, *God in Himself*, chap. 5.

and yet the glory of God becomes visible as a beauty among the world's beauties (Exod. 16:10; 24:16; 29:43; Num. 14:22; Deut. 5:24; 1 Kings 8:10; 2 Chron. 7:1-3; Ps. 97:6); when besought by Moses to show his glory, God answers, 'I will make my goodness (beauty, *tub*) pass by before thee, and I will proclaim the name of the LORD before thee' (Exod. 33:18-19).[145]

When it comes to beauty, this relationship, this 'analogy of being', can be seen from external expressions of divine beauty in the created order, as well as from the existential and subjective experience of beauty on the microlevel. An obvious biblical example of the former is found in Psalm 19:1-3: 'The heavens declare the glory of God, and the sky above proclaims his handiwork. Day to day pours out speech, and night to night reveals knowledge. There is no speech, nor are there words, whose voice is not heard.' Here the psalmist positively charges the reader to reason from creation's grandeur to the Creator's *glory* – insisting upon a real relationship between the two that is, in some sense, participatory. The telos of earthly beauty is 'the glory of God'. On this passage, Gregory of Nyssa writes:

> The heavens, showing the Maker's wisdom, practically shout with a voice, though silent, they declare the Creator's craftsmanship. We can hear the heavens teach us: 'O mortals, in looking on us and seeing our beauty and vastness, our incessant orbit with its orderly, harmonious movement, acting in one methodical direction, turn your thoughts to our Ruler! Through the beauty you see, envisage the beauty of the unseen Source!'[146]

Even more can be said about the relationship between *beauty* and God's beatitude. As we discussed in the previous chapter, 'what uniquely characterizes the subjectively experienced aspect of ... beauty ... is its effect of evoking pleasure or delight in the act of perceiving it.'[147] Beauty has an ineffable, self-authenticating character, such that its value is necessarily intrinsic rather than imposed from the outside. 'That characteristic to communicate delight as its own end,' observes Jonathan King, 'is correlative to the absolute self-delight that characterizes God's own eternal, internal, life as Father, Son and Sprit.'[148] This is Gregory of

---

145. Hart, *The Beauty of the Infinite*, 212.

146. Gregory, *Answers to Eunomius' Second Book*, 272-73.

147. King, *The Beauty of the Lord*, 58.

148. Ibid., 58-59.

Nyssa's very rationale in the fifth chapter of *The Great Catechism*: 'Thus, then, it was needful for man, born for the enjoyment of Divine good, to have something in his nature akin to that in which he is to participate.'[149]

Thus, '*the beauty of God ad extra as it is perceived and experienced by human beings is what most clearly evinces that perfection of beatitude and sense of delight that belongs to the Trinity ad intra*.'[150] 'Creation's being is God's pleasure,' says Hart, 'creation's beauty God's glory.'[151] It is no accident that the same patristic theologians who developed classical Trinitarianism (as described above) all come to agree on the analogous relationship between the Triune, harmonious glory of the Father, Son, and Spirit, creation's *beauty*, and the creature's *appreciation* (i.e., creaturely *beatitude*) for creation's beauty. They saw created beauty, and created beauty's aesthetic appreciation, as the fitting temporal corollary to the eternal, divine beauty of God's Triune beatitude. Thus 'beauty in the Christian intellectual tradition is most fundamentally a theological phenomenon – beauty has, that is, an inherent and essential association with God.'[152]

Bringing all themes together, by virtue of His simplicity, the eternal Triune God is perfectly, immutably, and gratuitously *of Himself*. As the eternal Father, Son, and Spirit, the Trinity is eternally the plenitude of perfection. He is the *a se* one, and as such He is the eternal and gratuitous source of life and love, and from this overflowing *ad intra* beatitude, He creates. All created life – including all the creaturely dimensions of goodness and truth and beauty – is derivatively participatory in this single Source. What we know to be beautiful, as finite creatures, is beautiful by divine derivation. Indeed, it is *at all* by divine derivation.[153]

---

149. Gregory of Nyssa, *The Great Catechism*, chap. V.

150. King, *The Beauty of the Lord*, 59 (emphasis original).

151. Hart, *The Beauty of the Infinite*, 252.

152. Brendan Thomas Sammon, *The God Who Is Beauty: Beauty As a Divine Name in Thomas Aquinas and Dionysius the Areopagite* (Eugene, OR: Pickwick, 2013), 356.

153. What Christopher R. J. Holmes, *The Lord is Good: Seeking the God of the Psalter* (Downers Grove, IL: InterVarsity Press, 2018), 38, says here about created and uncreated *goodness* applies also to *beauty*: 'The human spirit, precisely because it is created in God's likeness and image, shares in a manner appropriate to its creatureliness in God's goodness. Insofar as it simply is, the creature is good, which denotes a participatory goodness. Creatures by virtue of their being, by virtue of their participation in the pure act of existence itself, are good; what exists is good. Goodness, humanly speaking, and goodness, divinely speaking, are, however, infinitely distinct; the former is derivative, mixed (composite), and finite, whereas the latter is original, pure, simple, and infinite.'

The source of what the creature recognizes as beautiful is the simple Trinity's eternal beatitude. We might say, in other words, that divine *beatitude* and divine *beauty* describe the same reality of the divine nature from different vantage points. Divine *beatitude* is the divine attribute whereby God delights in Himself, and divine *beauty* is the divine attribute whereby creatures delight in God's self.[154]

The Analogy of Being

This language of 'participation', of course, calls to mind the oft debated doctrine of the *analogia entis* (the analogy of being).[155] To say that all created life is 'derivatively participatory in this single Source' is to say, with Matthew Levering, 'all finite beings theophanically disclose pure act as their glorious and incomprehensible source.'[156] The language of 'participation' is sure to put some on edge, in fear of an impending blur of the distinction between Creator and creature. But Hans Boersma is helpful to remind us that 'the doctrine of analogy does not just argue for similarity but also insists on the infinite *difference* between Creator and creature. In fact, *dis*similarity is the main point of the doctrine of analogy.'[157] John R. Betz makes a similar observation when he notes that in the Church's effort to 'defend its doctrine of creation, especially its ultimate goodness and peacefulness,' it has typically 'presented its doctrine of creation in terms of *analogy*.' This, argues Betz, 'has the advantage of allowing the Church to speak of the being, goodness and beauty of creation as a positive *participation* in the being, goodness and beauty of God, *while at the same time* affirming God's radical transcendence of creation and his abiding difference from it.'[158]

We have noted before how 'the church fathers were, by and large, not naïve about what to accept and what to reject from the Platonic

---

154. Many thanks to Craig Carter for his feedback on this topic and for this construction of 'blessedness' and 'beauty'.

155. John R. Betz makes the point in 'The Beauty of the Metaphysical Imagination,' in Peter M. Candler and Conor Cunningham, eds., *Belief and Metaphysics* (London, UK: SCM Press, 2007), 48-49.

156. Levering, *Doctrine of Creation*, 138.

157. Boersma, *Heavenly Participation*, 71 (emphasis original).

158. Betz, 'The Beauty of the Metaphysical Imagination,' 51 (emphasis original).

heritage.'[159] While they rejected outright Platonism's antipathy for creation, they critically appropriated its concept of 'Forms' and 'Ideas'. It may be tempting to assume that this, also, was a mistake, and a mistake destined to jeopardize the Creator-creature distinction. Indeed, this seems to be the suggestion from some evangelical quarters. But to assume as much is misguided, both because, on the one hand, it need not jeopardize the Creator-creature distinction (as we will show), and on the other hand, forfeiting such critical appropriation actually (ironically) jeopardizes crucial doctrines like the doctrine of Scripture itself (a cherished doctrine for many who might be inclined to criticize the patristics for their apparent insufficient emphasis on biblical authority). 'The Platonist-Christian synthesis,' notes Boersma,

> made it possible to regard creation, history, and Old Testament as sacra-mental carriers of a greater reality. Creation, history, and Old Testament had significance throughout most of the Christian tradition precisely because they pointed to and participated in a greater reality: what the Platonists called 'Forms' or 'Ideas,' and what Christians insisted was the Word of God himself.[160]

Which is to say, we forfeit the Platonist-Christian synthesis to our detriment. With that caution standing, let us look at one of the fruits of such a synthesis: the analogy of being. The doctrine of *analogia entis* traffics in the Platonic distinction between ἐχοντα ('having') and συμμετέχοντα (participating).[161] One may *have* a personal beauty, but not in an atomistic, nominalist fashion. Rather, one has beauty to the degree that she reveals or reflects or materializes the Form of *Beauty*. This seems to be what Aquinas is getting at when he insists that

> the beautiful and beauty are distinguished with respect to participation and participants. Thus, we call something 'beautiful' because it participates in some way in beauty. Beauty, however, is a participation in the first cause, which makes all things beautiful. So that the beauty of creatures is simply a likeness of the divine beauty in which things participate.[162]

159. Boersma, *Heavenly Participation*, 33.

160. Ibid., 38-39.

161. See, Lloyd P. Gerson, *Platonism and Naturalism: The Possibility of Philosophy* (Ithica, NY: Cornell University Press, 2020), chap. 4.

162. Aquinas, *Commentary on the Sentences*, 1252, quoted in Umberto Eco, *The Aesthetics of Thomas Aquinas*, trans. Hugh Bredin (Cambridge, MA: Harvard University Press, 1988), 27.

This emphasis particularly shines through in Aquinas' interactions with Pseudo-Dionysius. In his *Commentary on the Divine Names*, Aquinas makes great use of the transcendental equality of goodness and beauty. Their distinction is conceptual, and not substantive. 'Although the beautiful and the good are the same in subject,' writes Aquinas, 'because both clarity and consonance are included in the nature of the good – they are conceptually different. For beauty adds something to the good, namely an order which enables cognition to know that a thing is of such a kind.'[163] The substantive equality of beauty and goodness is not merely owing to their transcendental quality in the abstract (though we may say *at least* this much); we may go even further and say that their equality is owing to the fact that their archetypal form is found in the God who is simple. 'Everything is good according to its function. It is the nature of God, however, to be what he is; and so, he alone is his own goodness.'[164] Which is to say, God is goodness (and beauty) in Himself, while everything created is good (and beautiful) in relation to itself (i.e., its own telos instituted by God) and by derivation. In a particularly clear passage along these lines, Aquinas writes,

> Everything that exists comes from beauty and goodness, that is from God, as from an effective principle. And things have their being in beauty and goodness as if in [a] principle that preserves and maintains .... And all things are and all things become because of beauty and goodness, and all things look to them, as to an exemplary cause, which they possess as a rule governing their activities.[165]

When Aquinas writes that 'God is in all things; not, indeed, as part of their essence, nor as an accident; but as an agent is present to that upon which it works,' he is talking about this same all-good, all-beautiful God. The God who *is* Beauty is He who 'causes this effect in things not only when they first begin to be, but as long as they are preserved in being; as light is caused in the air by the sun as long as the air remains illuminated.'[166]

---

163. *Commentarium in Dionysii De Divinis Nominibus*, IV, 5 (hereafter, *Comm. Div. Nom*. Cited in Eco, *The Aesthetics of Thomas Aquinas*, 29.).

164. Aquinas, *Comm. Div. Nom.*, IV, 1.

165. Ibid., IV, 8.

166. Aquinas, *Summa*, I, 8, 1.

In this way, Aquinas stands 'firmly in the Greek intellectualist tradition, extending from Plato through Aristotle and Plotinus, and mediated to Aquinas principally by Augustine and Pseudo-Dionysius.'[167] Within this tradition, Beauty was considered not simply in an aesthetic category, but rather in an ontological or metaphysical one. 'Clearly,' writes Betz, 'for the Platonic tradition and its assimilation by the Church – from Augustine to Dionysius to the Chartres Platonists to Thomas – metaphysics and aesthetics go together, to the point of implying one another.'[168] 'Beauty' was a concept convertible to being itself,[169] and therefore, created beauty – and indeed, the created order – 'receives its being and significance from its participation in the eternal Word.'[170] But this participation is, as Boersma puts it, a *'mere'* participation. Aquinas notes how 'The creature does not have existence except as it descends from the first being, nor is it called a being except insofar as it imitates the first being.'[171] Thus, as Duby summarizes the point,

> Thomas's deployment of the analogy of attribution … (1) precludes any common factor in which God and creatures alike might participate, (2) assumes that the referring of created perfections back to God entails the presence of each perfection in a 'preeminent' or 'superexcellent' manner in God's own being, and (3) is built, at the predicative level, on the ontological relationship of creatures to God, a relationship explicative in terms of causality and participation.[172]

This, again, is why Boersma describes creation as 'merely a sacramental participation in the divine life'.[173] On the one hand, unless we are to swallow the *reductio* of nominalism and univocism, and conclude that God and creation exist on the same – or parallel – plain of being, we have to affirm that between creation and Creator there remains some

---

167. Eric D. Perl, '"All Men By Nature Desire to Know" The Classical Background of Aquinas on Beauty and Truth,' in Alice M. Ramos, ed. *Beauty and the Good: Recovering the Classical Tradition from Plato to Duns Scotus* (Washington, D.C.: The Catholic University Press, 2020), 70.

168. Betz, 'The Beauty of the Metaphysical Imagination,' 61.

169. Perl, 'All Men By Nature Desire to Know,' 70-71.

170. Boersma, *Heavenly Participation*, 50.

171. Thomas, *Sententiarum,* prol., q. 1, a. 2 ad 2 (10).

172. Duby, *God in Himself,* 250.

173. Boersma, *Heavenly Participation*, 70.

participatory relationship. Creation and Creator do not relate to one another as independent modes of being – the former derives its being in some way from the latter. On the other hand, unless we are to swallow the *reductio* of pantheism and deny either the infinite nature of God or the finite nature of creation, we must conclude that this 'participation is strictly a gift of grace and in no way erases the Creator-creature distinction'.[174] Indeed, Scripture itself confirms this notion. Levering helpfully gives us an example:

> As an example of all created things' theophanic analogicity, consider the praise that, according to Psalm 148, all the beings of the world offer to God. Angels and humans, of course, should praise God freely and intelligently, and Psalm 148 does not leave this out. But Psalm 148 also exhorts the sun, moon, stars, highest heavens, sea monsters, fire, hail, snow, wind, mountains, trees, beasts, insects and birds to praise the Lord. How could these irrational things praise God? The answer seems to be by simply existing, as actual things, in their wondrous diversity. Their praise of the creator is joined to the praise offered by 'all peoples, princes and rulers of the earth' (Ps 148:11).[175]

Therefore, joining Scripture, Aquinas, and his classical Platonist-Christian synthetic heritage, we affirm the *analogia entis* in general.

Still, we must determine the nature of this participation. Already, some might have anticipated a tension. How are we to conceptualize the Platonic relationship between 'Matter' and 'Forms' or 'Ideas' with the 'Good?' As Edward Feser points out, there are key distinctions between Plato, Aristotle and the Medieval scholastic theologians on the matter of realism.[176] For Plato, 'Forms' or 'Ideas' are not identical to the 'Good', nor are they an intrinsic part of 'Matter'. They exist in a third realm, somewhere between the 'Good' and 'Matter'. This ethereal third realm did not work for Aristotle,[177] who insisted instead

---

174. Ibid., 71.

175. Levering, *Doctrine of Creation*, 138.

176. Edward Feser, *Five Proofs of the Existence of God* (San Francisco, CA: Ignatius Press, 2017), 95-110.

177. Nor should it work for us, since, as Feser points out, it is rife with problems. This includes (a) the fact that this 'third realm' seems to pose no causal power, so it remains conceptually inert; (b) it seems to incoherently attempt to be a universal and a particular; and (c) it would seem to render individual material things *nothing* in themselves – if their essence exists in a third realm completely distinct from them, how can we say they are

that 'Forms' existed *within* their material manifestations in the world. The realist Scholastic theologians said, 'yes and no' to both Plato and Aristotle.[178] 'Like Aristotelian realism,' says Feser, 'Scholastic realism affirms that universals exist only either in the things that instantiate them, or in intellects which entertain them. It agrees that there is no Platonic "third realm" independent both of the material world and of all intellects.'[179] They did, however, recognize the limitations of Aristotle's view, acknowledging the necessity of some universals which do exist outside of *human* and other contingent intellects. So, they said 'yes' to the Aristotelian denial that universals exist outside of either material things or in the intellects that entertain them. But they said 'no' to the Aristotelian failure to account for a realm 'distinct both from the material world and from *human* and other finite intellects'.[180] Instead, the Scholastic realist tradition, following in the footsteps of Augustine,[181] relocated this realm of 'Forms' or 'Ideas', so that it no longer occupied a place of independent abstraction, but rather existed in the mind of God. 'In particular,' Feser notes, Scholastic realism 'holds that universals, propositions, mathematical and logical truths, and necessities and possibilities exist in an *infinite, eternal, divine* intellect.'[182]

So far, all well and good. But at this point another tension develops. How is one to conceive of these 'Forms' or 'Ideas', which are in the mind of God? The patristics had the instinctual move to associate Platonic 'Forms' with the divine Word – the Logos, the Son Himself.[183] This is fitting insofar as it goes, since the mind to which these 'Forms' belong is the *Triune God's*, wherein the divine life is ever *from* the Father, *through* the Son, and *in* the Spirit. But to make these ideas out to be identical with the Logos is less preferable than to conceptualize them as the

---

essentially real? 'So, what we call a tree seems at the end of the day to be no more genuinely treelike than a statue or mirror image of a tree is; what we call a human being seems no more genuinely human than a statue or mirror image of a human being is; and so forth. But that is absurd' (ibid., 99).

178. Or, as Feser puts it, their view is 'essentially Aristotelian in spirit, but gives at least a nod to Platonic realism' (Feser, *Five Proofs*, 102).

179. Ibid., 102.

180. Feser, *Five Proofs*, 102 (emphasis original).

181. See, Augustine, *Confessions*, books XI and XII.

182. Ibid., 102 (emphasis original).

183. See Boersma, *Heavenly Participation*, 38-39, 47-51.

Logos' ideas – He thinks them. Thus, it is right for our understanding of creation's mere participation in the divine life to be shaped by our understanding of divine ideas and the Logos as the Word who speaks creation into existence: creation reflects His ideas.[184]

In discussing 'divine ideas', we are, of course, coming into contact with Aquinas and his *exemplarism*. For Aquinas, exemplar ideas are 'the forms of things existing *apart* from the things themselves', and thus there is 'a distinction between the substantial form that is intrinsic to a thing and the form that is the thing's exemplar.'[185] It is not far from the truth to say (albeit in a simplified manner) that divine ideas are the blueprints for creation. It is through the imitation of divine ideas that a finite being participates in God. 'Because a finite essence is not its own act of being,' says Gregory Doolan, 'it exists only by participating in being (*esse*).'[186] Thus, Cornelio Fabro can insist that 'created essences derive from the divine essence by the intermediary of the divine Ideas, and this derivation formally follows the relationship of exemplarity.'[187] Creation participates in God by virtue of its reflection of divine ideas.

Tying the above discussion of the *analogia entis* with the topic of beauty is less of a burdensome task than one might assume. Betz succinctly summarizes:

> if we make a legitimate substitution of 'form' for 'essence;' since in the metaphysical tradition the two are more or less synonymous, we come up with the formulation: 'form in-and-beyond existence'. And if, following Thomas, we make the further substitution of 'beauty' for 'form', we suddenly come up with the formula, 'beauty in-and-beyond existence'. In other words, *what we discover is that what the* analogia entis *seeks to describe ... is altogether akin to what we feel in the face of beauty.*[188]

If the *analogia entis* is legitimate to any degree, it legitimately applies to beauty. Again, Betz helps to appropriately frame the issue when he asks, 'what are the aesthetic implications of Thomas's real distinction

---

184. For a thorough treatment on this topic, see Gregory T. Doolan, *Aquinas on the Divine Ideas as Exemplar Causes* (Washington, D.C.: The Catholic University of America Press, 2008).

185. Doolan, *Aquinas on the Divine Ideas*, 25 (emphasis original).

186. Ibid., 237.

187. Fabro, *Participation et causalité,* 630, quoted in Doolan, 237.

188. Betz, 'The Beauty of the Metaphysical Imagination,' 63 (emphasis added).

(which lies at the heart of the *analogia entis*), and what is added thereby to an otherwise strictly Platonic picture of finite reality participating in and showing forth a reality that exceeds it?'[189] His answer is that 'the *analogia entis* leads directly to a perception (to an aesthetics!) of creation *as creation*, which is to say, as a display of *gratuitous excess and depth* – gratuitous, inasmuch as its very reality is a gift; excess and depth, inasmuch as the essence of anything transcends its instantiation in any given moment.'[190]

With this all-too brief foray into metaphysics, let me offer this summary of the *analogia's* implication on created beauty in particular:

> *what Plato means by 'the Good' is the One who Christians worship as the Triune God – He is the* a se *and absolutely simple archetypical standard and source of Being; He is the ultimate True, the Good, the Beautiful. What Plato calls 'Forms' or 'Ideas,' Christians call essence, which is in-and-beyond creation, and is ultimately present in the divine intellect. Created essences find their archetypical exemplars in the form of 'divine ideas', which are thought and spoken by the Logos. The free, gracious and benevolent expression of these ideas is creation – which is teeming with being that* is *by virtue of its imitation of the divine ideas, and by virtue of imitation of them, it is a 'mere' participant of the Divine. If this is true for created being in general, it is true of created beauty in particular. Created beauty participates in the beatitude of the divine life by virtue of its being a reflection of the Logos's divine ideas.*[191]

(All of this, of course, gets at only one aspect of 'participation': the ontological aspect of derivative, creaturely being. There is another crucial aspect of 'participation' that remains to be discussed, which is at the very heart of this present project. Recall that in our thesis, we argue that 'in regeneration the Spirit communicates – or, sovereignly *brings the regenerate into participation with* – the glorious *a se* beatitude of the Trinity, mediated through Christ.' This is doxological, communal participation. It is the soteriological participation the Holy Spirit facilitates via union with Christ. A thorough elaboration of this kind of 'participation' can be found in chapter 4, but it is worth denying outright that what we

---

189. Ibid., 63.

190. Ibid., 63 (emphasis original).

191. This section is largely indebted to an email correspondence with Craig Carter.

have said up until this point requires that we conceive of it in a manner that conflates justification and sanctification – as in Roman Catholic soteriology – or in a manner that unites the divine to the human so as to lose sight of the latter as the former swallows it up – as in the theosis of Eastern Orthodox soteriology. Neither of these conclusions are necessary, as I will demonstrate emphatically in chapter 4.)

Divine Holiness, Goodness, Glory, and Beauty

If what we have seen thus far is true, one should expect to see various attributes of God overlapping in biblical descriptions of man's experience of the Triune God. In this concluding section, we explore the biblical relationship between God's holiness, goodness, glory, and beauty. This situates further discussions on soteriology within the context of God's *ad intra* beauty.

Yahweh is identified all throughout Scripture as 'the Holy One' or 'the Holy One of Israel' (e.g., Job 6:10; Jer. 50:29; 2 Kings 19:22; Hosea 11:9; Hab. 1:12; 3:3). Part of the difficulty of defining divine holiness is its conceptual proximity to divine simplicity – a concept altogether beyond human comprehension. Writes J. Alec Motyer, 'Holiness is supremely the truth about God, and his holiness is in itself so far beyond human thought that a "super-superlative" has to be invented to express it.'[192] As the opposite of 'common', it is the name that most directly points to the divine nature itself. This is why that which is not God, which Scripture designates as 'holy', is always and only holy in relation to God – the only one who is holy *ad intra*. God's holiness is His Godness, with particular attention to His unique goodness in contrast to all things common or unclean. Motyer notes how 'what it is that makes [Yahweh] unapproachable or what it is that constitutes his distinctiveness' is 'his total and unique moral majesty'.[193] This is why encounters with God's (minimally mediated) holiness are characterized by terror and dread. The archetypal biblical example of this is Isaiah 6:1-7. The display of God's majesty, high and lifted up, with the deafening ring of angelic declarations of 'Holy, holy, holy is the LORD of hosts; the whole earth is full of his glory!' elicited the unforgettable response of Isaiah, 'Woe

---

192. J. Alec Motyer, *The Prophecy of Isaiah: An Introduction and Commentary* (Downers Grove, IL: IVP Academic, 1993), 77.
193. Ibid. 77.

is me! For I am lost; for I am a man of unclean lips, and I dwell in the midst of a people of unclean lips; for my eyes have seen the King, the LORD of hosts!'

Within this passage there is a natural grouping of designations: 'holiness,' together with 'glory,' characterizing 'the King, the LORD of hosts.' 'Glory' as a manifestation of God's holiness that *fills* the 'whole earth' has a distinctly revelatory character to it. If holiness is the Godness of God in Himself, glory is the Godness of God (i.e., divine holiness) on display and experienced. Jason DeRouchie similarly calls 'glory' the encounter of 'holiness' (Exod. 28:22; Isa. 6:3; Pss. 29:2; 96:9).[194] He goes on to define holiness as 'the reality and value of God's fullness, expressed in his self-sustainability, his absoluteness and sole-ness, his excellence and worth, and the beautiful harmony of all his acts with that fullness.'[195]

This grouping of 'holiness' and 'glory' characterizing God's kingly authority makes fitting the association between divine 'glory' and royal imagery. His train 'filling the temple' parallels His glory 'filling the earth'. Thus, the sight that strikes the prophet with fear in Isaiah 6 finds its hopeful counterpart in the promise of Isaiah 33:17: 'Your eyes will behold the king in his *beauty*' (emphasis added). This is the very thing the psalmist pines after: 'One thing have I asked of the LORD, that will I seek after, that I may dwell in the house of the LORD all the days of my life, to gaze upon the beauty of the LORD and to inquire in his temple' (Ps. 27:4). An even clearer example of 'beauty' and its association to royal imagery is found in Psalm 96:6, where the psalmist writes: 'Splendor and majesty are before him; strength and beauty are in his sanctuary.'

If holiness is God's essential Godness, and glory is God's Godness on display, what affects if God's glory (i.e., His holiness on display and experienced) is received as a terror on the one hand (as in the beginning of Isaiah 6), or as a delightful enjoyment of divine beauty on the other (as in the case of Psalm 27:4)? On account of God's simplicity, we know that, ontologically speaking, God's beauty is always manifested

---

194. Jason DeRouchie, 'Seminary Lecture Notes on Leviticus, pt. 1,' JasonDeRouchie. com, 2020, 42, accessed August 27, 2020.

195. Ibid., 42-43.

in the display of His glory, whether it is received that way or not,[196] yet something must account for why this same, simple glory is sometimes received as the stench of death and at other times as the fragrance of life. Since the 'glory of the Lord' is the splendor and brilliance that is inseparably associated with all of God's attributes,[197] we know that its reception is not dependent on a change in God or some alien filter through which His glory runs to meet the creature.

In many ways, this question will take the rest of the present work to answer, but we can begin to grasp the answer by considering another conceptual cognate with holiness, glory, and beauty: *goodness*. In many ways, 'goodness' is a broader category than 'beauty'. They both fall under the umbrella of axiology – i.e., the philosophical branch that deals with rendering *value* judgments. Whereas 'beauty' bespeaks an aesthetic value judgment (i.e., the beautiful is the aesthetically excellent), 'goodness' presents itself to the mind as an ethical value judgment (i.e., the good is the morally excellent). Even still, 'goodness' does seem to have more versatility; it may associate with the ethical and moral dimensions of axiology, but it is not bound there.

While we cannot spend sustained attention on the divine attribute of goodness, we should note its similarity to divine beauty, not only as a conceptual and theological cognate but even in the *way* we talk about it. Consider, for example, the striking similarities between the way I have been describing divine beauty and Holmes' description of divine goodness here: 'God does not participate in something called goodness, as if goodness were some thing existing outside God, of which God was a part. Rather, goodness is God Himself. Goodness is indicative of God's "perfect existing".'[198] Together with divine beauty, divine goodness even shares an ineffableness – an abject transgression of linguistic boundaries and definition – which is in part, paradoxically, *definitional*. 'Yes, we cannot find words,' grants Holmes, 'and so on the one hand this study will fail, and that is fine; and yet, nonetheless, the utter delight to be had in the one who is good encourages us to persevere in receiving what the Lord is to himself.'[199]

---

196. 'The display of God's glory is thus always beautiful, always fitting, always entails an aesthetic dimension to it' (King, *The Beauty of the Lord*, 51).

197. Bavinck, *Reformed Dogmatics Volume 2*, 252.

198. Holmes, *The Lord is Good*, 12.

199. Holmes, *The Lord is Good*, 53.

There are several places in Scripture that link divine 'glory' and divine 'goodness' (2 Chron. 7:3; Jer. 33:9), but the most striking and relevant for our present purpose is in Moses' interaction with Yahweh on Sinai in Exodus 33:17–34:35. In this passage, Moses' request for Yahweh to 'show his *glory*' (emphasis added) is met with a qualified affirmative: 'I will make all my *goodness* pass before you and will proclaim before you my name "The LORD"' (Exod. 33:19).

The qualification comes in the form of God not allowing for Moses to see His face, since 'man shall not see [him] and live'; so instead Yahweh will place him in the cleft of a rock, with His own hand covering while His 'glory passes by' (Exod. 33:20-23). We will examine this passage at greater length in chapter 5, but for now the point to appreciate is that 'glory' and 'goodness' are used synonymously (cf. Zech. 9:17). God's refusal to let Moses see His face, since such a sight would kill Moses, calls to mind the dreadful experience of divine glory glimpsed in Isaiah 6. Yet, what Moses experienced was more akin to what the psalmist hopes for in Psalm 27:4, and the revelation of divine glory is received by Moses not as a terror but as a manifestation of God's 'goodness'. God's glory is the same, but when He sees fit to 'be gracious' and to 'show mercy' (Exod. 33:19), He can cause His beautiful holiness to be received as goodness.

As mentioned above, therefore, the thing that affects if God's glory is received as a terror or as a glimpse of divine beauty is not dependent on a change in God or some alien filter through which His glory runs to meet the creature. The 'filter' is God's own mediation, whereby He is 'gracious to whom he is gracious, and shows mercy to whom he shows mercy.'[200] Thus, to receive God's glory as 'goodness' and 'beauty' is to be graced by God and welcomed into His own ineffable enjoyment.[201]

That the Greek word καλο⊠ (*kalos*) is rendered as both 'good' and 'beautiful' in English is worthy of attention. In the Septuagint, then,

---

200. In a sense, even Isaiah 6 demonstrates this, for Isaiah did not see a completely unmediated display of God's glory. He did not, after all, die. Further, his lips – that which most offended his conscience and conspicuously bespoke uncleanness – were purified by divine intervention, so that he might be serviceable before this dreadfully holy God (Isa. 6:6-7).

201. 'God's beauty is delight and the object of delight,' says Hart, *The Beauty of the Infinite*, 177, 'the shared gaze of love that belongs to the persons of the Trinity; it is what God beholds, what the Father sees and rejoices in in the Son, in the sweetness of the Spirit, what Son and Spirit find delightful in one another, because as Son and Spirit of the Father they share his knowledge and love as persons.'

God promises to let His καλοσύνη pass before Moses (Exod. 33:19), and the psalmist seeks to dwell in the house of Yahweh to gaze upon His καλο☒ forever (Ps. 27:4), and in John 10:11 Jesus identifies Himself as the καλο☒ shepherd. It is no grammatical stretch, then, to designate the Lord Jesus Christ as 'the *Beautiful* Shepherd.' This does not mean that every biblical mention of divine 'goodness' is interchangeable with the divine 'beauty', but it does bespeak their conceptual and theological proximity. And here, with Christ in view as the manifestation of God's goodness and beauty, it is worth anticipating where we are going with our thesis. Moses required the mediation of God's accommodated goodness in order to receive His glory as a delight rather than a dread. This accommodation came in the form of the cleft of a rock in which Moses was to hide. We are standing on good ground to read this form of accommodation typologically as anticipating Christ – the Rock of Ages in whom New Covenant believers hide. In Christ, God accommodates His incomprehensible glory.

The Incarnation's Rationale

We are therefore standing on firm biblical ground in relating divine holiness, goodness, glory, and beauty, as conceptual cognates. These are all divine attributes that correlate, particularly as presented in special revelation. As we return now to our consideration of metaphysics, however, we begin to anticipate a problem. If what we have said about the *analogia entis* is true, and created goodness and beauty participates in an asymmetrical, gratuitous way with God (a 'mere' participation via reflecting divine ideas), what implications does sin have on this state of affairs? Can it really be said that creation is cursed and fallen and in need of redemption if its very being is a gracious participation in the holy, good, glorious, beautiful One? How can that which is ugly participate in Beauty? To bring matters even closer to home, how can we say that fallen man, who is dead in his trespasses, is in any way a participant in this 'sacramental tapestry'?[202]

It may be tempting for us to assume that the fall and corruption of man and creation, as a result of sin, must not therefore be total. In other words, we might want to affirm that a real fall from grace has occurred,

---

202. This, again, is Boersma's language in *Heavenly Participation*.

and that creation is indeed corrupted, but surely not to the degree that Calvin and his reformed compatriots maintain. Under this proposal, it seems we must choose between the metaphysics of the Great Tradition or the soteriology of the Reformed Tradition, but that we may not have both.

Indeed, Boersma says this explicitly. He blames the 'cutting' of the sacramental tapestry in the mind of the Church on the High Middle ages' two scissor-blades: Duns Scotus' univocism, and William of Ockham's nominalism.[203] Whether one rejects creation's analogous participation with the Creator by elevating it to the same plane of existence (Scotus), or by obliterating the concept of the universal (Ockham), the result was the same: from a historical point of view, the *analogia entis,* and therefore the sacramental tapestry of the cosmos, was effectively torn in the Church's imagination. And while Boersma grants that the reformers made a valiant effort at re-weaving the tapestry,[204] he maintains they ultimately fell short. It may seem as if this falling short was a foregone conclusion, given the reformers' rejection of Rome's sacramental soteriology (especially her conflation of justification and sanctification). In fact, Boersma will go so far as to indicate that Calvin's commitment to the Great Tradition's 'integrated cosmos' is internally inconsistent with his soteriology, when he says that 'this positive view of God's presence in and guidance of nature does not fit well with other elements of Calvin's thought.'[205] Among these 'other elements' are his 'emphasis on the pervasiveness of sin', and his 'teaching of justification by faith alone', which he attributes to a 'great deal of continuity with the nominalist tradition'.[206]

So, is the option truly that stark? Must we decide between embracing the metaphysics of the Great Tradition, and consequently own a Roman (or even an Eastern Orthodox) soteriology, or embracing the Reformed soteriology and, with a heavy and reluctant heart, bid farewell to the gorgeous metaphysic of Christian-Platonism and settle in with the drab and colorless metaphysic of nominalism? Fortunately, no such choice is

---

203. Boersma, *Heavenly Participation,* 68-81.

204. For example, Boersma is eager to emphasize that 'Calvin's view of grace overcoming the insufficiency of nature and of nature still forming the basis of redemption would not have been out of place in the integrated cosmos of the Great Tradition' (ibid., 91).

205. Boersma, Ibid., 92.

206. Ibid., 92.

necessary, because Boersma and others who would have us choose are mistaken to do so. For one thing, the choice is historically novel, since 'the early Reformed certainly drew on the resources of medieval philosophy and theology in an eclectic manner', but 'essentially stood in continuity with Thomas's approach [to metaphysics] and criticized Scotus's doctrine of univocity'[207] (and, we might add, Ockham's nominalism).[208] But even if this were not the case, Reformed theology has no necessary conflict with the Christian-Platonist metaphysic, whether the topic of sin or *sola fide* is concerned.

Answering the misguided charge of *sola fide's* necessary collusion with nominalism will have to wait until chapter 4. We can and must, however, say a bit about Calvin's view of sin here. Boersma says that 'Calvin's emphasis on the pervasiveness of human sin, on the radical dependency of the human will on divine grace, and especially, on the doctrine of double predestination meant that *Calvin did not share with the Great Tradition the view that human beings had a natural desire for the beatific vision*.'[209] But, of course, nothing of the kind is true. It is the case that the beatific vision featured a relatively small place of recognition in Calvin's Institutes *explicitly*, but Boersma himself will point out in another work how 'Calvin did treat the beatific vision as the end of the earthly pilgrimage', noting that 'we should not confuse Calvin's own theology with the impact it may have had in later Reformed (and evangelical) thought … he was … convinced that only God himself constitutes our final end, so that only our vision of him yields true happiness.'[210] In fact, it is precisely that 'natural desire for the beatific vision' (albeit, expressed through different language) that, for Calvin,

---

207. Duby, *Life in Himself*, 257.

208. Richard Muller, for example, shows how William Ames is decidedly Thomistic in his conception of divine ideas in chapter 6 of the first book of *The Marrow of Theology* (John Dykstra Eusden, trans., [Grand Rapids, MI: Baker Books, 1968], 91-100). While Ames offers a unique take in some respects, he is by no means a univocist, nor a nominalist. See, 'Calvinist Thomism Revisited: William Ames (1576–1633) and the Divine Ideas,' in Gary W. Jenkins, W.J. Torrance Kirby, and Kathleen M. Comerford, eds., *From Rome to Zurich, between Ignatius and Vermigli: Essays in Honor of John Patrick Donnelly, SJ* (Leiden, NL: Brill Publishers, 2017), 103-20.

209. Boersma, *Heavenly Participation*, 92 (emphasis added).

210. Boersma, *Seeing God The Beatific Vision in Christian Tradition* (Grand Rapids, MI: Eerdmans, 2018), 258-59.

makes sin so insidious, and idolatry so effective.[211] Idolatry would have no allure at all were it not for sin's utility – or rather, manipulation and perversion – of this natural desire. In other words, the desire for the beatific vision, God's manifestation of His presence in the natural world, and sin's effect of incapacitating man from satiating that desire in the God of heaven, all work to keep him in the suicidal idolatry of created things (including himself).[212] What Boersma seems to describe as contradictory strands in Calvin's thought (i.e., his Christian-Platonist cosmology, and his doctrine of sin), Calvin seems to have no problem weaving together as mutually reinforcing: 'This [the reality of idolatry preventing man from fulfilling his chief end] did not escape the observation even of philosophers. For it is the very thing which Plato meant (*in Phoed. et Theact.*) when he taught, as he often does, that the chief good of the soul consists in resemblance to God, i.e., when, by means of knowing him, she is whole wholly transformed into him.'[213]

By virtue of creation's mere participation in divine Beauty, the message of Psalm 19:1-6 still rings out. And man, by virtue of *his* mere participation in divine Beauty – his bearing the image of the divine[214] (or, in Calvin's words, his 'sense of deity') – still hears it ring out, and still desires it. But sin makes him incompetent at hearing it aright, and (to change metaphors) instead of following the sunbeams back up to the Sun, he worships them as if they were the source of light.[215] The tragedy

---

211. I would submit that the 'sense of deity' that Calvin points to as the root of false religion (*Institutes,* Book I:3:2.), which is 'indelibly engraved on the human heart' (ibid., I:3:3.) amounts to what Boersma identifies as the Great Tradition's belief in man's natural desire for the beatific vision. Such a conclusion seems difficult to avoid when Calvin describes this 'sense of deity' with the language he does: 'If all are born and live for the express purpose of learning to know God, and if the knowledge of God, insofar as it fails to produce this effect, is fleeting and vain, it is clear that all those who do not direct the whole thoughts and actions of their lives to this end *fail to fulfill the law of their being*' (ibid., I:3:3, emphasis added).

212. See Thomas H. McCall, *Against God and Nature: The Doctrine of Sin* (Wheaton, IL: Crossway, 2019), 301. More on this in chapter 5.

213. Calvin, *Institutes,* Book I:3:3.

214. See, especially, Richard Lints, *The Image of God and Its Inversion* (Downers Grove, IL: InterVarsity Press, 2015), 57-74.

215. McCall notes also how 'sin is *folly*; it is what is opposed to the natural order and *telos* of the universe. Sin is, thus, profoundly against *nature*.' McCall, *Against God and Nature*, 59.

of Romans 1:18-32 finds leverage in, and is made more tragic by, the splendor of the *analogia entis* in Psalm 19:1-6.

Depravity's totality – which is made *more* disastrous by the *analogia entis*, not less – is what makes the incarnation necessary. This is noteworthy, because so often the incarnation's rationale is considered exclusively within the conceptual realm of guilt and atonement. This is not wrong, of course, since that is where the emphasis lies in Scripture's depiction of the Son's mission. But the 'rescue mission' of the Son accomplishes more than justifying atonement. Christ not only overcomes the guilt of sin, but also (relatedly) the effects of sin, which includes the total inability to commune with God; his total incompetence to achieve his natural telos: doxological participation with the divine goodness and beauty of the Triune God. Because that telos is such a powerful driving force, and because sin is such a powerful obstacle, man's desire for the beatific vision is twisted and perverted into idolatry. Christ, the image of the invisible, beautiful God, became incarnate to rescue man's worship, and thus restore his proper participation with the divine. This rescue mission is not necessary *in spite* of the sacramental tapestry of the cosmos, but rather *because of* it. The point we are making is nothing new. Athanasius made it in the fourth century when he wrote:

> For since human beings, having rejected the contemplation of God and as though sunk in an abyss with their eyes held downwards, seeking God in creation and things perceptible, setting up for themselves moral humans and demons as gods, for this reason the lover of human beings and the common Savior of all takes to himself a body and dwells as human among humans and draws to himself the perceptible senses of all human beings, so that those who think that God is in the corporeal might, from what the Lord wrought through the actions of the body, know the truth and through him might consider the Father.[216]

Far from being a conceptual problem for the Great Tradition's metaphysic of creation's 'mere participation' with the divine, Calvin's view of sin is precisely what made the ultimate occasion for metaphysical participation – i.e., the incarnation – *necessary*. In the incarnation, divine Beauty came to sinful creatures *precisely because* they were so incapable of seeing and knowing Him any other way.

---

216. Athanasius, *On the Incarnation* chap.15.

Conclusion

In this chapter we have sought to give an account for God's divine beauty *ad intra*. We began with a brief apologetic for metaphysics in theology in order to establish precedence for placing 'divine beauty' in the context of 'divine simplicity' as understood in classical Christian Trinitarianism. We then traced 'simplicity' as the organizing principle for Trinitarian thought through Athanasius, Hilary, and the Cappadocians. Following this, we offered a defense of the doctrine of divine simplicity and from there, rooted beauty within God's aseity – His beatitude. This brought us into a discussion on the *analogia entis,* and its implications on the relationship between divine Beauty and created beauty. We then engaged in a biblical exploration of the concepts of holiness, glory, goodness, and beauty. We then dealt with the problem of sin in the world as the rationale for the incarnation. We are now ready to explore the apex of God's revelation of glory – and therefore, the sharpest manifestation of divine beauty – in the incarnation. 'Herein do we behold the glory of Christ himself,' says Owen,

> even in this life. This glory was given him of the Father, – namely, that he now should declare and evidence that 'God is love'; and he did so, 'that in all things he might have the pre-eminence.' Herein we may see how excellent, how beautiful, how glorious and desirable he is, seeing in him alone we have a due representation of God as he is love; which is the most joyful sight of God that any creature can obtain.[217]

---

217. Owen, *The Works of John Owen,* 1:301

CHAPTER THREE

Mediated Beauty

Thou hast but two rare cabinets full of treasure,
The Trinity *and* Incarnation.
Thou hast unlocked them both,
And made them jewels to betroth
The work of thy creation
Unto thyself in everlasting pleasure.

The statelier cabinet is the Trinity,
Whose sparkling light access denies
Therefore thou dost not show
This fully to us, till death blow
The dust into our eyes;
For by that powder thou wilt make us see.

But all thy sweets are packed up in the other;
Thy mercies thither flock and flow:
That, as the first affrights,
This may allure us with delights:
Because this box we know;
For we have all of us just such another.

GEORGE HERBERT[1]

---

1. George Herbert, 'Ungratefulness,' in *The Temple,* reprint ed. (Moscow, ID: Canon Press, 2020), 90.

Introduction

In the previous chapter I established that divine beauty is a particular expression of Triune beatitude; the brilliance of the Trinity's *a se* plenitude of life and love. Since God is the ontological source of everything, everything creaturely exists by virtue of an asymmetrical participation in the divine will; to be creaturely is to be fundamentally ectypal, which means all of creation's beauty is derivative. Everything is revelation. All beauty is revelatory of Triune beauty. John R. Betz is a help here when he observes,

> What is properly meta-physical about beauty ... is its display of depth, its revelation of something *in* a thing that at the same time *exceeds* or goes *beyond* the thing, so that the thing itself becomes a mysterious index of something beyond it ... so that the visible, as John Milbank has suggested, becomes a site of the appearing of the invisible – to the point that the visible is seen epiphenomenally (*sic*) for what it is: as the site of a 'wondrous exchange' between the visible and invisible.[2]

The 'beyond' source of all beauty is God, and thus this 'wondrous exchange' bespeaks a revelation of divine glory. And while God reveals His glory in every manifestation of divine revelation, the absolute apex of divine revelation is found in Christ, the image of the invisible God (Col. 1:15), which means this, too, is where the apex revelation of divine glory and beauty is to be found. We should be sure to stress this point of fundamental harmony: it is not merely that Christ happens to reveal the same divine beauty in which all creaturely beauty participates. It is also the case that, as the eternal Logos in which (or in whom) all creaturely beauty participates, all creaturely beauty points back to *Him*. 'Indeed,' says Betz,

> according to this rich image of 'wondrous exchange' (*commercium admirabile*), one could say that every experience of beauty bears a Christological stamp, whereby the perception of a mysterious reciprocity between the visible and the invisible, the immanent and the transcendent, points beyond itself, analogically, to an ultimate reciprocity of profundity and visibility in Christ, the primary analogate and measure of all beauty,

---

2. John R. Betz, 'The Beauty of the Metaphysical Imagination,' in Peter M. Candler and Conor Cunningham, eds., *Belief and Metaphysics* (London, UK: SCM Press, 2007), 60-61 (emphasis original).

indeed the measure of all creation whatsoever, since in him the resplendent *depths* of the Father (cf. James 1:17) are precisely and fully *seen* (John 14:7).[3]

In other words, in shifting topic of concern from the metaphysics of divine beauty in general to the incarnation of the Logos in particular, we are not at all changing the subject. We are zooming in on the same fundamental concern we explored in the previous chapter. In this chapter we will narrow in on one expression of this divine revelation of beauty. As the eternal Logos, then, Christ is the central point of integration for the metaphysical and aesthetic concerns of beauty we considered in the last chapter, and the soteriological concerns of saving faith, which we will consider in this and the following chapters.

The Incarnation: The Image of the Invisible (Beautiful) God

In the incarnation Christ reveals the glory of God. At the risk of being redundant, we should not miss the significant point that *Christ's* glory is *the glory of the Triune God* – it is the invisible θεός (*theos*) that Christ makes known (John 1:18; Col. 1:15). Gregory of Nazianzus makes this point when he describes the 'Word' as the 'definition' of the Father:

> He is 'Word,' because he is related to the Father as word is to mind, not only by reason of the undisturbed character of his birth, but also through the connection and declaratory function involved in the relationship. One could say too, perhaps, that his relationship is that of definition to term defined, since 'word' has the meaning in Greek of 'definition.' He who has known the Son ('seen' means 'known' in that context) has known the Father.[4]

When the 'Word became flesh', He was assuming the role of 'exegete of the Father'. 'The Fourth Evangelist,' writes Gerald O'Collins, 'develops the theme of the Son of God as the Revealer who communicates the divine self-manifestation (John 1:18) – the Logos as spoken word or relational utterance (rather than as thought or meaning that remains within the mind).'[5] Importantly, the entire event of the incarnation –

---

3. Ibid., 61 (emphasis original).

4. Gregory of Nazianzus, *Orations* 30.20.

5. O'Collins, *The Beauty of Jesus Christ*, 26.

from His Spiritual conception to His ascension – is revelatory. This point is often missed when Christ's divine and human natures are pitted against one another. The early fathers did not see these points as incommensurate; they insisted that the entire unity of Christ's person and work 'in the flesh' was a revelation of divine glory. For them, it was not simply the case that Christ revealed the glory of God when He performed the miraculous. The entirety of His enfleshed state was revelation. Thus, Athanasius says,

> For since human beings, having rejected the contemplation of God and as though sunk in an abyss with their eyes held downwards, seeking God in creation and things perceptible, setting up for themselves moral humans and demons as gods, for this reason the lover of human beings and the common Savior of all takes to himself a body and dwells as human among humans and draws to himself the perceptible senses of all human beings, so that those who think that God is in the corporeal might, from what the Lord wrought through the actions of the body, know the truth and through him might consider the Father.[6]

For Athanasius, the revelation of God's glory in Christ had a soteriological purpose; God intends to sweep up His creatures into the eternal beatitude of Triune love as an act of benevolent, gratuitous participation. And this sweeping process includes the crucial act of *revealing* His glory in Christ. Agreeing on this front, Calvin makes the point powerfully:

> Because God's majesty, which is far removed from us, would be like a secret and hidden spring, he has revealed himself in Christ. And so we have an open fountain at hand to draw from. The words mean that God did not want to have the life hidden and as it were buried within himself, and therefore he transfused it into his Son that it might flow to us.[7]

In their own ways, Athanasius and Calvin point to the existential plight of fallen man, which the incarnation answers. Both because of his sinful preoccupation with idols (Athanasius)[8] and his creaturely limitations and inaccessibility to God's unapproachable beatitude (Calvin), man remains cut off from even an awareness of 'the fullness of joy' and 'pleasures

---

6. Athanasius, *On the Incarnation* chap.15.

7. John Calvin, *The Gospel according to St. John 1–10* (Edinburgh: St. Andrew Press: 1995), 131.

8. More on this point in chapter 4.

forevermore' (Ps. 16:11), let alone access into that light. But in the incarnation Christ brings that light into the view of sinful man (John 1:5).[9]

Further, it is worth stressing the point of the incarnation's complete integrity. Christ does not simply reveal God from time to time while in His 'corporeal' (i.e., human) nature. God's revelation in Christ does not merely *occur* in His earthly ministry. His corporeal nature *is* divine revelation. The revelation of the incarnation is a total event, represented in the whole of His life. Every second of His enfleshed state is revelation. 'There really is no other instance of a figure like Christ,' notes David Bentley Hart, 'in whom attributions of such extravagance and details of such mundane particularity not only coincide, but indeed inhere in one another.'[10] In the incarnation God speaks with flesh and bones. And since all divine revelation is a manifestation of divine glory, and since all manifestation of glory entails a manifestation of divine beauty (see chapter 2), the whole of Christ's person and work is the apex of the divine revelation of beauty. This point Augustine eloquently makes:

> Let us therefore, who believe, run to meet a Bridegroom who is beautiful where he is. Beautiful as God, as the Word who is with God, he is beautiful in the Virgin's womb, where he did not lose his godhead but assumed our humanity. Beautiful he is as a baby, as the Word unable to speak because while he was still without speech, still a baby in arms and nourished at his mother's breasts, the heavens spoke for him, a star guided the magi, and he was adored in the manger as food for the humble. He was beautiful in heaven, then, and beautiful on earth: beautiful in the womb, and beautiful in his parent's arms. He was beautiful in his miracles but just as beautiful too in not shrinking from death, beautiful in laying down his life and beautiful in taking it up again, beautiful on the cross, beautiful in the tomb, and beautiful in heaven .... Do not allow the weakness of his flesh to blind you to the splendor of his beauty. The supreme and most real beauty is justice: if you can catch him out in any injustice, you will not find him beautiful in that regard; but if he is found to be just at every point, then he is lovely in all respects. Let him come to us, so that we may gaze on him with the eyes of our spirit.[11]

9. Again, see Athanasius, *On the Incarnation* chap.15.

10. Hart, *The Beauty of the Infinite*, 328-29.

11. Augustine, *Exposition of Psalm 44* in *Expositions of the Psalms 33–50*; cited in King, *The Beauty of the Lord*, 211.

In his recent work *The Beauty of Jesus Christ: Filling out a Scheme of St. Augustine*, O'Collins draws on this passage from Augustine and considers how Christ manifests divine beauty in various aspects of His person and work. 'As the Revealer par excellence,' he notes, 'Christ communicates the divine beauty and loving goodness. Since God is love and beauty, Jesus is that love and beauty in person.'[12]

The glory Christ manifests is not simply unique to His person; it is the glory of the divine nature, epistemologically mediated. John Owen makes this point with (surprising) brevity: 'He is the complete image and perfect representation of the Divine Being and excellencies.'[13] In a characteristically longer statement, Owen writes:

> He 'is the image of the invisible God.' In him God was, in him he dwelt, in him is he known, in him is he worshipped according unto his own will, in him is there a nearer approach made unto us by the divine nature than ever could enter into the heart of man to conceive. In the constitution of his person – of two natures, so infinitely distinct and separate in themselves – and in the work it was designed unto, the wisdom, power, goodness, love, grace, mercy, holiness, and faithfulness of God, are manifested unto us. This is the one blessed 'image of the invisible God,' wherein we may learn, wherein we may contemplate and adore, all his divine perfections.[14]

For Owen, the mediatory role of Christ as divine revelation is crucial. The Christian who looks longingly upon Jesus – the two-natured God-man who comes to us as an earth dweller among earth dwellers – is not settling for an inferior object of affection. Jesus' human nature, for Owen, does not dilute the glory of His divine nature but rather *translates* it. 'The self-revelatory nature of God's actions in Christ during his earthly career,' Jonathan King points out, 'means that the essential nature of God – and thus the glory of God – is in fact revealed.'[15] Since God's glory is the majesty and perfection of all divine attributes,[16] one cannot associate it, in an idiosyncratic sense, with a single divine person;

---

12. O'Collins, *The Beauty of Jesus Christ*, 136.

13. Owen, *The Works of John Owen*, 1:69.

14. Ibid., 1:73.

15. King, *The Beauty of the Lord*, 168. Cf., Henry's affirmation that 'the *incarnate* Christ is the revelation of God's essential glory and redemptive grace' (*God, Revelation, and Authority*, 3:205-6).

16. Bavinck, *Reformed Dogmatics Vol. 2*, 252

it is constituent to the divine nature.[17] Thus, when Christ reveals glory, it is not Christ's glory alone but rather the Trinity's glory – the glory of the divine nature the Father, Son, and Spirit share (John 17:5). Thus, Boersma can say, 'God always and forever manifests himself in and through the humanity of Jesus Christ.'[18] As we will see in chapter 6, the language of 'always and forever' is no hyperbole. Let us not imagine man would be able to bear unmediated sight of God's essential glory were it not for his sin, and thus will be able to bear such a sight in the new heavens and the new earth. While the sight of divine glory is hampered and impaired by sin, this fact alone does not quite tell us enough. Unmediated divine glory is outside of man's possible comprehension not strictly on account of his sinfulness but rather on account of his creatureliness. The mediatory revelation of Christ does not simply make the *beatific vision* possible for sinners. More fundamentally, it makes such a vision possible for finite creatures. Again, Owen says this powerfully:

> In his incarnation, the Son was made the representative image of God unto us – as he was, in his person, the essential image of the Father, by eternal generation. The invisible God – Whose nature and divine excellencies our understandings can make no approach unto – does in him represent, exhibit, or make present unto our faith and spiritual sense, both himself and all the glorious excellencies of his nature.[19]

This point of Christ's revelation of divine glory was of no small concern for the fathers, who made great use of it in their reverent musings on Christ. Hilary of Poitiers, speaking of John's prologue, notes how 'the eternity and infinity and beauty which, by the light of natural reason, [my soul] had attributed to its Creator belonged also to God the Only-begotten.'[20] He later says plainly, 'Thus in the Son of God we behold the true Divine nature. He is God, He is Creator, He is Son of God, He is omnipotent.'[21]

---

17. The incomprehensibility of God and analogical use of language must here be acknowledged, for language is intrinsically unable to communicate this point in full. Even the term 'constituent' is misleading, since it denotes being part of the whole – an idea unbecoming of the Triune God who is simple, as we shall explore below.

18. Boersma, *Seeing God*, 134.

19. Owen, *The Works of John Owen*, 1:72

20. Hilary, *De Trinitate* 1.11.

21. Ibid., 4.5.

Likewise, in his thirtieth oration Gregory of Nazianzus notes, 'The Son is the concise and simple revelation of the Father's nature – everything born is a tacit definition of its parent .... Here we have a living image of a living being, indistinguishable from its original.'[22] Gregory of Nyssa says it starkly: 'Through the covering of the flesh the divine power is made accessible, so that the enemy will not take fright at God's appearing and so thwart his plan for us.'[23] The striking, paradoxical nature of Gregory's wording should not be missed. 'The divine power is made accessible' not *in spite* of the 'covering of the flesh', but rather, it is through *covering* Himself with flesh that the divine Son makes the divine power *accessible*. He goes on to insist that 'all God's attributes are at once displayed in this ['the covering of the flesh,' i.e., the incarnation] – his goodness, his wisdom, and his justice.'[24] Commenting on this passage, Carnes rightly concludes, 'the incarnation, then, is and was intended as a profound act of disclosure, teaching us the abiding goodness, wisdom, and justice of God.'[25]

The 'radiance' imagery of which the author of Hebrews makes use seems to confirm this point as well (Heb 1:1-3). Not only does it contribute to the Bible's overall testimony of the Son's eternal generation, it also drives a communicative point. John Webster points this out: 'Put in formal terms, the metaphor attests a double reality of *filiation* and of *manifestation*: of how the Son has his being in relation to the Father, and of how the Son radiates the presence of God's majesty.'[26] This is precisely what John's prologue communicates as well. What Moses was prohibited from seeing in Exodus 33:20 was God's divine glory. The Fourth Evangelist calls attention to this same glory with his words, 'No one has ever seen God' (John 1:18a). But, as Henri Blocher points out, 'What corresponds to the mysterious passing by and the hand protecting is now the coming of the Word in the flesh of the Son become one of us.' He goes on to say,

> We know God when Jesus Christ has passed and we follow him; we know
> him in truth, for he is God, and whoever has seen him has seen the Father;

---

22. Gregory of Nazianzus, *Orations* 30.20.

23. Gregory of Nyssa, *Address on Religious Instruction* sec. 23.

24. Ibid.

25. Carnes, *Beauty*, 149.

26. Webster, 'One Who Is Son,' in *God Without Measure*, 73.

we know him by grace, and we marvel not only that we escaped destruction by the blaze of the Glory, but that in him, through faith in his name, we receive eternal life as sons and daughters of God.[27]

As an aside, we should note this does not mean that every moment of Christ's life is divine revelation in exactly the same way or with the same intensity. There are punctuated moments in the life of Christ, wherein His glory is more apparent. The time that lapses in Jesus' life between Luke 2:52 and 3:1 is, in light of what we have explored above, *revelation*. But we are not then required to insist that this revelation is as clear or potent as, for example, Christ's baptism (Matt. 3:13-17; Mark 1:9-11; Luke 3:21-22), His sermon on the mount (e.g., Matt. 5:1-7:29) and other teachings, His miraculous works, His calming of the storm (Mark 4:35-41; Luke 8:22-25), His transfiguration (Matt. 17:1-8; Mark 9:2-8; Luke 9:28-36; cf., 2 Pet. 1:16-18), His crucifixion (Matt. 27:22-50; Mark 15:21-39; Luke 23:26-46; John 19:1-28), His resurrection (Matt. 28:1-10; Mark 16:1-8; Luke 24:1-35; John 20:1-29), or His ascension (Luke 24:50-53; Acts 1:6-11). Always, Christ is the supreme revelation of divine glory, but on occasion more readily perceived as such.

One may acknowledge this much, but the Word's being made flesh raises the question: is the divine nature's glory that is revealed in the incarnation a *result* of the incarnation? Is this a glory that did not exist prior to the incarnation? Is this, in other words, a *new* glory? 'No' is our short response, which we will unpack in the form of a meditation on the doctrine of divine immutability in light of the incarnation.

The Incarnation of the *Immutable* Son of God

On its surface the incarnation – wherein the Second Person of the Trinity 'became' man – itself appears to make short work of the previous chapter's defense of divine immutability.[28] Surely the incarnation must

---

27. Henri Blocher, 'John 1: Preexistent Logos and God the Son,' in *Theological Commentary: Evangelical Perspectives*, ed. R. Michael Allen (New York: T&T Clark, 2011), 128.

28. Graham A. Cole, *The God Who Became Human: A Biblical Theology of Incarnation*, New Studies in Biblical Theology 30 (Downers Grove, IL: IVP Academic, 2013),145, helpfully frames this discussion: 'If we indeed live on a visited planet, then did that even change God, and if so in what ways? After all, John 1:14 claims that the Word (*logos*) became (*egeneto*) something other than the Word, namely flesh (*sarx*). There are several

denote mutability in the divine nature, must it not?[29] The answer to this quandary is, in truth, mere Chalcedonian Christology. For example, in answer to Moltmann and other critics of divine immutability who object to its validity on the grounds of the incarnation, Blocher writes,

> The force of Moltmann's argument really hinges on his rejection of the Chalcedonian two natures. He obviously distastes the distinction in the Symbol: unconfusedly, unchangeably. For him, the *human* history of Jesus enters God's being and thus determines Trinity. *We* would maintain the Chalcedonian scheme as not only indispensable if deity and humanity are to be confessed with their Scriptural value, but, as such, already discernable in the New Testament. The logic of Hebrews 1 and 2, and of Paul in Romans 9:1-5, so implies …. Turretin's reply to those who argue for divine mutability on the basis of the incarnation, that the *Person* of the Son, the *Logos*, became flesh, took on human nature, and not *deity* as such, has solid biblical foundations.[30]

Central to a Chalcedonian conception of Christology is Christ's two-nature distinction predicated upon the one person.[31] The divine nature did not add to itself a human nature; rather the divine Son – who has a divine nature – added to Himself a human nature. This means, while the Son reveals the shared divine nature of the Trinity in the incarnation (i.e., the glory and beauty of the Trinity), the assumption of a human nature was predicated on the *person* of the Son and not the *divine nature* He reveals. In other words, the incarnation added nothing whatsoever to the divine nature. Rather, the Son humbled Himself by taking on a

---

logical possibilities here. One is that the incarnation changed the very being of God …. The better answer is the classical one.' Though on this matter we should do as Cole says and not as he does, for the answer Cole adopts cannot be properly understood as the 'classical' one. He writes that the 'Trinity *now relates to itself qua Trinity in a new way* through the humanity of Christ …. The plus is the new way the Father, Son and Holy Spirit relate through the assumed humanity of the Son. Rather we are speaking of the Trinity and plus. The change is relational and permanent' (ibid., 145-46).

29. See Jürgen Moltmann, *The Crucified God* (Minneapolis: Fortress, 2015); Moltmann, *The Trinity and the Kingdom*; Isaac A. Dorner, *Divine Immutability: A Critical Recon-sideration*, trans. Robert R. Williams and Claude Welch (Minneapolis, MN: Fortress Press, 1994).

30. Henri Blocher, 'Divine Immutability,' in *The Power and Weakness of God*, ed. Nigel M. de S. Cameron (Edinburgh: Rutherford House, 1990), 120 (emphasis original).

31. See Stephen J. Wellum, *God the Son Incarnate: The Doctrine of Christ*, Foundations of Evangelical Theology (Wheaton, IL: Crossway, 2016), chap. 13.

human nature in addition to *His* untouched, immutable, eternal divine nature in such a way that the two natures remain 'without confusion, without change, without division, and without separation.'[32] Adonis Vidu points out that the doctrine of inseparable operations implies that 'the incarnation-assumption belongs to the Trinity as a whole', such that 'Father, Son, and Holy Spirit are together *causing* the assumption' from the perspective of action. Nevertheless, the action terminates 'in the Son … in a state that characterizes the Son alone.'[33] The incarnation is a Trinitarian act, which terminates in the Son. Thus, it is the subject of the divine person of *the Son*, and not the divine nature as such, that 'becomes man.'

Further, it is not as though the Son toggles back and forth between His divine nature and His human nature as if they were vehicles; one He leaves vacant while occupying the other. For the divine nature to be vacant of a divine person (or, for a divine person who neglects to act within a divine nature) is an incoherent concept.[34] A divine person is 'divine' by virtue of His divine nature. Further, there is no divine nature back of the divine persons; to be the one, simple, divine being is to be the Father who eternally begets the Son, and in that begetting, together with the Son, eternally spirates the Spirit.[35] Since the divine nature is, by definition, simple and pure Triune act, it cannot be anything other than itself eternally.

To suggest that a divine person can voluntarily suspend the very attributes (e.g., immutability, impassibility, omniscience, etc.) that make Him divine without compromising either His divine personhood or the divine nature itself is self-defeating. On the one hand, He cannot be

---

32. 'The Chalcedonian Decree' in Edward Rochie Hardy, ed., *Christology of the Later Fathers* (Louisville, KY: Westminster John Knox Press, 2006), 372-374.

33. Adonis Vidu, *The Same God Who Works All Things: Inseparable Operations in Trinitarian Theology*, Grand Rapids, MI: Eerdmans, 2021), 162.

34. This seems to be the implication of the proposal by some evangelicals who argue that Christ, while retaining access to His divine nature during the incarnation, chose not to exercise divine attributes through it. E.g., Bruce A. Ware, *The Man Christ Jesus: Theological Reflections on the Humanity of Christ* (Wheaton, IL: Crossway, 2013).

35. See Lewis Ayers, 'Augustine on the Trinity,' in Emery and Levering, *The Oxford Handbook of the Trinity*; and Stephen R. Holmes, 'Trinitarian Action and Inseparable Operations: Some Historical and Dogmatic Reflections,' in *Advancing Trinitarian Theology: Explorations in Constructive Dogmatics*, ed. Oliver Crisp and Fred Sanders (Grand Rapids, MI: Zondervan, 2014).

called divine if His attributes are not eternal (i.e., if His attributes are not characterized by the essential divine attribute of eternity).[36] On the other hand, if a true subject of the divine nature can suspend attributes of said divine nature (e.g., immutability), such attributes are not essential. This, however, is an oxymoron since the divine nature cannot be a composite of essential and accidental properties.[37]

Safeguarding against this kind of reductionism is precisely what the concept of the *communicatio idiomatum* (communication of attributes)[38] is for. Working together with that cherished misnomer, the *extra calvinisticum*,[39] we can affirm that Christ operates fully through both His natures. What can be said about either nature of Christ can be said about His person precisely because *He* does not cease to occupy His divine nature when He assumes His human nature. This seems to be a necessary implication from various New Testament passages. For example, in Colossians 1:15-18 and Hebrews 1:1-3, the Son of God is credited not only for the origin of the created universe but also its continual maintenance ('... and in him all things hold together' [Col. 1:17b]; '... and he upholds the universe by the word of his power' [Heb 1:2b]). If this is true at any point of creation's existence, it is true for every point, including those days in which the earth enjoyed the physical presence of Jesus Christ of Nazareth. The cosmos are upheld by the *Son*: this is how creation continues to exist moment by moment. At the risk of redundancy: to be creation is to be upheld by the *Son*. Were the Son to ever cease upholding the cosmos by His powerful word,

---

36. Thomas Aquinas, *Summa Theologiae* I.3. Anselm, *Monologion* chap. 15, in *The Major Works*. Dolezal, *All That Is in God*, 31-66. Dolezal, ibid., 39, states, 'The reason God actively operates is because all that is in him is perfect and thus actual.'

37. See Anselm, *Monologion* chap. 25.

38. Wellum summarizes this in *God the Son Incarnate*, 424-25.

39. This is the concept that the Son of God, while assuming a human nature, never ceased to utilize the fullness of His divine attributes; He never ceased to have 'purely actual' nature. See Calvin, *Institutes*, Book II:13. Although, as E. David Willis points out in *Calvin's Catholic Christology: The Function of the So-Called Extra Calvinisticum in Calvin's Theology* (Leiden: Brill, 1966), the doctrine did not originate with Calvin. Of course, this doctrine was the centerpiece of the Christological controversies between the Reformed churches and the Lutheran churches in the sixteenth and seventeenth century, but these issues do not concern the present work. For an overview of that controversy, see Andrew M. McGinnis, *The Son of God Beyond the Flesh: A Historical and Theological Study of the Extra Calvinisticum* (New York, NY: T&T Clark, 2014), chap. 4.

the cosmos would cease to exist, since their continued existence is His divine prerogative. Therefore, Athanasius is more than justified to write:

> For he was not enclosed in the body, nor was he in the body but not elsewhere. Nor while he moved that [body] was the universe left void of his activity and providence. But, what is most marvelous, being the Word, he was not contained by anyone, but rather himself contained everything. And, as being in all creation, he is in essence outside of everything by his own power, arranging everything and unfolding his own providence in everything to all things, and giving life to each thing and to all things together, containing the universe and not being contained, but being wholly, in every respect, in his own Father alone. So also, being in the human body, and himself giving it life, he properly gives life to the universe also, and was both in everything and outside of all.[40]

Not only does this doctrine seem to be a necessary extrapolation from passages like Colossians 1 and Hebrews 1, it seems to be stated explicitly elsewhere in Scripture: 'He was foreknown before the foundation of the world but was made manifest in the last times for the sake of you who through him are believers in God, who raised him from the dead and gave him glory, so that your faith and hope are in God' (1 Pet. 1:20-21). Reflecting on this passage, Steven Duby notes that 'we believe in God through Christ in that what God does in Christ is the culminating revelation of God in the economy and is the greatest assurance that we can trust in the benevolence and power of God, whose own life nevertheless does exceed what takes place in the economy.'[41]

The incarnation, then, poses no threat to the doctrine of divine immutability. Even the κενωσι (*kenosis*) and ταπεινωσι (*tapeinosis*) of the Son in Philippians 2:4-8 does not jeopardize this confession. Christ's 'emptying' is 'explained by the instrumental participles that follow it: Christ empties himself *by* taking the form of a servant and *by* being made in the likeness of human beings .... [K]enosis here is not subtraction by addition.'[42] By taking on a mutable human nature as the instrumentality for translating divine infinitude for finite creatures, Christ reveals the immutable divine nature precisely by means of

---

40. Athanasius, *On the Incarnation* chap. 15.

41. Duby, *God in Himself,* 17.

42. Ibid. 159.

κενωσι☒ (*kenosis*).[43] 'The act by which the form of God appears in the form of a slave,' notes Hart, 'is the act by which the infinite divine image shows itself in the finite divine image: this then is not a change, but a manifestation, of who God is.'[44]

In fact, the incarnation needs the doctrine of immutability for its authenticity; for the Son to be both fully and truly God as well as fully and truly man, the divine nature must be immutable. Without immutability, the incarnation would denote a blended-natured God-man who is neither God nor man. Such a being would be impotent for the work of salvation on account of its failure to represent God (i.e., He could not reveal the divine nature in an aesthetic-soteriological sense because He would not have it) or any actual human. Thus, as Weinandy points out, 'God's immutability must be maintained not only for theological reasons, i.e., in order to protect God as God; but also for incarnational reasons, i.e., God must remain immutable in becoming man if it is really and truly *God* who is man.'[45]

Further, it is not simply the Son's immutability that renders the kenotic and semi-kenotic readings of Philippians 2:4-8 an impossibility, however. Maintaining the integrity of Trinitarian theology also necessitates that we refuse this standard reading of the text. The doctrine of the incarnation must never be detached from an understanding of divine appropriations, in light of the doctrine of inseparable operations, or else the Triune *processions* and *missions* are destined for confusion. Vidu frames the issue well:

> The incarnation only appears to present to us *just* one of the divine persons, the eternal Word. Such an appearance is fitting, for the end of the incarnation pertains to the illumination of humanity, leading to the restoration of the divine image in man. And yet this ascription should not be understood in a strict sense, to the exclusion of the presence of the Father and the Spirit in the incarnation. Since the triune persons are inseparable from each other in substance, *the sending forth of the Son cannot entail his becoming untethered from the Father.*[46]

---

43. Bavinck, *Reformed Dogmatics, Volume 3*, 259, stresses the importance of this point in terms of worship, safeguarding against idolatry.

44. Hart, *The Beauty of the Infinite*, 375.

45. Weinandy, *Does God Change?*, 187 (emphasis original).

46. Vidu, *The Same God Who Works All Things*, 65 (emphasis mine).

There is simply no reason to assume that Christ's 'self-emptying' in Philippians 2:4-8 (or, for that matter, His 'impoverishment' in 2 Corinthians 8:9) entails His giving up anything related to His divine nature unless the distinction between *procession* and *mission* is blurred. But to blur such a distinction is a fatal mistake. True, they are not *unrelated*, but they necessarily relate in an indicating way: to equate the Trinity's existence *ad intra* with His actions *ad extra* – or Triune *procession* with Triune *mission*, or to flatten the difference between the *immanent* Trinity and the *economic* Trinity – is to circumscribe the infinite into the finite. Trinity may not be less truly present in what is revealed, but Trinity is certainly more.

While the divine mission of the Son following the Father's sending in assuming a human nature, and the Spirit following the Father and Son's sending in applying the work of redemption, do not bespeak univocal movement in the Trinity's timeless eternal life, they do *fittingly correspond* to that timeless eternal pure act of filiation and procession. The Son, not the Father nor the Spirit, is *fittingly* sent by the Father to assume a human nature, and to send the Spirit *with* the Father to apply their Triune love to the elect – such a work is only appropriate for He who receives life in Himself eternally from His begetting Father, a life that includes the shared act of spiriting the Holy Spirit eternally. Again, Vidu is helpful here:

> Since God does not become a finite cause, since he has not exhausted himself in finite reality, but remains transcendent, the nature and reality of the divine acts in history is not fully expressed by what may be experienced .... There is a depth to this divine activity that may only be contemplated from above, so to speak, or from the direction of the immanent Trinity, or the processions .... the divine operations *ad extra* follow from, and are grounded in, the immanent processions.[47]

Unless we maintain this much with Vidu, we are forced to conclude the absurd statement that the eternal processions of eternal generation, filiation, and spiration were (at least) temporarily suspended while the Son impoverished Himself of His divine glory. For His divine glory is none other than His eternal filiation from the Father, and their eternal spiration of the Spirit. But 'temporary' and 'suspend' are time- and

---

47. Ibid., 95.

space-bound words that ought never approach the eternality of Triune processions. Trinitarian missions and processions must be held together without confusion in a way similar to how Christ's two distinct natures must be held together without confusion.

The importance of maintaining the hypostatic union of these two distinct natures – truly immutable and infinite *God*, truly mutable and finite *man* – in the one divine person of the Son has been articulated by few people better than Francis Turretin. We quote him at length here:

> The work of redemption could not have been performed except by a God-man associating by incarnation the human nature with the divine by an indissoluble bond. For since to redeem us, two things were most especially required – the acquisition of death for satisfaction and victory over the same for the enjoyment of life – our mediator ought to be God-man to accomplish these things: man to suffer, God to overcome; man to receive the punishment we deserved, God to endure and drink it to the dregs; man to acquire salvation for us by dying, God to apply it to us by overcoming; man to become ours by the assumption of flesh, God to make us like himself by the bestowal of the Spirit. This neither man nor God alone could do. For neither could God alone be subject to death, nor man alone conquer it. Man alone could die for men; God alone could vanquish death.[48]

Likewise, musing on these very matters, Hilary goes to ask, in doxological fashion:

> What worthy return can we make for so great a condescension? The one Only-begotten God, ineffably born of God, entered the Virgin's womb and grew and took the frame of poor humanity. He who upholds the universe, within Whom and through Whom are all things, was brought forth by common childbirth: He at Whose voice Archangels and Angels tremble, and heaven and earth and all the elements of this world are melted, was heard in childish wailing. The Invisible and Incomprehensible, Whom sight and feeling and touch cannot gauge, was wrapped in a cradle. If any man deem all this unworthy of God, the greater must he own his debt for the benefit conferred the less such condescension befits the majesty of God. He by Whom man was made had nothing to gain by becoming Man; it was our gain that God was incarnate and dwelt among us, making all flesh His home by taking upon Him the flesh of One. We were raised because He was lowered; shame to Him was glory to us. He, being God,

---

48. Turretin, *Institutes*, 2:XIII.xix.

made flesh His residence, and we in return are lifted anew from the flesh to God.[49]

Note: whether these truths are affirmed by post-Reformation theologians or early church fathers, the point is not to explain or resolve the mystery of the incarnation. Rather, the concern is to describe the mystery in a way that befits and honors God. Describing so as to revere God, rather than explaining God, is the goal of the pious in every age.

Cruciform Beauty: Glory in the Cross

All of this, however, creates an uncomfortable tension: the 'gospel of the glory of Christ', wherein the Son reveals the beautiful glory of the Triune God, centers on a grotesque crucifixion scene (1 Cor. 2:2; Gal. 6:14).[50] 'Surely,' one might argue, 'such a spectacle cannot be reconciled to any notion of beauty.'[51] The problem is set forth succinctly by O'Collins: 'The terrible ugliness of the crucifixion appears to rule out any talk of Christ's being attractively beautiful in "laying down his life".'[52] Yet, according to Jonathan Edwards, the very essence of saving faith's aesthetic impetus is *cruciform beauty*. One of the precise places wherein the sinner sees the beauty of the divine at its clearest is in the person of Christ, bloodied and hanging on a cross:

> It is by seeing the excellency of Christ's Person that the saints are made sensible of the preciousness of His blood, and its sufficiency to atone for

---

49. Hilary, *De Trinitate* 2.25.

50. A fuller treatment of what follows can be found in John-Mark Hart, 'Triune Beauty and the Ugly Cross: Towards a Theological Aesthetic,' *Tyndale Bulletin* 66 (2015): 293-312. This is the central tension featured in Hart's article.

51. An example of this kind of rationale may be found in the work of Brian Zahnd. E.g., Brian Zahnd, *Beauty Will Save the World: Rediscovering the Allure and Mystery of Christianity* (Lake Mary, MO: Charisma House, 2012); Brian Zahnd, *Sinners in the Hands of a Loving God: The Scandalous Truth of the Very Good News* (Colorado Springs, CO: WaterBrook, 2017). Though Zahnd is perfectly content with identifying the crucifixion as a display of divine beauty in some respect, the notion that *retributive justice*, whereby Christ satisfies the wrath of the Father on the cross, is, for him, appalling. Thus he writes, 'The cross is a cataclysmic collision of violence and forgiveness. The violence part of the cross is entirely human. The forgiveness part of the cross is entirely divine' (*Sinners in the Hands of a Loving God*, 101). Also, 'In the parable of the prodigal son, the father doesn't rush to the servants' quarters to beat a whipping boy and vent his anger before he can forgive his son. Yet Calvin's theory of the cross would require this ugly insertion into Jesus's most beautiful parable' (ibid., 103).

52. O'Collins, *The Beauty of Jesus Christ*, 100.

sin; for therein consists the preciousness of Christ's blood, that it is the blood of so excellent and amiable a Person .... By this sight of the moral beauty of divine things is seen the beauty of the way of salvation by Christ; for that consists in the beauty of the moral perfections of God, which wonderfully shines forth in every step of this method of salvation from beginning to end.[53]

The Fourth Evangelist connects Jesus' revealed glory and His crucifixion as well. At the close of the book of signs in the Gospel of John, the evangelist gives an account for the widespread rejection of Jesus' ministry (which will eventually culminate with crucifixion), quoting two passages from Isaiah (John 12:36-43; cf., Isa. 6:10; 53:1).[54] Speaking of both passages (i.e., the heavenly throne room scene of Isaiah 6 and the suffering servant scene of Isaiah 53), John writes, 'Isaiah said *these things* when he saw his glory and spoke of him' (John 12:41, emphasis added).[55] According to John, the same glory Isaiah describes seeing in the heavenly throne room is manifested in the sufferings of the Messiah in Isaiah 53.[56] The grotesque crucifixion of Christ is what divine beauty looks like when grace towards sinners is in view.[57] Jonathan King makes this point well,

> In his crucifixion as a convicted criminal, and his placement in the prominent center between two other convicted criminals, Christ's ignominy becomes both an iconic and ironic dramatization of his majesty. It is because the form ... and content ... of God's self-revelation in Christ

---

53. Jonathan Edwards, *Works of Jonathan Edwards*, 2:274-75. Cf., King, *The Beauty of the Lord*, 209.

54. For a full treatment on John's use of these Isaianic passages, see, Andreas J. Köstenberger, 'John,' in *Commentary on the New Testament Use of the Old Testament*, ed. G. K. Beale and D. A. Carson (Grand Rapids, MI: Baker Academic, 2007), 476-83.

55. We are not immediately concerned with whether the glory Isaiah sees in chapter 6 is Jesus' glory or if the glorious one sitting on the throne is in fact Jesus. For more on this topic, see Köstenberger, 'John,' 479-80; D. A. Carson, *The Gospel according to John* (Grand Rapids, MI: Eerdmans, 1991), 449-50; Herman N. Ridderbos, *The Gospel according to John: A Theological Commentary*, trans. John Vriend (Grand Rapids, MI.: Eerdmans, 1997), 445-46; Andreas J. Köstenberger, *John* (Grand Rapids, MI: Baker Academic, 2004), 390-93. What primarily concerns us at present is the relationship John sees between the glory of Jesus, His crucifixion, and the Jews' rejection.

56. 'In the wake of the *two Isaianic quotes* in 12:38 and 12:40, the evangelist concludes that "Isaiah saw Jesus' glory"' (Köstenberger, *John*, 391, emphasis added).

57. See, King, *The Beauty of the Lord*, 220.

– that is, the character of the Son within the form of Christ – are perfectly united, that the essential nature of God – and thus glory of God – is truly and properly revealed.[58]

Furthermore, this cruciform display of glory seems to be the very thing the Jews reject.[59] In this way, the crucifixion not only displays divine glory, it results from divine glory; God blinds the eyes and hardens the hearts of unbelieving Jews by sending a Messiah whose divine glory they reject as apparent un-glory (more on this in chapter 5). Only with the eyes of faith, therefore, can one reconcile the seeming contradiction of Christ's beauty and His grotesque death on the cross. This is nothing new. As we shall see in the coming chapters, perception judgment is typical in God's saving economy. The natural man cannot consider the bloody cross beautiful any more than the natural Greek can consider the gospel *wise*, or the natural Jew consider it a *powerful sign*. The apparently ugly, foolish, weak gospel is considered beautiful, wise, and powerful only to 'those who are called' (1 Cor. 1:18-25). At present, it is crucial to emphasize simply that in the objective estimation of God's word, the cross reveals the glory (and, thereby, *beauty*) of God, regardless of how that revelation is perceived at the subjective level.

Before concluding this section, we should recognize that Christ reveals this divine glory in far more places in His life and ministry than the crucifixion. Indeed, the transfiguration, the benevolent life and miraculous works of Christ, and the ascension all prove to be fruitful events for theological contemplation of divine glory.[60]

The disproportionately high attention I have given to the glory of Christ in the crucifixion should not be read as an implicit assumption that the glory Christ reveals at these other moments in the *historia salutis*

---

58. Ibid., 222.

59. Thus a parallel seems to be drawn with Jesus' prophetic message and Isaiah's, in that both serve as the judicial hardening instrument God uses. See Carson, *John*, 448.

60. See Aquinas, *Summa Theologiae Tertia Pars* Q.45; Michael Ramsey, *The Glory of God and the Transfiguration of Christ* (Eugene, OR: Wipf & Stock, 2009); Dorothy Lee, *Transfiguration* (London: Continuum, 2004); O'Collins, *The Beauty of Jesus Christ*; Patrick Schreiner, *The Ascension of Christ: Recovering a Neglected Doctrine* (Bellingham, WA: Lexham, 2020); Peter Orr, *Exalted above the Heavens: The Risen and Ascended Christ*, New Studies in Biblical Theology 47 (Downers Grove, IL: IVP Academic, 2018); Michael Dawson, *Jesus Ascended: The Meaning of Christ's Continuing Incarnation* (London: T&T Clark, 2004).

are somehow less important. Nothing could be further from the truth. I focus here on the crucifixion for two practical reasons.

First, the thesis of this project is concerned with the role of Christ's beauty in conversion, and while the revelation of Christ's glory in His life, transfiguration, resurrection, and ascension are all essential aspects in the gospel, the cross does seem to be the conceptual center – wherein every other moment is heading *toward* or extending *from*. The crucifixion's conceptual centrality does not make it more important than these others (indeed, the cross is rendered incoherent apart from the miraculous conception of Christ, His sinless life, His resurrection, and His ascension), but it does provide a point of focus for a limited project such as this one. Since I have to make some choice for what to focus on in this work on *conversion*, the cross of Christ seems appropriate.

Second, and related, the crucifixion's centrality as such does not intuitively cohere with the thesis that Christ attracts sinners with His *beauty*. Whereas few would object to the claim that Christ's benevolent life, transfiguration, victorious resurrection, or glorious ascension reveal divine beauty, it is almost instinctual to protest calling the bloody cross *beautiful*. Therefore, in light of the role of *beauty* in this project, sustained attention on its chief apparent obstacle (the ugly cross) is fitting.

Conclusion

The whole incarnation of Christ constitutes the absolute apex of God's self-disclosure. In Christ are creatures able to behold the divine glory of the Triune God. The whole of Christ's person and work, therefore, is the zenith of transcendent beauty accommodated for earthlings like us. Accommodated, but not dumbed down, for the Triune glory that Christ reveals is not exhausted in the incarnation, because it is, in fact, inexhaustible. Apart from Christ, as Mediator, the inaccessible light of the divine would remain forever inaccessible. But through His person and work – the highs and the lows, from the transfiguration to the crucifixion – we can see incomprehensible beauty in truth. On this point Hart writes,

> The form of Christ inhabits at once a province of shadows and a region of glorious light, he is at once nocturnally and diurnally beautiful, his is simultaneously a way of abasement and a way of exaltation. And these two ways are one: not a before and after, but a venturing forth from and return to

the Father that is one motion, one life, one dramatic action that overcomes totality's defining horizon – death – not through reconciliation with the limits it marks but through the infinite act of *kenosis* and glorification that transgresses it, passes it by as though it were nothing.[61]

Here, the question arises: if in Christ God reveals His absolute beauty, why do so many persist in their insistence that He is unworthy of adoration? Why do not all who hear of Christ's person and work worship Him immediately with abandon? This question brings us to our central soteriological concerns. And it is at this juncture that this present work must part ways with many of the Roman Catholic dialogue partners who have appeared thus far. Therefore, before beginning to answer these narrow questions with a chapter on the existential realities of idolatry, illumination, regeneration, and faith, I wish to distinguish my own Protestant and Reformed soteriological convictions over and against others who have wrestled with this topic. The following chapter is an excursus of sorts laying out a broad Reformed affirmation of the *ordo salutis* in order to situate the rest of this work, methodologically, within a thoroughgoing Protestant context.

---

61. Hart, *The Beauty of the Infinite*, 322.

CHAPTER FOUR

Soteriological Foundations

THE *pactum Salutis*, THE *historia salutis*, AND THE *ordo salutis*

> *He swore but once, the deed was done*
> *'Twas settled by the Three-in-One*
> *Christ was appointed to redeem*
> *All that the Father loved in Him*
>
> *Hail sacred union, firm and strong*
> *How great Thy grace, how sweet the song*
> *That rebel worms should ever be*
> *One with incarnate Deity*

JOHN KENT[1]

Introduction

Properly speaking, this project concerns soteriology. We are interested in discerning what aesthetic dimensions are present in salvation, with particular attention to regeneration and saving faith. Within the process of salvation, I argue that the omni-beautiful Christ is the object of regenerated vision. What newly regenerated believers see when they see Christ is *divine beauty* – divine beauty intrinsically desirable and extrinsically apprehended by the instrument of faith.

This way of discussing divine beauty in the realm of soteriology is not new, which is both an advantage and a disadvantage to this project. The disadvantage comes on account of Roman Catholic presentations,

---

1. John Kent (1766–1843) "Twixt Jesus and the Chosen Race,' Hymn, public domain.

which unite justification and sanctification under the category of 'faith working through love', or charity, as the product of infused grace, perfecting faith so as to make the believer meritoriously righteous. This is not what I intend when I say that regeneration involves the restoration, creation, and activation of spiritual sense properties to recognize Christ's divine beauty and that faith involves the glad-hearted apprehension of Christ, who is desirable in part because He is beautiful. What concerns this chapter is the crucial distinction between 'hearty faith' – faith characterized by *fiducial*, heart-felt persuasion of Christ's worthiness – and 'faith perfected by charity'. Therefore, before turning our attention to the aesthetic dimensions of the *ordo salutis* in general, and regeneration and saving faith in particular, we will articulate in broad fashion the Reformed conception of the *ordo salutis* over and against the Roman Catholic conception.

In doing so, I have the opportunity to insist that what we said in chapter 2 about the metaphysics of divine beauty and, in particular, the *analogia entis*, is not out of step with a Reformed soteriology. There, we made a distinction between ontological participation and doxological or stereological participation. Remember, Hans Boersma claimed that accepting the Platonist-Christian account of the former must mean rejecting the Reformed account of the latter. The Reformed forensic account of justification by faith alone, and the Reformed conception of depravity's totality, Boersma has said, is out of step with the Great Tradition's 'sacramental tapestry'.[2] We saw in chapter 2 how sin's totalizing devastation does not conflict with the Great Tradition's metaphysic – its 'sacramental ontology' – but is rather punctuated by it: the incarnation is made more necessary – and thereby, in the end, more glorious – when sin's presence is cast within the context of a Christian-Platonist cosmos. Now the task remains to demonstrate how (contra Boersma's claim) the forensic nature of justification is not an attempt to weave a nominalist fabric with a Christian-Platonist one.

Is it possible to harmonize the Great Tradition's metaphysic of 'participation' with a Reformed soteriology? Answering this question clearly is certainly not made easier by the fact that some within the Reformed camp agree with Boersma about the harsh choice between the metaphysic

---

2. Hans Boersma, *Heavenly Participation: The Weaving of a Sacramental Tapestry* (Grand Rapids, MI: Eerdmans, 2011), 92.

of the Great Tradition and the soteriology of the Reformed tradition.[3] In truth, however, the Reformed tradition has always had a category for soteriological participation, which comfortably harmonizes the forensic character of justification by faith alone with the metaphysic of the Great Tradition discussed thus far. This category is hidden in plain sight, silently calling out and inviting contemporary adherents of Reformed theology to reunite with their catholic heritage. We are, of course, talking about *union with Christ*. This we shall discuss in due course.

The *pactum salutis* and Election

God's work of salvation, like all His works, began in the timeless eternity of His single, undivided, Triune will. To note this fact is not only to tip my hat to the intention of 'keeping theology theological', it is to note an important point about God's *ad intra* beauty. What unfolds in the *historia salutis* is a work of magnificent loveliness, but only when seen as a whole, originating within the timeless setting of God's eternal presencing. The work of salvation is no salvage project wherein God responds to the careless debacles of man. From beginning to end, the history of salvation is a beautiful story perfectly told, extending from and revealing the infinite beauty of the Trinity.

We are, of course, affirming here the doctrine of the covenant of redemption, succinctly defined by J. V. Fesko as 'the pre-temporal, intra-trinitarian agreement among Father, Son, and Holy Spirit to plan and execute the redemption of the elect.'[4] Fesko points out, 'theologians

---

3. E.g., see John M. Frame's comments on early and Mediaeval Christian thought in *A History of Western Philosophy and Theology* (Phillipsburg, NJ: P&R Publishing, 2015), 86-163. See also, Cornelius Van Til, *The Defense of the Faith;* Van Til, *A Christian Theory of Knowledge* (Phillipsburg, NJ: Presbyterian and Reformed Publishing, Co. 1969); and Jeffrey D. Johnson, *The Failure of Natural Theology: A Critical Appraisal of the Philosophical Theology of Thomas Aquinas* (Conway, AR: Free Grace Press, 2021). For two splendid critiques of the position articulated by these figures, specifically with regard to natural theology, see J. V. Fesko, *Reforming Apologetics: Retrieving the Classical Reformed Approach to Defending the Faith* (Grand Rapids, MI: Baker Academic, 2019); and David Haines, *Natural Theology: A Biblical and Historical Introduction and Defense* (Landrum, SC: The Davenant Press, 2021).

4. J. V. Fesko, *The Trinity and the Covenant of Redemption* (Ross-Shire: Christian Focus, 2016), 131. The proceeding section is indebted largely to this excellent work. In his thorough treatment, Fesko demonstrates that while few Reformed theologians have contested the biblical or orthodox legitimacy until recently, the specifics surrounding the *pactum* differ from theologian to theologian. For one thing, 'there does not appear

repeatedly appeal to the idea that the *pactum* is a manifestation of intra-trinitarian love, one that overflows to the elect.'[5] As we established in chapter 2, the Trinity's essential beauty is a necessary conceptual subset of God's *a se* eternal *beatitude*, which means creation is an overflowing and generous expression thereof. All created beauty has an analogical (and asymmetrical) participatory relationship to God's beauty. If this is true for creation in general, it is true for the *pactum salutis* in particular.[6]

The question of the relationship between the *pactum salutis* and election has been a question of no small debate in Reformed circles.[7] Involved in this debate are other intermural disputes regarding the timing of imputation and justification and infralapsarian vs. supralapsarian accounts of predestination.[8] While these questions are important, and my own inclinations regarding some of them are sure to become apparent in the proceeding discussion, they are not in themselves of first importance in this project. What I wish to emphasize at this point is that election and the *pactum salutis* involve one another. In insisting that they involve one another, we maintain a real distinction between the *pactum salutis* and election. Whereas the *pactum salutis* involves the 'pre-temporal, intra-trinitarian agreement … to plan and execute

---

to be one set exegetical path to establishing the doctrine of the *pactum*' (ibid., 46). The most important and highly contested question regarding the covenant of redemption, however, involves the parties involved. Is it an agreement between the Father and the Son exclusively (i.e., the Christological model), or is it an agreement reached and a plan hatched amongst all three divine persons (i.e., the Trinitarian model)? Fesko demonstrates how the predominant historical view is the Christological model, advocated by the likes of David Dickson, Jacob Arminius, Herman Witsius, Franciscus Gomarus, Gilbert Voetius, Patrick Gillespie, Samuel Rutherford, John Owen, Jonathan Edwards, Charles Hodge, Geerhardus Vos, and Louis Berkhof (ibid., 129). Notwithstanding such an impressive and wide-ranging list of thinkers, I agree with Fesko that the minority position – advocated alike by James Durham, Thomas Goodwin, Abraham Kuyper, and Herman Bavinck – is the preferable model, since it most naturally harmonizes with the doctrine of *inseparable operations*, and places the arrival of the Comforter (John 14:16; cf., 16:7) in 'the original plan', so to speak (see ibid., 130).

5. Ibid., 47-48.

6. As we saw in chapter 2, 'the Triune God reveals the eternal processions in their covenantal missions. The trinitarian processions become manifest in time through creation and especially redemption' (ibid., 169).

7. Fesko, *The Trinity and the Covenant of Redemption*, 195-244

8. Particularly helpful is Fesko's analysis of Geerhardus Vos, Jan van Genderen and William Hendrik Velema on the issue (Fesko, *The Trinity and the Covenant of Redemption*, 209-14).

the redemption of the elect,' as Fesko has pointed out, election is that work in which God determines who the elect *are*. As Berkhof notes, the *pactum salutis* is 'that eternal act of God whereby He, in His sovereign good pleasure, and on account of no foreseen merit in them, chooses a certain number of men to be the recipients of special grace and of eternal salvation.'[9] Election is a part of the beautiful Trinity's self-revelation in redemption, which is summarized succinctly in the covenant of redemption. As Fesko notes,

> The *pactum* is the anchor or eternal foundation of the covenant of grace, that which establishes the Son's voluntary obedience to secure eternal life for those who are united to Him by the Father's divine election – to obey the Father's will in the power of the Spirit, to fulfill the law, and thereby to secure both eternal life and the forgiveness of sins. It is here in the decree of election where the *pactum*, covenant of grace, Christology, and the active obedience meet.[10]

This conclusion seems unavoidable from Scripture, not only from hotly contended passages like Zechariah 6:13, which tells of Yahweh's 'Branch' who will 'build the temple of the LORD' where He will reign in royal authority, sharing 'the counsel of peace' with 'a priest';[11] or Psalm 2:7-8, where Yahweh says, 'You are my Son; today I have begotten you,' and subsequently invites His Davidic audience to ask of Him to receive the 'nations' as an inheritance and 'the ends of the earth' as His possession.[12]

The exegetical force for the *pactum salutis* is felt most strongly from three passages: Psalm 110, Ephesians 1:3-14, and 2 Timothy 2:9-10.[13] Despite the objections of those who have an allergic reaction to any hint of a *sensus plenior* in biblical interpretation,[14] there can be little doubt that the New Testament authors, and Jesus Himself, apply Psalm 110 to the work of Christ (cf., Matt. 22:44; Mark 12:36; Luke 20:42-43; Acts 2:34-35; Heb. 1:13; 7:1-22; 10:13). However David understood

---

9. Berkhof, *Systematic Theology*, 114.

10. Fesko, *The Trinity and the Covenant of Redemption*, 241.

11. For a defense of this passage as support of the *pactum salutis*, see ibid., 53-77.

12. Again, see Fesko, *The Trinity and the Covenant of Redemption*, 79-94.

13. See ibid., 107-22.

14. See excursus in chapter 2.

this conversation between 'the LORD' and 'my Lord',[15] Christ and His followers purport that, at the deepest level, it is a covenant conversation between the Father and the Son.[16] The 'priest forever' who is 'a guarantor of a better covenant' is Jesus Himself.[17]

Even if hermeneutical foul play is called on this reading of the New Testament's use of the Old, there seems to be little solace for those who would deny the biblical warrant of the *pactum salutis* in Ephesians 1:3-14. Within this passage Paul weaves a marvelous Trinitarian tapestry of salvation wherein those who are blessed by 'the God and Father of our Lord Jesus Christ' are blessed '*in* Christ' and are 'sealed with the promised Holy Spirit, who is the guarantee of our inheritance until we acquire possession of it, to the praise of his glory' (1:3, 13-14). Those whom the Father blesses *in Christ* receive in Christ 'every spiritual blessing', which includes the position of holiness and blamelessness before Him (1:4), spiritual adoption as sons (1:5), redemption through His blood, which is the forgiveness of sins (1:7), revealed knowledge of the mystery of His will (1:9), and the inheritance of glory, sealed and secured by the Holy Spirit (1:13-14).

Not only does this passage offer an impenetrable defense of monergism (i.e., those for whom Christ purchases redemption and the forgiveness of sins are those who are blessed by the Father in predestination and sealed by the Holy Spirit – to introduce a separation between election, atonement, or conversion is to introduce a separation in the Trinity's will to save sinners 'to the praise of his glory'), it also offers cogent summary

---

15. David W. Pao and Eckhard J. Schnabel argue that in its original context the psalm would have been understood by its early readers as 'celebrating David's conquest of Jerusalem and his accession to the throne, highlighting the implication of these events as divine pledges of universal dominion.' 'Luke' in Beale and Carson, *Commentary on the New Testament Use of the Old Testament*, 371.

16. 'Yahweh swears a covenant-oath to the Christ in eternity which establishes His priestly office according to the order of Melchizedek and appoints Him the guarantor or surety of the new covenant' (Fesko, *The Trinity and the Covenant of Redemption*, 106; see 95-106 for a full discussion on this psalm).

17. See, Beale, *A New Testament Biblical Theology*, 319. Additionally, despite the sustained sneer the term seems to receive from certain quarters, there is something to be said for the prosopological exegesis that would see Christ's relationship to this text not strictly in typological perspective but as an *actual* speaker in this dialogue between Himself and the Father. For a cogent perspective on this reading of Psalm 110:1, see Matthew W. Bates, *The Birth of the Trinity: Jesus, God, and Spirit in New Testament and Early Christian Interpretations of the Old Testament* (New York: Oxford University Press, 2016), 47-56.

of the *pactum salutis*. Though these things surely occur in time, they are all a singular work, προορισμένος ('predestined') πρὸ καταβολῆ⬚ κόσμου ('before the world began'). 'By placing God's choice of the elect before the foundation of the world, into the realm where only the Triune God existed,' observes Fesko, 'Paul locates the divine intra-trinitarian deliberations regarding the redemption of the elect completely out of man's reach – the Triune God chooses the church, the church does not choose the Triune God.'[18]

Despite the strong exegetical ground for affirming the *pactum salutis*, some criticize the doctrine on the dogmatic grounds that it (a) introduces multiple wills within the Trinity and thereby leads inevitably to tritheism, or (b) that such a notion simply falls outside of creaturely limitation and squarely into the realm of fruitless speculation.[19] But neither of these criticisms are good reason for rejecting the doctrine.

In terms of the latter criticism, we have already examined the necessity of philosophical contemplation of divine operations in chapter 2. Scripture itself invites and necessitates that we affirm not only what Scripture explicitly states but also what it affirms 'by good and necessary consequence'. Consequently, objections to Trinitarian formulae that insist upon a real distinction between the immanent Trinity and the economic Trinity are not limited to this discussion on the *pactum salutis*. Rahner's Rule is no better applied here than anywhere else, and the response from orthodox quarters is always the same: 'the Triune God reveals the eternal processions in their covenantal missions.'[20] While the divine mission of the Son following the Father's sending in assuming a human nature, and the Spirit following the Father and Son's sending in

---

18. Fesko, *The Trinity and the Covenant of Redemption*, 111.

19. The most prominent contemporary Reformed theologian who rejects the doctrine is Robert Letham who argues that 'inevitable problems arise in applying covenant concepts to God' since 'applied to the Trinity, it implies that the Trinitarian persons each have their own will, entailing something approaching tritheism.' Robert Letham, *The Holy Trinity: In Scripture, History, Theology, and Worship*, rev. and exp. ed. (Phillipsburg, NJ: P&R Publishing, 2019), 319. Karl Barth, too, raised a similar charge. See Karl Barth, *Church Dogmatics, Vol. IV/1: The Doctrine of God*, ed. G. W. Bromiley and T. F. Torrance, trans. T. H. L. Parker et al. (Edinburgh: T&T Clark, 1957), 65. The increasing designation of 'speculative' theology (or, as the Westminster divines would have put it, theology by 'good and necessary consequences') as a self-evident slur is owing to the increasing reductionism of late, encapsulated well by Rahner's Rule. See chapter 2.

20. Fesko, *The Trinity and the Covenant of Redemption*, 169.

applying the work of redemption, do not bespeak univocal movement in the Trinity's timeless eternal life, they do *fittingly correspond* to that timeless eternal movement of filiation and procession. It is fitting for the Son, not the Father nor the Spirit, to be sent by the Father to assume a human nature, and to send the Spirit *with* the Father to apply Their Triune love to the elect – such a work is only appropriate for He who receives life in Himself eternally from His begetting Father, a life that includes the shared act of spiriting the Holy Spirit eternally.

In terms of the former criticism (i.e., that the *pactum salutis* necessitates three wills and thereby logically concludes in tritheism), critics would do well to remember that the *pactum salutis*' being situated 'before the foundations of the world' does not require that we abandon all distinctions between 'processions' and 'missions', or 'appropriations,' or any of the other categories of which we make use. In other words, the *pactum salutis* poses no more of a problem for the undivided, simple will of the Triune God than any expression of God's covenantal movement toward sinners. The fact that we are talking about the 'covenant' of redemption should signify in no uncertain terms that what we intend to communicate is a description of divine appropriation – the one, undivided will of the Trinity is the work of redemption whereby the Father, Son, and Spirit agree to save the elect in the form of the Father electing in Christ and sending Christ to accomplish the work of redemption, the Son being sent by the Father and fulfilling the work of redemption, and the Spirit being sent by the Father and Son to apply the work of redemption.

The preceding discussion has been to establish that the work of redemption is a work originating within (and revealing and reflecting) the timeless eternity of the Trinity's *a se beatitude*. We now turn our attention to this work itself. Specifically, the redemption accomplished by Christ in the *historia salutis* and applied by the Spirit in the *ordo salutis*.

Redemption Accomplished

When the apostle Paul reminded the Corinthians that upon his initial arrival to their city he had decided 'to know nothing among [them] except Christ and him crucified' (1 Cor. 2:1), he was championing a distinct simplicity. Having no interest in pampering to their taste for sophistry and rhetorical flourish, he preached as if he really did believe that *the gospel* – to the exclusion of all else – was the power of God unto salvation (Rom. 1:16). He preached a mere gospel.[21] Much depends, however, on how one defines 'mere'. In many a pulpit this summary statement can be read as, 'I determined to know nothing among you except the crucifixion.' Not a little evangelical preaching centers on a bloody cross, and rightly so, for without a bloody cross there is no gospel. Nevertheless, much evangelical preaching abstracts one particular benefit of this bloody cross from others: the forgiveness of sins. Such a conception of the gospel may leave the listener with the impression that the sinner's only need – and Christ's only provision – is forgiveness.[22] I contend that while Paul's summary statement to the Corinthians includes nothing less than the forgiveness of sins, it certainly contains more. For Paul did not decide to know nothing among the Corinthians except the crucifixion; he decided to know nothing among them except *Christ*, and *Him* crucified. The linguistic difference is minimal, but jots and tittles here contain galaxies.

We begin with some overall definitions. My contention here is that *justification requires both the passive and active obedience of Christ, and imputed righteousness cannot be therefore abstracted from Christ's person and work.* Necessary for arguing this point is a clear understanding of each of these key terms.

Justification refers to the overall category for God's judicial declaration of the sinner's innocence before Him. 'In a word,' writes John Murray, 'justification is simply a declaration or pronouncement respecting the relation of the person to the law which he, the judge, is required to administer.'[23] Justification presupposes, therefore, many ideas, including that of God's

---

21. This is a major emphasis for Paul when addressing the Corinthians (2 Cor. 2:17; 4:2, 5). Apparently, they needed frequent reminders that the gospel is the power of God unto salvation (Rom. 1:16), since the Corinthians were wont to find power elsewhere. See, Timothy B. Savage, *Power through Weakness: Paul's Understanding of the Christian Ministry in 2 Corinthians* (New York: Cambridge University Press, 1996).

22. Schreiner's New Testament theology has this kind of tincture. See Thomas R. Schreiner, *New Testament Theology: Magnifying God in Christ* (Grand Rapids, MI: Baker Academic, 2008), 351-62. Although Schreiner makes imputed righteousness explicit and argues that such 'righteousness is a forensic declaration' and is thereby the 'link between righteousness and forgiveness', he nevertheless fails to account for the nature of the righteousness (i.e., Christ's active obedience and meritorious fulfillment of the law).

23. John Murray, *Redemption Accomplished and Applied* (Grand Rapids, MI: Eerdmans, 2015), 125.

law and the transgression thereof.[24] All that goes into the final declaration of justification can scarcely be exaggerated,[25] but the idea of justification itself refers to God's judicious declaration of innocence and righteousness.

The *passive obedience* of Christ has popularly been understood simply as the death of Christ, but this is a mistake. In truth, Christ's *passive obedience* refers to His lifelong work of bearing up under the curse of sin on humanity's behalf. This means that everything Christ suffered as a human in a fallen world is part of passive obedience's edifice, the culmination of which is the crucifixion.[26] Christ passively obeys when He experiences the consequences of sin, including the wages thereof: death. Propitiation, as the work of satisfying the wrath of God on behalf of sinners, is an essential aspect of this passive obedience.[27] Christ's

---

24. This seems like as good a place as any to flag my position on what has been called the new perspective on Paul. While there are certainly valuable insights to glean from the likes of N. T. Wright, James Dunn, E. P. Sanders, Douglas A. Campbell, and others, I remain unpersuaded by the variegated versions of 'new perspectives' to date (though, of course, who can keep up with all of them?). To put the matter crassly, the new perspectives on Paul remain, in my estimation, woefully inferior to the old, Reformed perspective on Paul. In signaling my intention to virtually ignore the new perspective, I wish to voice my agreement with those who have waded through the material carefully and have concluded in favor of the Reformers' understanding of Paul. See Guy Prentiss Waters, *Justification and the New Perspectives on Paul: A Review and Response* (Philadelphia: P&R Publishing, 2004); Robert J. Cara, *Cracking the Foundation of the New Perspective on Paul: Covenantal Nomism versus Reformed Covenantal Theology* (Ross-Shire: Christian Focus, 2017); Cornelis P. Venema, *The Gospel of Free Acceptance in Christ: An Assessment of the Reformation and New Perspectives on Paul* (Edinburgh: Banner of Truth, 2006); D. A. Carson, Peter Thomas O'Brien, and Mark A. Seifrid, eds., *Justification and Variegated Nomism*, 2 vols. (Grand Rapids, MI: Baker Academic, 2001, 2003); Matthew Barrett, ed., *The Doctrine on Which the Church Stands or Falls: Justification in Biblical, Theological, Historical, and Pastoral Perspective* (Wheaton, IL: Crossway, 2019); Mark A. Seifrid, *Christ, Our Righteousness: Paul's Theology of Justification* (Downers Grove, IL: InterVarsity Press, 2000); Michael Scott Horton, *Justification*, 2 vols. (Grand Rapids, MI: Zondervan, 2018); Graham A. Cole, *God the Peacemaker: How Atonement Brings Shalom* (Downers Grove, IL: InterVarsity Press, 2009); Brian S. Rosner, *Paul and the Law: Keeping the Commandments of God* (Downers Grove, IL: InterVarsity Press, 2013); Simon J. Gathercole, *Defending Substitution: An Essay on Atonement in Paul* (Grand Rapids, MI: Baker Academic, 2015).

25. This can be demonstrated by the sheer magnitude of recent works like Barrett, *The Doctrine on Which the Church Stands or Falls*.

26. See Brandon D. Crowe, *The Last Adam: A Theology of the Obedient Life of Jesus in the Gospels* (Grand Rapids, MI: Baker Academic, 2017).

27. Gathercole, *Defending Substitution*; Steve Jeffery, Michael Ovey, and Andrew Sach, *Pierced for Our Transgressions: Rediscovering the Glory of Penal Substitution* (Wheaton, IL: Crossway, 2007).

passive obedience is *on behalf of* sinners who cling to Him by faith. The forgiveness of sins is granted by this passive obedience. Those in Christ are in no threat of the judgement of God since Christ – in His passive obedience – received that judgement in their stead and on their behalf in His sacrificial life and death.

Just as Christ's passive obedience has been misunderstood as His death, many mistakenly understand Christ's *active obedience* merely as His life.[28] But this cannot be the case, since, as we have observed, Christ passively obeys throughout His entire incarnation. Rather, Christ's active obedience refers to the judicial righteousness He earns on behalf of His people.[29] If passive obedience refers to Christ fulfilling the law by suffering the law's penalty, His active obedience refers to His fulfilling the law by obeying the law's commands. This is what provides the tail side of justification's coin. Justification is God's judicial declaration that a sinner is no longer guilty (thanks to passive obedience) and is now righteous (thanks to active obedience). On account of Christ's passive obedience, a believer has a blank slate – i.e., no longer does he owe the wages of sin since Christ has paid them and has canceled the record of debt that stood against the believer with its legal demands (Col. 2:13-14). However, a blank slate is no grounds for eternal life. 'No longer deserving death and hell' does not automatically entail 'deserving eternal life'. The ground for the latter is not merely for a person to be 'not guilty' but rather for them to be *righteous*. Michael Horton notes how 'justification is not only forgiveness of sins (i.e., not imputing our sins to us), but the positive imputation of Christ's merits.'[30] Or, as Turretin puts the matter, 'the obedience of Christ has a twofold efficacy, satisfactory and meritorious; the former by which we are freed from the punishments incurred by sin; the latter by which (through the remission of sin) a right to eternal life and salvation is acquired for us.'[31]

---

28. See, Richard N. Longenecker, 'The Obedience of Christ in the Theology of the Early Church,' in *Reconciliation and Hope: New Testament Essays on Atonement and Eschatology Presented to L. L. Morris on His 60th Birthday*, ed. Robert Banks (Grand Rapids, MI: Eerdmans, 1974), 142-52.

29. See Calvin, *Institutes* Book II:16:6.

30. Horton, *Justification*, 1:275.

31. Turretin, *Institutes*, 2:XIV.x.

In Christ's active obedience, Jesus recapitulates humanity – God's covenantal, image-bearing creature – and is faithful where Adam and his progeny were unfaithful. 'All of history can be summarized by two Adams,' writes Matthew Barrett, 'a first Adam, whose covenant representation resulted in the condemnation of humanity, and a second or last Adam, whose covenant representation results in the justification of the ungodly.'[32]

Moving on in defining our terms, *imputed righteousness* refers to God's act of imputing Christ's obedience to believers.[33] This is a crucial point to make, for without Christ's active obedience, imputed righteousness is rendered ambiguous at best and groundlessly arbitrary at worse.[34] Something characteristically human is being attributed to Christians in the act of imputed righteousness; otherwise it could be received by no human.[35] The righteousness imputed to the believer is the righteousness of perfect obedience to the law.[36] Without the active

---

32. Barrett, *Canon, Covenant and Christology*, 206.

33. This is why Beale, *A New Testament Biblical Theology*, 476, has described imputed righteousness as 'attributed righteousness'.

34. The latter seems to be the outcome from Wright's reasoning in N. T. Wright, *The New Testament and the People of God* (Minneapolis: Fortress, 1992).

35. T. F. Torrance and his followers have made much use of this concept and in their appeal to Gregory of Nazianzus's dictum, 'the unassumed is the unhealed.' E.g., T. F. Torrance, *Incarnation: The Person and Life of Christ* (Downers Grove, IL: IVP Academic, 2015); John C. Clark and Marcus Peter Johnson, *The Incarnation of God: The Mystery of the Gospel as the Foundation of Evangelical Theology* (Wheaton, IL: Crossway, 2015). Not only do they get far more mileage out of Nazianzus' words than he intended, they commit the following crucial errors in insisting upon Christ having a fallen human nature: (a) they invent a distinction between a 'fallen human nature' and a 'sinful', or rather, 'guilty' human nature; (b) they fold the atonement entirely into the incarnation; (c) they sacrifice Christ's impeccability and thus misconstrue the hypostatic union; (d) they functionally turn sinful temptation into fundamental human nature, so much so that it would appear to be a now essential aspect of the *imago Dei*; and most importantly, (e) they misconstrue the nature of original sin and federal headship – the virgin birth, in this construction, becomes a superfluous display of power and, even worse, implies that the Holy Spirit conceived in Mary a sinful human nature. If Christ assumed a fallen nature in the incarnation, He would be disqualified as the spotless Lamb to take away the sins of the world before He was even born. 'Spotless' and 'fallen' cannot meaningfully coexist as descriptions of Christ's human nature. In his recent work Rafael Bello refutes this 'fallen Christology' with force. See Rafael Nogueira Bello, *Sinless Flesh: A Critique of Karl Barth's Fallen Christ* (Bellingham, WA: Lexham, 2020).

36. For a great summary of this aspect of Christ's earthly ministry, see Barrett, *Canon, Covenant and Christology*, chap. 5.

obedience of Christ, we are left scratching our heads as to how such a perfect obedience could be rightly ours, or else we are left to conclude that the Father has agreed to pretend that we were obedient when in fact we were not. Christ's active obedience secures a concrete righteousness, and there is therefore nothing imaginary about it. It is not as if God looks at believers and pretends that they are righteous; rather, in Christ they *are* righteous (2 Cor. 5:21). What God imputes to those in Christ is an earthy, profoundly human obedience – an obedience that can truly be theirs because it was achieved by the human head of their (new) human race.

Before moving on, it is important to stress the interconnectedness of Christ's passive and active obedience. Construed in this way, passive obedience makes little sense without active obedience, and vice versa. Christ's perfect, actively obedient life fits Him as the Lamb of God (Heb. 2:10-11; 5:9). Standing as the great high priest, Christ offers up the sacrifice of Himself as the spotless Lamb (Heb. 7:23-28), and His spotlessness (active obedience) is what fits Him as the sin-atoning offering that satisfies divine wrath (passive obedience) (Heb. 9:25-28; 10:11-14). 'Unless both active and passive obedience are present,' observes Matthew Barrett, 'justification is incomplete.'[37] It is worth taking some time to biblically substantiate this claim. We turn now to three passages: Romans 5:12-21; 2 Corinthians 5:21; and Romans 8:1-4.

Romans 5:12-21. In Romans 5 Paul introduces the idea of recapitulation, with Christ arriving as the Second Adam – a new federal head over a new humanity.[38] This concept comes on the heels of a lengthy discourse on justification by faith (Rom. 3:21–5:11) as its elaboration. Paul marshals Abraham as evidence that 'justification by faith' is no new Pauline aberration to Scripture's teaching; those who seek justification by faith alone are in good company, following in the footsteps of their father Abraham (4:13-16). Paul reveals how God is still righteous for having so consistently granted justification to sinners who look to Him in faith.

---

37. Matthew Barrett, 'Raised for Our Justification: The Christological, Covenantal, Forensic, and Eschatological Contours of an Ambiguous Relationship,' in Barrett, *The Doctrine on Which the Church Stands or Falls*, 401.

38. While many today reject the notion of imputation and federal headship (e.g., N.T. Wright, Peter Enns), Fesko has given a convincing defense of the doctrine in historical, exegetical, and theological perspective in J. V. Fesko, *Death in Adam, Life in Christ: The Doctrine of Imputation* (Ross-Shire: Christian Focus, 2016).

All this raises a difficult question, however. How could God be righteous for overlooking trespasses and granting justification to sinners before Christ? Answer: because every sinner God justifies is justified on account of the propitiatory work of Christ (3:21-26). Abraham and company looked to God in faith that He would *somehow* remain just and yet declare them righteous. Paul reveals that this 'somehow' is Christ Jesus, 'whom God put forward as a propitiation by his blood to be received by faith' (3:25). Having established the mechanics of justification by faith (i.e., one is justified by faith in Christ, whose propitiatory work grounds such justification), Paul then begins to explain how Christ is fit to fulfill such a role.

In 5:12 Paul identifies Adam as the federal head of humanity and the one responsible for introducing sin into creation. The consequence of this sin is death, and so where there is death, there is also sin. Likewise, where there is sin, there is also the law (and the transgression thereof) (5:13), which means it is a mistake to assume that the law handed down at Sinai exhausts the meaning of 'God's law'. If it did, the consequences of breaking the law (i.e., death) would not be present until after the law at Sinai was revealed, 'yet death reigned from Adam to Moses' (5:14). Sin and death are therefore personified as reigning slave masters, co-lording in their tyranny from Adam onward and witnessing to humanity's transgression in Adam.

Romans 5:15-21 features a comparison and contrast between two 'Adams'.[39] 'Many died' through Adam (i.e., many received the penalty for sin); many have received 'the grace of God and the free gift of that grace' (i.e., life) through the Second Adam (5:15). Judgment and condemnation followed the trespass of Adam, such that death reigned through him and his posterity (5:16-18). Justification and righteousness followed the act of the Second Adam, such that life now reigns through Him and His posterity (5:16-18). Adam's disobedience made many sinners, the Second Adam's obedience makes many righteous (5:19).[40] Sin reigns in death through Adam; grace reigns in righteousness leading to eternal life through the Second Adam, 'Jesus Christ our Lord' (5:21). All this introduces several implications.

---

39. See Crowe, 'The Active and Passive Obedience of Christ,' 447.

40. See ibid., 448.

First, this passage implies that imputation and federal headship pre-suppose one another.[41] There is a parallel between the works of Adam, the federal head of humanity, being imputed to his posterity, and the works of Jesus, the federal head of a new humanity, being imputed to *His* posterity. Adam stands in for all of humanity when he transgresses God, and his transgression is imputed to all those he represents. Likewise, Christ stands in for all of His new humanity when He obeys God, and His righteousness is imputed to all those He represents. This passage makes little sense without a conception of federal headship and imputation together.

Second, this passage implies that man is a covenantal creature. He is created responsible to God. His being human means man is legally answerable to the God in whose image he is made. This is the inescapable conclusion of 5:13-14 and is verifiable all throughout Scripture.[42]

Third, this passage instructs us on the concept of recapitulation.[43] Christ is not merely offering a parallel alternative to Adam as another option. Rather, Christ is recapitulating humanity as it was intended. Adam's failure was a failure to obey and to thereby achieve the righteousness leading to eternal life.[44] Therefore, when Jesus arrives as the sinless one, He is succeeding precisely where Adam failed. Further, like how Adam's failure is consequential for all his posterity, the Second Adam's success is consequential for all His posterity. Calvin sums up nicely,

> Accordingly, our Lord came forth as true man and took the person and the name of Adam in order to take Adam's place in obeying the Father, to present our flesh as the price of satisfaction to God's righteous judgment, and, in the same flesh, to pay the penalty that we had deserved.[45]

Romans 5:12-21 gives a fuller account to Paul's teaching on justification, which he began in 3:21. Christ's obedience on behalf of the justified

---

41. See, Crowe, *The Last Adam*; Calvin, *Institutes of the Christian Religion*, Book II:17:1-6.

42. On man's covenantal ontology, see, Horton, *Lord and Servant*; Van Til, *The Defense of the Faith*; Herman Bavinck, *Reformed Ethics*, ed. John Bolt, vol. 1: *Created, Fallen, and Converted Humanity* (Grand Rapids, MI: Baker Academic, 2019).

43. See, Cole, *God the Peacemaker*, 103-19.

44. For a recent description and defense of this doctrine, see J. V. Fesko, *The Covenant of Works: The Origins, Development, and Reception of the Doctrine* (New York, NY: Oxford University Press, 2020).

45. Calvin, *Institutes* Book II:12:3.

is a fully integrated obedience. Jesus passively obeys as He receives the condemnation for sin (Rom. 8:3), propitiating wrath and securing the forgiveness of sins (3:25). He likewise actively obeys as He succeeds where Adam failed, achieving righteousness and securing eternal life (5:21). This passage thus confirms that 'forgiveness of sins corresponds to Christ's passive obedience, and the securing of eternal life corresponds to Christ's active obedience.'[46] 'As with Adam's guilt,' says Fesko, 'God employs the same mechanism to give believers the last Adam's righteousness.'[47]

2 Corinthians 5:21. Apart from the above discussion on Romans 5, the integrated obedience of Christ may be confirmed elsewhere as well. Second Corinthians 5:21, for example, is as succinct a passage as any to convey the double imputation presupposed in the concepts of active and passive obedience. 'For our sake [God] made [Christ] to be sin who knew no sin' is a perfect summary of Christ's passive obedience. Being free from sin, Christ is yet made to be sin 'for our sake'.[48] This, Paul continues, happens 'so that in him we might become the righteousness of God' (2 Cor. 5:21). In whom? In He who knew no sin. Our being made the righteousness of God, according to Paul, is on account of our being in Christ, who knew no sin. Thus, the ministry of reconciliation has two requirements. First, it requires that trespasses are not counted against its ministers (2 Cor. 5:19). This Christ accomplishes in His passive obedience where trespasses are counted against *Him*, who was made to be sin, instead of them (2 Cor. 5:21). Second, it requires that its ministers become the righteousness of God.[49] Christ accomplishes this in His active obedience whereby He is 'without sin', and it is attributed to such ministers when they are 'in him' (2 Cor. 5:21).

Romans 8:1-4. Likewise, Romans 8:1-4 contains a powerful attestation to the benefit of Christ's passive obedience, and an implicit attestation to His active obedience as well. Answering the question rhetorically asked

---

46. Crowe, 'The Passive and Active Obedience of Christ,' 445.

47. Fesko, *Death in Adam, Life in Christ*, 263.

48. See George H. Guthrie, *2 Corinthians* (Grand Rapids, MI: Baker Academic, 2015), 315.

49. See, Murray J Harris, *The Second Epistle to the Corinthians: A Commentary on the Greek Text* (Grand Rapids, MI: Eerdmans, 2013), 430-45; Mark A. Seifrid, *The Second Letter to the Corinthians* (Grand Rapids, MI: Eerdmans, 2014), 257-59; Guthrie, *2 Corinthians*, 308-10.

in Romans 7:24 ('Who will deliver me from this body of death?'), Paul begins chapter eight by reveling in his liberty afforded by Christ. Those who are 'in Christ Jesus' are now freed from condemnation, and the Spirit has set them free 'in Christ Jesus from the law of sin and death' (8:1-2). How have those 'in Christ' been liberated from condemnation and the law of sin and death? Paul answers that God has accomplished this, by 'sending his own Son in the likeness of sinful flesh, and for sin he condemned sin in the flesh' (8:3). This is a definitive case for Christ's passive obedience. Those in Christ are free from the condemnation sin brings because Christ bore that condemnation for them. Paul has already explained how sin turns the righteous Law of God into a law of sin and death (Rom. 7:8), which means sin coupled with the Law brings about condemnation. When Christ was sent in the likeness of sinful flesh and for sin, He was taking on that which occasions condemnation, thereby bearing the condemnation due those who are 'in him'.

This much is clear to most when considering Romans 8. What often goes unnoticed, however, is Paul's implicit instruction on Christ's active obedience. Paul explains how God condemned sin in the flesh of Christ 'in order that the righteous requirement of the law might be fulfilled in us who walk not according to the flesh but according to the Spirit' (8:4). In other words, it is not merely the penalty of the law that is satisfied for those in Christ but also the fulfillment of the law's 'righteous requirements'.

Some may object that this reading is invalid, since Paul primarily has the believer's obedience in view here and not Christ's active obedience on behalf of the believer. While it is true the believer's obedience is primarily in view, I would contend that the bifurcation between the two (i.e., the believer's obedience and Christ's) is unnecessary. The law of the Spirit of Christ is inextricably linked to union with Christ (8:2); the obedience of the believer is rooted in his union with Christ, such that his obedience is an acting out of that which is 'in Christ'. This point thus highlights the relationship between imputation and union with Christ, to which we now turn.

Union with Christ and Imputation

The believer's union with Christ and Christ's forensic imputation of righteousness are often pitted against one another as irreconcilable concepts.[50] In truth there is no need to reconcile one to the other because 'they are mutually determining and illuminating'.[51] This point becomes clear once one grasps that justification is included in 'every spiritual blessing in the heavenly places', which belong to all those whom the Father has blessed 'in Christ' (Eph 1:3-10).[52] Tensions arise when Christ's benefits are abstracted from His person. With regard to this debate, this abstraction happens (a) when justification is depicted as a benefit that might be received outside of – and apart from – union with Christ, (b) when union with Christ is depicted in a purely mystical and existential way, and (c) when the relationship with these realities are strictly related on existential terms on the one hand or strictly logical terms on the other. These mistakes are understandable, as they are misled by genuine truths about both doctrines. Justification *is* a forensic benefit that has implications beyond existential, felt realities, and union with Christ *is* certainly no less than mystical and experiential. Yet neither is complete without the other.

While it is true that 'in some texts, Paul speaks about believers becoming righteous "in Christ" without mentioning imputation explicitly,' and 'Paul speaks of God imputing righteousness to believers without using language of union or participation,' VanDrunen points out how 'neither set of texts should control the other'. They are rather 'mutually defining and illuminating'.[53]

Without union with Christ, the active obedience of Christ offers little comfort for the believer. What good does it do a guilty sinner to know that someone else has achieved perfection? The success of the former means nothing to the latter until it is somehow imputed thereunto. Conversely, union with Christ, abstracted from the forensic dimension

---

50. David VanDrunen puts his finger on several figures for whom this bifurcation functions: 'I consider, first, those who use union with Christ to jettison the substitutionary atonement as the ground of justification, as represented by Daniel Powers; second, those who use union to jettison the solely forensic character of justification, as represented by Michael Gorman; and third, those who use union to jettison or at least enervate the imputed active obedience of Christ as an aspect of justification, as represented by N. T. Wright and Michael Bird.' David VanDrunen, 'A Contested Union: Union with Christ and the Justification Debate,' in Barrett, *The Doctrine on Which the Church Stands or Falls*, 471.

51. Ibid., 469.

52. See Billings, *Union with Christ*, 27.

53. VanDrunen, 'A Contested Union,' 496.

of imputed righteousness, offers little solace to the covenant breaker. He may hope to enjoy unprecedented communion with Christ in present, existential ways, but it is groundless without imputation. Calvin makes this point well: 'We do not, therefore, contemplate him outside ourselves from afar in order that his righteousness may be imputed to us but because we put on Christ and are engrafted into his body – in short, because he designs to make us one with him.'[54] Likewise, Turretin makes this point powerfully. We quote him here at length:

> As long as Christ is outside of us and we are out of Christ, we can receive no fruit from another's righteousness. God willed to unite us to Christ by a twofold bond – one natural, the other mystical – in virtue of which both our evils might be transferred to Christ and the blessings of Christ pass over to us and become ours. The former is the communion of nature by the incarnation. By this, Christ, having assumed our flesh, became our brother and true Goel and could receive our sins upon himself and have the right to redeem us. The latter is the communion of grace by mediation. By this, having been made by God a surety for us and given to us for a head, he can communicate to us his righteousness and all his benefits. Hence it happens that as he was made of God sin for us by the imputation of our sins, so in turn we are made the righteousness of God in him by the imputation of his obedience (2 Cor 5:21).[55]

Forensic imputation brings girth to the promise of union with Christ. It communicates that when a person is united to Christ by faith, they are united to rock-solid hope: a real, perfect, active and passive obedience, which guarantees propitiation and righteousness, i.e., full justification. Further, union with Christ personalizes imputed righteousness. It communicates that the perfect active and passive obedience of Christ is not an abstract garment that Christ weaves and the Father drapes onto the believer – Christ Himself *is* the garment. There is no receiving Christ's robes of righteousness without being received into Christ Himself. 'The fact that imputation occurs through union with Christ,' observes VanDrunen,

---

54. Calvin, *Institutes*, Book III:11:10. Horton, *Justification*, 1:207, thus rightly observes how 'Calvin's judicial emphasis with respect to *justification* is complemented by the organic imagery of union and ingrafting in relation to the *inner renewal* and communion with Christ, including his holiness' (emphasis original).

55. Turretin, *Institutes*, 2.XVI.v.

indicates that the righteousness imputed is not abstract or impersonal but a personal righteousness that guarantees God's justice when he justifies … . Believers are personally united to the one whose righteousness appears in their account …. There is no fiat money or debased currency involved. This is a real righteousness that believers claim as their own through an everlasting union with the one who was obedient unto death.[56]

To put matters more concisely, union with Christ is *how* the great exchange happens (2 Cor. 5:21).[57]

When Paul asks the Church in Rome, 'Do you not know that all of us who have been baptized into Christ Jesus were baptized into his death?' (Rom 6:3), he expected his readers to remember what he just said about this Christ in the preceding sections of his letter. Christians are baptized *into* Christ, the Second Adam who succeeds where the first Adam failed. Like how Adam's failure was accounted to His posterity by virtue of their *being in him*, Christ's obedience is accounted to his posterity by virtue of their *being* (baptized) *in(to)* Him. In other words, Paul's discussion on union with Christ in Romans 6 does not merely root sanctification in union with Christ (though it certainly does not do less than that); it roots the *application* of the justification of chapter 5 in union with Christ as well.

This does not mean, however, that union with Christ has logical priority to the forensic realities of justification and imputation. It is true that the believer has no justification outside of Christ, but the forensic reality of justification is *logically* and *legally* prior to the believer's union to Christ. The believer's union to Christ is not a-legal. This, of course, thrusts us into a debate between those who would affirm the importance of a logical *ordo salutis* that roots sanctification and the relational dynamics of mystical union in the legal verdict of justification logically[58] and those who

56. VanDrunen, 'A Contested Union,' 496.

57. See Horton, *Justification*, 1:216-17.

58. These would include J. V. Fesko, J. Todd Billings, Michael Horton, Geerhardus Vos, and Louis Berkhof. See Fesko, *The Covenant of Works*; Louis Berkhof, *Systematic Theology*; Horton, *Justification*, vols. 1 and 2; Geerhardus Vos, 'The Alleged Legalism in Paul's Doctrine of Justification,' in *Redemptive History and Biblical Interpretation: The Shorter Writings of Geerhardus Vos*, ed. Richard B Gaffin Jr. (Phillipsburg, NJ: Presbyterian and Reformed, 1980); J. Todd Billings, *Calvin, Participation, and the Gift: The Activity of Believers in Union with Christ* (New York: Oxford University Press, 2007); J. Todd Billings and I. John Hesselink, eds., *Calvin's Theology and Its Reception: Disputes, Developments, and New Possibilities* (Louisville: Westminster John Knox, 2012).

would (in some cases) minimize the importance of a logical *ordo salutis* and would instead put union with Christ as the 'basis' for justification.[59]

Though there is much we could say to sort this debate out, we might be benefited by looking at the issue from two separate vantage points: the man's-eye perspective and the God's-eye perspective. From the man's-eye perspective, justification is by faith alone, but not merely faith in a proposition. Justification is by faith alone *in Christ alone*. He is the object of the believer's faith. But the object of the believer's faith is not 'Christ unaccompanied by propositions'. The reason He is a *saving* object of faith is that He has *objectively achieved* justification outside of the believer's union with Him. The believer has faith alone in Christ, *who* accomplished redemption with His passive and active obedience, substitutionary death, etc. It is upon the basis of this legal work – the work the Son was sent to accomplish – that the believer finds in Christ a justifying object of faith. This is the God's-eye view. The Father sends the Son to legally purchase the right for the believer to cling to Him by faith in union. Thus, Fesko is right to summarize,

> To say, then, that union with Christ is the basis for a person's justification lacks specificity and is misleading. If *basis* means that one cannot be justified apart from union with Christ, then such a statement is true. Justification requires faith in Christ, and only one who is in union with Him can exercise faith. But if by *basis* the legal ground for justification is intended, then, no, union with Christ, the personal indwelling, is not the legal basis of justification.[60]

While the man's-eye perspective views justification as that which is rendered his *through Christ* (i.e., justification *received*; redemption *applied*), the God's-eye perspective – the perspective of the logical priority of the *ordo salutis* as rooted in the *pactum salutis* – places

---

59. Included in this group we might place N. T. Wright, Kevin J. Vanhoozer, Richard Gaffin Jr., Sinclair Ferguson, and David B. Garner. See, N. T. Wright, *Justification: God's Plan & Paul's Vision* (Downers Grove, IL: IVP Academic, 2016); Kevin Vanhoozer, 'Wrighting the Wrongs of the Reformation? The State of the Union with Christ in St. Paul and Protestant Theology,' in *Jesus, Paul, and the People of God: A Theological Dialogue with N. T. Wright*, Nicholas Perrin and Richard B. Hays (Downers Grove, IL: IVP Academic, 2011); Richard Gaffin, 'The Work of Christ Applied,' in Allen and Swain, *Christian Dogmatics*; Sinclair B. Ferguson, *The Holy Spirit*, Contours of Christian Theology (Downers Grove, IL: InterVarsity Press, 1996); David B. Garner, *Sons in the Son: The Riches and Reach of Adoption in Christ* (Phillipsburg, NJ: P&R Publishing, 2016).

60. Fesko, *The Trinity and the Covenant of Redemption*, 299 (emphasis original).

justification as the legal grounds for union with Christ (i.e., justification *achieved*; redemption *accomplished*).

Thus, it is the *historia salutis* that grounds the *ordo salutis*. Christ accomplishes redemption with His perfect life, death, resurrection, and ascension. This accomplished redemption is applied to the believer in Christ through the ministry of the Holy Spirit when He unites the believer to Christ. While the *ordo salutis* does not necessarily imply hard and fast time distinctions in the application of redemption, it does nevertheless imply a causal or logical order. Because of the objective judicial work that Christ accomplishes on behalf of the elect, the legal stage is set for the Holy Spirit to apply the work of redemption to the believer in time.

Before examining the *ordo salutis* in more detail, it is worth explicitly tying the above discussion back to the earlier inquiry about the language of 'participation'. It is not uncommon to criticize Protestant Reformed soteriology as *merely* forensic, and therefore a far cry from the kind of participatory soteriology embraced by the church fathers. For example, commenting on Athanasius' statement that 'God became man so that man might become God', Robert Letham notes how Athanasius was affirming that 'all things receive the characteristics of that in which they participate. Hence, by participating in the Holy Spirit, we become holy; by participating in the Logos, we are able to contemplate the Father.'[61] Critics of Reformed theology in general, and Calvin in particular, are not lacking in their claim that Reformed soteriology neglects this participatory element of Christ's person and work, which seems to be so clearly central for so much of the Church's history.[62]

J. Todd Billings has convincingly argued, however, that this narrative is profoundly misguided.[63] Rather, 'the images of union with Christ, ingrafting into Christ, partaking of Christ, and adoption were drawn from Paul and Johannine writings in the New Testament and were deeply woven into the fabric of [Calvin's] soteriology.'[64] Billings does

---

61. Robert Letham, *Union with Christ: In Scripture, History, and Theology* (Phillipsburg, NJ: P&R Publishing, 2011), 93.

62. See Billings, *Union with Christ*, 64.

63. See Ibid., 63-75; *Calvin, Participation, and the Gift*, 68-104; 'United to God through Christ: Calvin on the Question of Deification,' *Harvard Theological Review* 98, no. 3 (July 2005); 315-34.

64. Billings, *Union with Christ*, 65.

acknowledge that 'while the critics … are mistaken in thinking that Calvin does not have a theology of salvation as restoration, communion, and union with God,' differences do remain between Calvin and other theologies of 'participation', namely and chiefly the fact that 'Calvin's account of justification is deeply forensic in orientation'.[65]

As we have seen, however, this is a *feature* of Calvin's notion of union with Christ, not a bug. Rather than conflating justification with sanctification – i.e., conflating the root with the fruit – Calvin and other Reformed theologians distinguish between the two, even while both are connected intimately to the believer's union with Christ. 'Reformed theology has generally used the term *union with Christ* to refer to this comprehensive sense of salvation,' notes Letham, 'taking the form of both forensic and transformational elements.'[66] In Christ, the believer is legally justified – by the Spirit, he *already* participates with God in Christ; he is seated with Christ in the heavenly places (Eph. 2:6), and he sits there *legally*. And in Christ, by the Spirit, the believer is progressively becoming on earth who he is in heaven. In Christ, he is justified; in Christ, he is sanctified.

The Protestant Reformed (and, we may be so bold as to say, *biblical*) imperative associated with sanctification, can be summarized as 'be who you are' (e.g., Rom. 6; Gal. 6; Col. 3). Within this framework, the communal participation believers enjoy with God in Christ is *legal*; it is purchased by the blood of Christ, and is enjoyed (a) *already*, (b) in a *progressively increasing* sense on this side of the believer's resurrection, and will be enjoyed (c) in a *consummated* way in the beatific vision on the other side of the resurrection.[67]

In describing the believer's union with God in Christ in this way, we are not turning away from the Christian-Platonist metaphysic of the Great Tradition. In fact, what other metaphysic could possibly account for a mystical union that bridges so many metaphysical gaps than that of the Great Tradition? The temporal gap of *now* and *then*; the cosmological gap of a *corrupt creation* and a *glorified creation*; the anthropological gap of a *sinful humanity* and a *resurrected humanity* – all of these are traversed

---

65. Ibid., 66, fn. 17.

66. Letham, *Union with Christ*, 102.

67. It is true that saints who are departed from their bodies are present with Christ, and experience the beatific vision now, but the full consummation of the beatific vision is a resurrection-reality. See chapter 6.

by the believer's union with Christ. In Christ, he is *then* and *now, there* and *here, already sanctified* and *becoming sanctified*. Only the thick realism of a Christian-Platonist metaphysic has room enough for such a splendid depiction of salvation, and the forensic element strengthens – rather than contradicts – this vision.

Redemption Applied

As noted above, the Holy Spirit's work in the *ordo salutis* is *legal*, in the sense that it is above board – it is not a-legal, it is blood bought and right. Additionally, the unfolding application of redemption in the life of a believer happens in an orderly manner. It is not as though salvation is dropped into the lap of the believer as one jumbled lump sum. There is a logic to the relationship between these salvific gifts. I now take some time to reflect on this logical order.

Effectual calling

The elect are called by God to Christ through the Spirit. Scripture is manifestly clear that this kind of 'calling' is effectual and wrought by God (Rom. 1:6-7; 8:30; 11:29; 1 Cor. 1:2, 7:18; 2 Thess. 2:13-14; Heb. 3:1-2; 2 Pet. 1:10). Perhaps nowhere is this point stated more succinctly than in Romans 8:30: 'And those whom he predestined he also called, and those whom he called he also justified, and those whom he justified he also glorified.' 'Paul does not say that out of all those whom God calls some are justified and then glorified,' notes Matthew Barrett. 'No, Paul is clear: those God calls are indeed justified and also glorified.'[68] Robert Letham points out that while Murray specifically identifies the Father as the principle agent in effectual calling[69] and Hodge argues instead that the work ought to be attributed to the Holy Spirit,[70] insisting on either to the exclusion of the other is an unnecessary choice. 'Strictly,' Letham notes, 'the Father calls us by the Spirit; calling is the work of the Spirit, although the author is the Father (John 14:26; 15:26; 16:7).'[71]

---

68. Matthew Barrett, *Salvation by Grace: The Case for Effectual Calling and Regeneration* (Phillipsburg, NJ: P&R Publishing, 2013), 87.

69. Murray, *Redemption Accomplished and Applied*, 88-90.

70. Charles Hodge, *Systematic Theology*, 2:639-41, 675-77.

71. Robert Letham, *Systematic Theology* (Wheaton, IL: Crossway, 2019), 658. This makes Letham's rejection of the *pactum salutis* all the more unfortunate, since it serves

Regeneration

This effectual calling involves the Holy Spirit's sovereign work of regeneration whereby He restores and imparts the faculties necessary for the elect to repent and believe in Christ (Deut. 30:6; Jer. 31:33; 32:39-40; Ezek. 36:26-27; John 3:3-8; 1 Pet. 1:3-5). This is why Barrett observes that 'a discussion of regeneration flows naturally from effectual calling'.[72] Barrett's definition of regeneration is strong, and so we quote it here in full:

> Regeneration is the work of the Holy Spirit to unite the elect sinner to Christ by breathing new life into the dead and depraved sinner so as to raise him from spiritual death to spiritual life, removing his heart of stone and giving him a heart of flesh, so that he is washed, born from above and now able to repent and trust in Christ as a new creation. Moreover, regeneration is the act of God alone and therefore it is monergistic in nature, accomplished by the sovereign act of the Spirit apart from and unconditioned upon man's will to believe. In short, man's faith does not cause regeneration but regeneration causes man's faith.[73]

There are many aspects of this definition we may focus on, but here I wish to highlight the restorative character of regeneration. Crucial here is the relationship between regeneration and faith; the faculties with which the believer lays hold of Christ in faith are, apart from regeneration, unresponsive, broken, and, in fact, dead (Eph. 2:1). Regeneration, therefore, is 'a change or renovation of nature, it ought to be the work of God alone and not of man.'[74]

Faith and Repentance

The Spirit's work in regeneration restores and enables the faculties of the heart to exercise faith and repentance – this is the fruit of regeneration. 'This divine action,' says Turretin,

> does not injure but strengthens the liberty of the will, and nothing hinders the same action from being performed freely ... and yet being done by

---

such a formulation with strong conceptual backbone. It would seem that the Father's authoring effectual calling, and the Spirit's working thereof, would fit well with the idea that the economic work of the Trinity in the *pactum salutis*, the *historia salutis*, and the *ordo salutis* are fitting appropriations of the Trinity's eternal modes of subsistence.

72. Barrett, *Salvation by Grace*, 126.

73. Ibid., 127.

74. Turretin, *Institutes*, 2:XV.x.

the invincible grace of God, which in the highest degree reconciles the infallibility of the event with the liberty of the will. For God so acts in us as not to overturn the singular nature of things, but to leave to each its proper method of acting.[75]

Turretin argues that faith is constituted in three acts, or aspects – knowledge (*notitia*), assent (*assensus*), and trust (*fiducia*). Simply knowing about Christ, or giving bare mental assent to His person and work, is not enough; true faith also lays hold of Christ with trusting conviction.[76] In saving faith, in other words,

> we judge the gospel to be not only true, but also good and therefore most worthy of our love and desire; also the promises of grace to be most certain concerning the remission of sins and the bestowal of salvation upon all believers and penitents and so also upon me if I shall believe and repent.[77]

We should not miss that Turretin sees desire as a part of the mix in those faculties renovated and activated in regeneration; Christ, the object of faith presented to us in the gospel, is desirable to the newly renovated eyes of faith. Unsurprisingly, Owen makes this point powerfully:

> The essence of faith consists in a due ascription of glory to God, Romans 4:20. This we cannot attain unto without the manifestation of those divine excellencies unto us wherein he is glorious. This is done in Christ alone, so as that we may glorify God in a saving and acceptable manner. He who discerns not the glory of divine wisdom, power, goodness, love, and grace, in the person and office of Christ, with the way of the salvation of sinners by him, is an unbeliever.[78]

This, of course, is close to the heart of this present work as a whole. With Owen, I argue that faith which neglects to discern the 'glory of divine wisdom, power, goodness, love, grace,' and we might add, *beauty*, 'in the person and office of Christ' is deficient. While we do not wish to delve headlong into how *divine beauty* plays into this discussion, it is worth flagging here in anticipation.

Importantly, I link faith and repentance here because, while 'faith' and 'repentance' may be distinguished from one another in some sense,

---

75. Ibid., 2:XV.xvii.

76. Ibid., 2:XV.vi-vii.

77. Ibid., 2:XV.vii.

78. Owen, *The Works of John Owen*, 1:295.

their existence in a believer is coterminous. They are distinguished in terms of the object they concern – repentance is a turning away *from sin*, and faith is a turning *to Christ* – but they are comprehended in the same movement. The one is the tail side to the other's head. It is not possible, for example, to turn to Christ by faith and turn to sin by faithlessness at the same time and in the same way.

Justification

Spirit-wrought regeneration enables Spirit-enabled faith in Christ, which is the instrument for justification. In the reception of Christ by faith, the convert is accounted as righteous and is justified. His forensic status in Christ is no longer 'guilty' but rather 'righteous' on account of an alien righteousness imputed to him.[79] By faith, says Turretin, we 'betake ourselves by an act of desire to Christ thus known by us',[80] and by this 'act of adhesion' and from this 'union of persons arises the participation in the blessings of Christ, to which (by union with him) we acquire a right (to wit, justification, adoption, sanctification and glorification).'[81] Thus, whereas we established above how justification is *accomplished* by Christ in the *historia salutis*, it is *applied* by the Holy Spirit through faith in Christ in the *ordo salutis*.

Adoption

The familial dimension of this judicial conversion is adoption. One must never separate the relational dimension of adoption from its judicial dimension, for the believer's communion with God as a beloved child is not illegitimate or a-legal. We may say even further that that the relational is *grounded* on the forensic element. There is no enjoying the familial benefits of adoption apart from the legal benefits of justification. This said, to be in the family of God is not *strictly* a legal matter. In fact, we might go so far as to say that adoption is the

---

79. Consider, for example, Turretin's statements here about imputation: 'Although God justifies us on account of the imputed righteousness of Christ, his judgment does not cease to be according to truth because he does not pronounce us righteous in ourselves subjectively (which would be false), but in another imputatively and relatively (which is perfectly true). Thus God truly estimates the thing and judges it as it is; not in itself and in its own nature, but in Christ' (Turretin, *Institutes*, 2:XVI.xxvi).

80. Ibid., 2:XV.viii.

81. Turretin, *Institutes*, 1:XV.x.

relational telos of the work of redemption. This seems to be what Paul says in Galatians 4: 'But when the fullness of time had come, God sent forth his Son, born of woman, born under the law, to redeem those who were under the law, *so that we might receive adoption as sons* (ὥστε να λάβουμε την υιοθεσία ως τέκνα)' (4:4-5, emphasis added). We should not miss this purpose clause (ἵνα); Christ redeemed those under the law, not simply to free them from their condemnation – a negative statement about that which they are *no longer* – but also that they might receive adoption as sons – a positive statement about that which they now *are*. This is clear from verses 6 and 7: 'And because you are sons, God has sent the Spirit of his Son into our hearts, crying, "Abba! Father!" So you are no longer a slave, but a son, and if a son, then an heir through Christ.' Few places summarize the condition and benefits of adoption better than the twelfth article of the Westminster Confession of Faith. We quote it in full here:

> All those that are justified, God vouchsafeth, in and for his only Son Jesus Christ, to make partakers of the grace of adoption, by which they are taken into the number, and enjoy the liberties and privileges of the children of God, have his name put upon them, receive the Spirit of adoption, have access to the throne of grace with boldness, are enabled to cry, Abba, Father, are pitied, protected, provided for, and chastened by him, as by a father: yet never cast off, but sealed to the day of redemption; and inherit the promises, as heirs of everlasting salvation.[82]

Sanctification and Glorification

Once he/she has been justified, God continues to sanctify the believer progressively in this age, as he becomes (progressively) who he is (definitively) in Christ. While the term 'sanctification' is used broadly throughout Scripture, we use it here, with Turretin, in the narrow sense of 'a real and internal renovation of man by which God delivers the man planted in Christ by faith and justified (by the ministry of the word and the efficacy of the Spirit) more and more from his native depravity and transforms him into his own image.'[83]

While sanctification is inseparable from justification, it is nevertheless strictly distinct from it. This is no more of a contradiction than to say

---

82. Westminster Confession of Faith, article XII.
83. Turretin, *Institutes*, 2:XVII.iii.

that the root of a tree is inseparable, though strictly distinct from, its fruit. Justification and sanctification do certainly agree on many things. Turretin points out how they share the same author (i.e., God), the same meritorious cause (i.e., the righteousness of Christ, purchased by His blood), the same general purpose (i.e., the glory of God), and the same instrumental cause (i.e., faith – faith *receives* justification and *produces* sanctification).[84] Nevertheless, they are not the same thing. Justification is a forensic rendering whereby God declares a believer – on account of the imputation of Christ – no longer guilty, and now righteous. It is on account of this forensic rendering that the Holy Spirit progressively works on such a believer in the purification of sanctification. To put the matter plainly, a person is never justified on account of having been sanctified; rather, a person is sanctified on account of having been justified.

This sanctification occurs through a variety of means, but ultimately it is a gift of God that culminates in glorification, the final state of sinless resurrection and the ever-increasing beatific vision. This ever-increasing beatific vision will be the subject of our final chapter, so we will not delve too deeply into the matter here. We should note that sanctification is often discussed in Scripture in tandem with suffering and the hope of heaven – suffering being the vehicle of sanctification which culminates in glory (2 Cor 4:16–5:10).

Before moving on, it is worth lingering on what has been said thus far in this chapter in light of the project as a whole. This project is concerned with the aesthetic dimensions of soteriology in general, and regeneration and faith in particular. *Something*, I will argue in the next chapter, is happening with the convert's 'heart eyes' (Eph. 1:18) in relation to the beauty of Christ. What the eyes of faith see when they behold Christ is the unparalleled beauty of the Triune God. Before arguing for what I *do* mean by this, however, the muddied waters of theological language surrounding 'beauty' and 'love' and 'affections' require that I take time to emphasize what I *do not* mean. The preceding sections of this chapter have been an effort to insist that what I argue in the next chapter is *not* a deviation from, or modification of, the traditional Reformed understanding of monergistic salvation. I affirm this understanding wholeheartedly and do not wish it changed. In the remainder of this

---

84. Ibid., 2.XVII.ix.

chapter, I am more direct in my denials and self-consciously break paths with both Roman Catholic and Edwardsian conceptions of soteriology, which both use language strikingly similar to what I employ in this book.

Justification According to Rome

The differences between Rome's soteriological conception and the Reformation model articulated above are numerous.[85] The starkest difference is Rome's insistence that justification and sanctification are indistinguishable – they are flattened into the same sweep of salvation.[86] Conflating the formative aspects of salvation (sanctification) with the judicial aspects (justification),[87] Rome is unable to affirm with the Reformers that God declares a saint righteous strictly on the merits of the imputed righteousness of Christ; an alien righteousness counted as theirs.[88] Rather, Rome conceptualizes grace as a substance, whereby faith, hope, and love are *infused* in the sinner over a lifetime of 'faith working through love'.[89] This notion of 'faith working through love' is a description of 'unformed faith' becoming 'formed faith'.[90]

---

85. For a recent thorough treatment on an evangelical assessment of Roman Catholic soteriology, see Gregg R. Allison, *Roman Catholic Theology and Practice: An Evangelical Assessment* (Wheaton, IL: Crossway, 2014), 413-50.

86. 'This disposition, or preparation, is followed by Justification itself, which is not remission of sins merely, but also the sanctification and renewal of the inward man, through the voluntary reception of the grace, and of the gifts, whereby man of unjust becomes just, and of an enemy a friend, that so he may be an heir according to hope of life everlasting.' Council of Trent, Session 6, 'Council Concerning Justification, 13 January, 1547,' in *Decrees of the Ecumenical Councils*, 2 vols., ed. Norman P. Tanner, (London: Sheed & Ward, 1990), volume 2. Cf., *Catechism of the Catholic Church: With Modifications from the Editio Typica* (New York: Random House, 1995), Article Two: 'Grace and Justification,' chap. 1.

87. 'Justification *detaches man from sin* which contradicts the love of God, and purifies his heart of sin. Justification follows upon God's merciful initiative of offering forgiveness. It reconciles man with God. It frees from the enslavement to sin, and it heals' (*Decrees of the Ecumenical Councils,* emphasis added).

88. 'Justification has been *merited for us by the Passion of Christ* who offered himself on the cross as a living victim, holy and pleasing to God, and whose blood has become the instrument of atonement for the sins of all men. Justification is conferred in Baptism, the sacrament of faith. It conforms us to the righteousness of God, who makes us inwardly just by the power of his mercy. Its purpose is the glory of God and of Christ, and the gift of eternal life' (ibid. emphasis added).

89. 'With justification, faith, hope, and charity are poured into our hearts, and obedience to the divine will is granted us' (ibid.).

90. 'Sanctifying grace is an habitual gift, a stable and supernatural disposition that perfects the soul itself to enable it to live with God, to act by his love. *Habitual grace*, the

The point at which faith constitutes as 'formed faith', or, when the formative aspect of justification has reached its proper end, corresponds with a 'moral fitness'. This is final justification. To be sure, Rome insists, within this conception, all of this is resourced by *grace* – an infusion of grace made possible by the atonement of Christ – but in the end, the *grounds* for final justification are a 'cooperation'.[91] Final justification results from both the merit of Christ, appropriated by faith in Christ, and the merits of the individual (and the treasury of merit, for that matter) wrought by 'faith working through love' – that is, the acts of charity, made possible by infused grace, whereby faith is 'formed'.[92] Grace, in this instance, does not refer to the kindness of God given as the gift of salvation through faith in Christ (cf., Rom. 3:24); grace is rather a formative *substance*, which may be increased or decreased.[93] Union with Christ, in this articulation, is rendered a reward for faith and obedience.[94] God, in a true sense, is *responding* to the saint in final justification.

So much of Rome's theology of beauty in soteriology comes through squarely from within this notion of *charity*. Many of the insights

---

permanent disposition to live and act in keeping with God's call, is distinguished from actual graces which refer to God's interventions, whether at the beginning of conversion or in the course of the work of sanctification' (ibid., chap. 2).

91. 'Justification establishes *cooperation between God's grace and man's freedom*' (ibid., chap. 1 emphasis added).

92. 'Moved by the Holy Spirit and by charity, *we can then merit* for ourselves and for others the graces needed for our sanctification, for the increase of grace and charity, and for the attainment of eternal life. Even temporal goods like health and friendship can be merited in accordance with God's wisdom. These graces and goods are the object of Christian prayer. Prayer attends to the grace we need for meritorious actions' (*Decrees of the Ecumenical Councils*, chap. 3, emphasis added).

93. 'Since the initiative belongs to God in the order of grace, *no one can merit the initial grace* of forgiveness and justification, at the beginning of conversion. Moved by the Holy Spirit and by charity, *we can then merit* for ourselves and for others the graces needed for our sanctification, for the increase of grace and charity, and for the attainment of eternal life. Even temporal goods like health and friendship can be merited in accordance with God's wisdom. These graces and goods are the object of Christian prayer. Prayer attends to the grace we need for meritorious actions' (ibid., chapter 3, emphasis added).

94. 'Spiritual progress tends toward ever more intimate union with Christ. This union is called "mystical" because it participates in the mystery of Christ through the sacraments – "the holy mysteries" – and, in him, in the mystery of the Holy Trinity. God calls us all to this intimate union with him, even if the special graces or extraordinary signs of this mystical life are granted only to some for the sake of manifesting the gratuitous gift given to all' (ibid., chap. 4).

Roman Catholic theologians have contributed on beauty in the role of sanctification are quite helpful; the problem is that because Rome conflates justification with sanctification,[95] these insights are sullied because they conceptualize an increasing affection for God's beauty as a justifying reality. The lifelong gaze of God's beauty results in the onlooker becoming, by virtue of this activity of gazing, morally fitted for final justification. While I agree that gazing at the beauty of God results in one's sanctifying conformity, 'from one degree of glory to another,' to the image of Christ (cf. 2 Cor. 3:18), I deny that this conformity amounts to 'moral fitness' for eternal life. Therefore, Rome's contribution to theological aesthetics is quite strong with respect to theology proper and revelation (specifically, Christology), but her theological aesthetics falls woefully short on the topic of soteriology.

Justification According to Edwards

In his own estimation, Edwards stands within the Protestant Reformed tradition. Faith, for Edwards, is not a virtue that makes the believer fit for justification in any judicial or meritorious way. This does not mean that Edwards simply co-signs what his Reformed forefathers maintained. He has no problem, for example, with self-consciously parting ways with Calvin and Turretin and others when they describe faith as the 'instrument' of justification and insists instead on calling it justification's mediatorial 'qualification'.[96]

Again, Edwards is not saying that faith is a virtue that qualifies the believer for justification on meritorious grounds – this he positively denies.[97] Rather, Edwards is concerned to avoid the impression that justification is somehow abstracted from Christ. Faith grasps not onto an abstract thing called 'justification'; faith grasps onto Christ, and justification is rendered the believer's via *real union* with Christ.[98] In

---

95. E.g. Aiden Nichols writes, '[In] the humanity of the Word incarnate, God has made his supreme self-communication, such that in gazing on this artwork we are ourselves transformed by what we see – judged, engraced, and ushered into the world of the divine life itself.' Aiden Nichols O.P., 'Sketch for a Christological Aesthetics,' *Logos* 1, no. 1 (1997): 46.

96. Edwards, *Works of Jonathan Edwards Online*, 19:153.

97. Ibid., 19:155.

98. Ibid., 19:156-59.

a recent article analyzing Edwards' doctrine of justification by faith, Gary Steward sums up Edwards' position thusly: 'Because faith actually unites a believer's soul to Christ, and because a corresponding legal union with Christ is so derived (flowing out of God's "love of order"), faith "qualifies" a believer for justification.'[99] Steward does grant that the concern for refusing to abstract Christ's benefits from Christ Himself is shared by those in the Reformed tradition, with strikingly similar articulations by the likes of Calvin and Turretin. The differences between Edwards and his Reformed predecessors are, nevertheless, significant.

For one thing, Edwards' definition of 'faith' differs strongly from the Reformed tradition in that Edwards – with Rome – sees 'love' not as proceeding from faith, but as forming part of its essence. Turretin, for example, explicitly distinguishes between faith and love, with faith as 'concerned with the promises of the gospel', and love 'with the precepts of the law'.[100] Justifying faith, for Turretin and others in the Reformed tradition, resources love as obedience to the law, but they remain distinct and related as cause and effect, the root and the fruit. Not so for Edwards, who insists that 'Faith is a duty required in the first table of the law, and in the first commandment; and there it will follow that it is comprehended in the great commandment, "Thou shall love the Lord thy God with all thy heart, and with all thy soul, and with all thy mind."'[101] 'Love,' Edwards goes on to say, 'is the very life and soul of a true faith.'[102]

Such an articulation bears remarkable resemblance to the Roman Catholic conception of 'formed love'. In fact, in his *Reformed Dogmatics,* Geerhardus Vos answers the question, 'Does the essence of faith then consist in love for the Mediator?' in the negative on account of the affirmative answer's resemblance to Rome: 'To maintain this would bring us onto Roman Catholic terrain, because, as has already been noted, for Rome love is seen as the "form" of faith – that is, love is what gives faith its distinguishing character.'[103] I agree with Steward when he

---

99. Gary Steward, 'Jonathan Edwards's Reception and Alteration of *Sola Fide*,' a paper delivered at the annual Evangelical Theological Society (2017), 5.

100. Turretin, *Institutes*, 2:XV.x.

101. Edwards, *Works of Jonathan Edwards Online*, 8:140.

102. Ibid.

103. Geerhardus J. Vos, *Reformed Dogmatics (Single Volume Edition): A System of Christian Theology*, ed. Richard B. Gaffin (Bellingham, WA: Lexham, 2020), 741.

grants that something called 'love' could be included in the essence of faith in such a way as to harmonize with the Reformed tradition (i.e., within the *fiducia* dimension of saving faith – there is a willingness to receive Jesus because Jesus is *desirable*). But 'love in this sense would need to be carefully distinguished from the love which is the greatest commandment of the law (Matt. 22:36) and which fulfills the law (Rom. 13:10).'[104]

Because Edwards parts ways with the Reformed tradition on the question of whether 'obedience' and 'love' should be included in the essence of faith, he opens himself to possibilities he would have otherwise had to exclude. This includes the notion that God's act of justifying sinners is on some level merited – the righteousness of Christ being the reward of faith and God's 'naturally fitting' response to obedient faith.[105] Edwards' move to flatten justifying faith and its fruits causes a wedge, not only between himself and his Arminian or Roman adversaries – as were his intentions – but also between himself and his Protestant Reformed forefathers. Thus, Steward can conclude,

> Although Edwards held to the imputation of Christ's righteousness as the sole formal basis for our justification, and although he sought to exclude all personal merit from justification, the Reformed understanding of *sola fide* is so re-worked in Edwards that it becomes virtually unrecognizable. Though adopting the Reformation slogan and using it in his macro-structure, the details of Edwards's position at this particular point significantly undermine the Reformed position he sought to defend.[106]

As it relates to this present volume, we should point out the relevance of Edwards' theological aesthetics in this whole discussion. Beauty, for Edwards, is inseparable from the notion of 'harmony' or 'fittingness'. Insofar as it goes, we should point out that justification, in God's economy, *is* fitting and harmonious and beautiful. God is Beauty, and all He does is beautiful, and in accordance with His simplicity, all His demonstrations of justice and goodness are demonstrations of His beauty. When Paul insists that God is 'the just and the justifier' (Rom. 3:26), we may safely conclude that His essential justness is beautiful, and the act

---

104. Steward, 'Jonathan Edwards's Reception and Alteration of *Sola Fide*,' 9 n 41.

105. Edwards, *Works of Jonathan Edwards Online*, 19:236.

106. Steward, 'Jonathan Edwards's Reception and Alteration of *Sola Fide*,' 19.

of justifying is beautiful. All well and good. The problem with Edwards' conception is that he confuses characteristic for motivation. He is not concerned with simply saying that God's justifying sinners is fitting; he insists rather that God's justification is *motivated* by the fittingness of faith. Faith renders the faithful *naturally* fitted for justification. This is a bridge too far, for it both commits the error we described above (i.e., the error of confusing the God's-eye view with the man's-eye view order; the error of insisting that God's *foundation* for justifying sinners is their union with Christ), and it renders the judicial motivation behind God's act in justifying sinners secondary to an aesthetic motivation. While both divine righteousness and divine beauty are irreducibly manifested in justification (by virtue of God's simplicity), justification is nevertheless a judicial category, not an 'artistic' one.

Conclusion

In this chapter I have sought to signal that what follows will articulate regeneration and faith from an aesthetic point of view, but from an aesthetic point of view that differs strongly from others like it. Much of the language in the following chapter will utilize language that might ring familiar to Roman Catholics or Jonathan Edwards, but I intend to contribute my voice to the chorus of Reformed theologians within the Protestant tradition. My contribution of 'regeneration and faith' as 'recognition and apprehension of divine beauty' is not a deviation of the Reformed conception of soteriology but rather an accentuation thereof through the lens of aesthetics. Accordingly, this chapter laid out a Reformed account of the *pactum salutis* in its relation to the *historia salutis* and the *ordo salutis*. I then compared this with soteriology from a Roman Catholic conception on one hand and an Edwardsian account on the other, noting my rejection of both. The next chapter develops the crux of this volume: in regeneration the Holy Spirit endows the sense perception faculties necessary for the newborn Christian to recognize the beauty of God in the face of Jesus Christ, which he subsequently apprehends by faith.

CHAPTER FIVE

Veiled and Unveiled Beauty

What has stripped the seeming beauty
From the idols of the earth?
Not a sense of right or duty,
But the sight of peerless worth.

Not the crushing of those idols,
With its bitter void and smart;
But the beaming of His beauty,
The unveiling of His heart.

ORA ROWAN[1]

Introduction

We have arrived now to the crux of this work: the consideration of the relationship between Christ's divine beauty, regeneration, and faith. Far from being a detached and esoteric concern, this question is of immanent practical concern. The problem of unbelief is, after all, a perennial mystery for the Christian. Dispatched into a sin-marred world, Christians carry the antidote for the spiritually sick and dying, and against all reason and good sense, some prefer death over life. The same aroma of Christ to God that some receive as a pleasing fragrance, others rebuff as an offensive stench (2 Cor. 2:15-16). Unbelief in neighbour often confounds the Christian, who considers Christ an altogether worthy object of faith.

---

1. Ora Rowan (1834–1879), 'Hast Thou Heard Him, Seen Him, Known Him,' Hymn. Public domain.

The manner in which one addresses the problem of unbelief has everything to do with where the question is situated. For example, from the vantage point of God's eternal decree, the topics of election and reprobation elbow their way to the fore (as we saw in the previous chapter).[2] Another vantage point from which to consider unbelief is at the individual, experiential level. At this level, the relevant questions are, 'What is the unbeliever experiencing in his rejection of the gospel?' and 'What is the convert experiencing in his acceptance of this gospel he once rejected?' In 2 Corinthians Paul delves into these existential concerns and concludes that the problem of unbelief is a spiritual eyesight problem. Unbelief, we will see, results from the inability to see Christ's glory aright.

This chapter will examine the Christological and soteriological implications of Paul's use of 'δόξα' (glory) in 2 Corinthians 3:12–4:6. Consequently, I will show that Christ's revealed glory is the glory of the divine nature (per chapter 3), and thereby has an aesthetic character (per chapter 2) that is at once attractive to some and repulsive to others, depending on the Holy Spirit's regenerating and illuminating ministry. Unbelief persists until the Spirit enables one to see Christ's glory aright.

I will advance this argument in the following stages: first, we will consider the context of 2 Corinthians 3–4 as it relates to the letter as a whole; second, we will exegete 2 Corinthians 3:12–4:6 with special attention to Paul's use of 'δόξα (doxa)'; third, we will compare our findings with John 12:36b–43; and fourth, we will conclude by summarizing the Christological and soteriological implications of our study, with particular attention given to *regeneration* and *faith*. In the end, we will show that unbelief results from the inability to appreciate the beauty of Christ's cruciform glory. According to the unbeliever's aesthetic criteria, nothing lovely can be found in Christ. Once perceived rightly, however, Christ's beauty is irresistible and is therefore soteriologically effective.

---

2.   Jonathan Hoglund, *Called by Triune Grace: Divine Rhetoric and the Effectual Call* (Downers Grove, IL: IVP Academic, 2016); Matthew Barrett, *Salvation by Grace: The Case for Effectual Calling and Regeneration* (Phillipsburg, NJ: P&R Publishing, 2013); Matthew Barrett and Tom J. Nettles, eds., *Whomever He Wills: A Surprising Display of Sovereign Mercy* (Cape Coral, FL: Founders, 2012), 16-76; Herman Bavinck, *Reformed Dogmatics* Volume 2, 337-405.

2 Corinthians 3–4 in Literary and Historical Context

Outlining 2 Corinthians is far from easy since its occasion is birthed out of Paul's history with the Christians in Corinth, which is long and colored. 'The Paul-Corinthian relationship,' Linda Belleville comments, 'spanning seven years, three personal visits and four letters, is one of the most complex topics in New Testament studies.'[3] Paul shifts to various topics (e.g., from travel plans in 1:12–2:4 to instructions on church discipline in 2:5-11), often abruptly (e.g., Paul's shift in and out of instructions for the collection for Jewish believers in 8:1 and 9:15), which is indicative of the various conversations he and the Corinthians had.[4]

The longest uninterrupted flow of Paul's thought in 2 Corinthians begins in 2:14 with a series of metaphors he strings together in defense of his new covenant ministry,[5] feeding into his argument that concludes in 7:16. Our passage (3:12–4:6) contains two of these metaphors (i.e., the metaphors of a 'veil' and of 'light'). Before examining this passage, however, we must consider Paul's broader purpose of defending his ministry as a whole. Why was a defense necessary at all? Of what was Paul accused? Further, why were the Corinthians influenced by these particular accusations?

---

3. Linda L. Belleville, *2 Corinthians* (Downers Grove, IL: IVP Academic, 1996), 15. Belleville outlines this relationship in ten stages (ibid., 15-19). See also Murray J. Harris, *The Second Epistle to the Corinthians: A Commentary on the Greek Text* (Grand Rapids, MI: Eerdmans, 2013), 101-05; Mark A. Seifrid, *The Second Letter to the Corinthians*, xxii–xxviii; George H. Guthrie, *2 Corinthians* (Grand Rapids, MI: Baker Academic, 2015), 17-22.

4. This volume assumes the basic unity of 2 Corinthians as a single letter, including chapters 10–13, contra Rudolf Bultmann, Roy A. Harrisville, and Rudolf Karl Bultmann, *The Second Letter to the Corinthians* (Minneapolis: Augsburg, 1985); F. F. Bruce, *1 and 2 Corinthians* (Grand Rapids, MI: Eerdmans, 1992); Savage, *Power through Weakness*. It may be that Paul wrote the letter in two settings, with an intermission and new information between the end of chapter 9 and the beginning of 10 (so says Harris, *The Second Epistle to the Corinthians*; D. A. Carson and Douglas J. Moo, *An Introduction to the New Testament*, 2nd ed. [Grand Rapids, MI: Zondervan, 2005]; Andreas J Köstenberger, L. Scott Kellum, and Charles L Quarles, *The Cradle, the Cross, and the Crown: An Introduction to the New Testament* [Nashville, TN: B&H Academic, 2016]), but we maintain that Paul intended for all thirteen chapters to be delivered as a single address.

5. Christopher P. Azure, 'A New Humanity in the Risen Christ: Paul's Use of KAINH KTIΣIΣ in 2 Corinthians 5:17 as a Metaphor from New Foundations' (PhD diss., Midwestern Baptist Theological Seminary, 2017), 201-49.

Literary Context

Since Paul's opponents are nowhere named explicitly, and since the nature of their criticism is nowhere disclosed in full, we must read between the lines. Paul's heartache over the Corinthians is near audible in this letter (cf. 6:13; 7:2; 10:1-2).[6] The central tragedy that animates Paul's emotive language is the Corinthians' lack of loyalty.

A class of teachers critical of Paul had infiltrated the Corinthian church with no apparent objection from the believers there (e.g., 'you put up with it readily enough,' 11:4).[7] Their central message is not certain, but the mood and general thrust of their ministry is apparent from Paul's response. They carried themselves with a swagger and built their platform largely by putting Paul down, stepping on him to elevate themselves. Boasting of super-apostolic status (11:5), they placed a high premium on letters of recommendation (3:1), physical professionality (10:10), and rhetorical showmanship (11:6).[8] Calling attention to Paul's apparent lack of these qualities served to both belittle him and elevate themselves.[9] As the Corinthians grew increasingly sour toward Paul, his disappointment understandably occasions words of exhortation and rebuke (chaps. 10–13).

It would be a mistake to assume, however, that Paul's defense of his ministry is a reactionary expression of hurt feelings. Second Corinthians contains a calculated defense aimed at the Corinthians' good. Their abandonment of Paul reflected a deeper problem. Paul was far more concerned with repudiating the Corinthians' idolatry than with preserving his own reputation. This becomes clear when the social dynamics of first-century Corinth are taken into consideration.

Historical Context

Corinth was fertile soil for criticism against Paul of this kind to flourish. Timothy Savage notes that 'the criticisms have cultural

---

6. See Köstenberger, Kellum, and Quarles, *The Cradle, the Cross, and the Crown*, 541.

7. Seifrid, *The Second Letter to the Corinthians*, 407-11.

8. Savage, *Power through Weakness*, 12, summarizes the elements of the opponents' criticisms of Paul as '*Boasting* ... they seem to be critical of his refusal to boast'; '*Physical presence*'; '*Speech*'; and '*Support* ... the Corinthians disapprove of the refusal to accept monetary support.'

9. Ibid., 55-56.

overtones. They reflect the social prejudices of the day.'[10] Corinth was no different than any other city in first century Rome in the sense that it 'cultivated a rigorous self-sufficiency (αὐτάρκεια).'[11] Savage points out that, influenced by the philosophers of the day, 'people began to focus on themselves and in particular on cultivating their self-worth.'[12] This influenced everything from social status[13] to religious practice.[14] Everything in which the Hellenist participated was calculated for maximal self-aggrandizement.

If this much was true for Rome in general, it was doubly so for first century Corinth, a city 'at the height of its glory' and 'a tribute to human-made splendor'.[15] Corinth was a city perhaps destined for prosperity by virtue of its two major ports, which 'served as a unique crossroads, providing Rome with a shortcut to the ports of Asia and the Eastern Mediterranean.'[16] Yet there were times in its history in which Corinth faced uncertainty: established in the seventh century B.C., she was fought over for centuries, sacked and burned by Rome in 146 B.C., and then repopulated by freshly liberated slaves a century later.[17]

By the time Paul arrived in Corinth, the city was an economic powerhouse, electric with possibilities for those seeking to become self-made people. Unlike many other places in the Greco-Roman world, Corinth was a city of unlimited social opportunity. In the 'Corinthian dream', a freshly freed slave could make his way to Corinth and begin to ascend the ladder of social upward mobility to make a name for himself.[18] It was customary – even socially orthodox – to climb this ladder with grandiose self-exaltation and boasting. 'Putting oneself on show was not a ritual reserved for the elite. It was a passion played out at every level, though on lesser scales. In Corinth, perhaps more than

---

10. Ibid., 12-13.
11. Ibid., 19.
12. Ibid., 19.
13. Ibid., 20.
14. Ibid., 25-26.
15. Ibid., 36.
16. Guthrie, *2 Corinthians*, 12.
17. Ibid., 9-10.
18. Ibid., 11-16.

anywhere else, social ascent was the goal, boasting and self-display the means, personal power and glory the reward.'[19]

This historical backdrop brings tremendous clarity to Paul's opposition in 2 Corinthians and helps to explain why criticism of him and his message was taken up so readily by the church in Corinth. Nothing about Paul's ministry lends itself naturally to Corinthian sensibilities. He preaches a 'foolish' gospel of a crucified Savior who accomplished salvation by – in the estimation of competitive Corinthian culture – losing (1 Cor. 1:18-31).[20] Paul represented this gospel as one who refused to boast in anything but his own weakness (2 Cor 2:17; 11:30-31; 12:9-10), who embodied unassuming meekness (2 Cor. 10:10), who refrained from flourishes of rhetorical showmanship (2 Cor. 10:10; 11:6; 1 Cor. 2:1-5), and who insisted on remaining in a state of poverty, refusing opportunities afforded him to increase his wealth (2 Cor. 11:7-11). For a city that prized strength, victory, boasting, beauty, impressive speech, and financial self-advancements, Paul was not merely an oddity, he was a stigma.

This all being the case, it becomes obvious that Paul is not firstly concerned with defending his ministry for his own sake. If he were, he would boast in a fashion similar to his critics. He would play to his audience, who have by now made it quite clear that they desired self-promotion. They wanted braggadocious self-exaltation. They wanted high credentials and respectability. In short, the Corinthians wanted strong leaders who boasted in their strength. It would not have been difficult for Paul to turn on his rhetorical flourish and smooth talk himself back into their good graces on their own terms. He could have simply given them what they wanted.

Instead, Paul doubles down in the opposite direction. Recognizing that their cultural sensibilities led to self-worship, Paul defended his ministry in a way that intentionally offended those sensibilities, in the hopes that the Corinthians would see their idolatry. Paul knew that boasting of his weakness was not the way to restore his injured

---

19. Savage, *Power through Weakness*, 41.

20. In this way, Paul simultaneously exalts the grace of God and insults the sinful arrogance of the Corinthians. As if to say, 'The proof that God is actually confounding the wisdom of the wise by saving those who are too stupid to save themselves, dear Corinthians, is your own salvation. Exhibit A: the Corinthian church.'

reputation among the Corinthians on their terms, but it could possibly awaken them to the error of those very terms. Thus, Paul defends his ministry by doing the very thing the Corinthians despised: highlighting his weakness. They wanted glory; he gave them shame.

This, however, was not because he wanted to deprive the Corinthians of all forms of glory. To the contrary. In Paul's estimation the irony of the Corinthians' situation was that their rejection of Paul's weakness was the rejection of a glory greater than the glory they prized. Savage summarizes,

> Not only that his converts are drawing inspiration from the social outlook of the day but also that Paul responds by adopting a position that represents the exact antithesis of what they would have desired in a religious leader. While the Corinthians will find his position offensive, Paul insists that it actually works for their good. The reason for this fundamental disagreement between Paul and his converts would seem to boil down to a conflict between two opposing perspectives: the worldly outlook of the Corinthians and Paul's own Christ-centered viewpoint.[21]

What the Corinthians perceived as undesirable and pathetic was in fact irresistibly beautiful, once perceived aright. Their problem was that they viewed Paul, his ministry, and his message 'according to the flesh' and, therefore, inaccurately. According to Paul, the way of weakness is the way of vision correction. The weakling whom God delights to make strong can behold Christ's transformative glory, the quality of which dwarfs every other.

Exegesis: δόξα (doxa) in 2 Corinthians 3:12–4:6

By the time Paul comes to 2 Corinthians 3:12, he has already begun the work of contrasting his divinely sanctioned new covenant ministry with his opponents. Paul describes his ministry with a series of interconnected metaphors: triumphal procession (2:14-16), street peddling (2:17), letters of commendation and their couriers (3:1-11), veiling (3:12–4:6), and light (4:4-6).[22]

Paul introduces the idea of δόξα in 3:7, where he grants that the ministry of Moses – the ministry of death – came with a degree of glory,

---

21. Savage, *Power Through Weakness*, 99.
22. See, Azure, 'A New Humanity in the Risen Christ,' 206-20.

though a kind inferior to his own ministry – the new covenant ministry of life. In Exodus 34:29-35, after ascending Sanai, Moses received a revelation of God's glory, and the result was a luminous glow in Moses' own face that made Israel afraid. To accommodate the people's dread, Moses put a veil over his face to hide the glory that radiated from his face (2 Cor. 3:13). This level of divine experience made Moses an attractive figure for the Corinthians, who considered this great leader of Israel to be an exemplary model of strength and spiritual achievement. 'In an age obsessed with magic and the supernatural,' writes Savage, 'it is not surprising that Moses attracted so much attention. Indeed no other name in antiquity is more revered for its wonder-working powers.'[23]

The Inferior Glory of Moses

Yet, despite the greatness of Moses' glory – which was great enough for Israelite onlookers to consider unbearable – Paul estimates that it is excelled by the glory of his own ministry, 'the ministry of the Spirit' (3:8). In contrast to Moses' letters carved on stone (3:3, 7), Paul's ministry includes Spirit-penned letters on flesh (3:3). In contrast to Moses' message of death (3:6, 7), Paul's message of the Spirit brings life (3:6). In contrast to Moses' message, which brings condemnation (3:9), Paul's message of the Spirit brings righteousness (3:10). If the stone-written, condemning message of death brings a degree of glory, Paul reasons, surely the glory of the Sprit's heart-written, righteousness-granting message of life far surpasses it in splendor.

Yet Paul goes even further, suggesting that the glory of his new covenant ministry surpasses Moses' glory of the old covenant ministry not only for the above qualitative difference but also for the quantitative difference of *longevity*. Azure makes this clear:

> Moses, suggests Paul, knew that, upon seeing the glory of his face fade, the Israelites would lose hope because of their hardened understanding (ἐπωρώθη τὰ νοήματα αὐτῶν). Therefore ... Moses placed a veil on his face so that the Israelites would not see that the glory (light) on his face faded (καταργουμένου) between visits with the Lord (cf. 2 Cor. 3:13). The effect of Moses's behavior was that the children of Israel thought that Moses face, and thus the Old Covenant, did not fade, and was permanent.[24]

---

23. See Savage, *Power through Weakness*, 109.
24. Azure, 'A New Humanity in the Risen Christ,' 222.

In other words, Moses protected the people not only from the unbearable glory of his face but also from the disillusioning realization that his glory – and the glory of the old covenant – was *fading*. The same precautions are not necessary for Paul, however (cf. '*not* like Moses,' 3:13). There is not the slightest worry that the glory he represents will begin to fade. There is one more layer to Paul's 'veil' metaphor, but before addressing it we must clarify the sharpness of this contrast. To do so, we turn our attention to the superior glory of Christ.

The Superior Glory of Christ

This glory, with which Paul contrasts Moses', is at once clear when Paul reveals its owner: 'And we all, with unveiled face, *beholding the glory of the Lord*' (3:18a). Whereas Moses' ministry showed God's glory through the mediation of his luminous face – which radiated with a *reflection* of the glory only he saw – Paul insists that his ministry was characterized by direct vision of 'the glory of the Lord'. In this sense, everyone who 'turns to the Lord' is positioned alongside Moses: beholding the glory of the Lord.[25] Indeed, we can lean in on the parallels even further. Recall how Moses required mediation in order to behold the glory of the Lord. God could not allow the brilliance of His glory to befall on Moses without some sort of mediation, lest Moses be completely consumed by divine holiness. This mediation came by way of God's own goodness in the form of (a) His hand covering Moses' face, and (b) Moses' hiding in the cleft of the rock. It is not as if New Covenant saints no longer require mediation: God's holiness is still just as threatening to our creaturely limitations. Therefore, for the believer experiencing faithful vision of the glory of God in the face of Jesus Christ, *Jesus* is the mediation. We hide, like Moses, in the cleft of the Rock, who is Christ Himself.

This point becomes increasingly clear when we consider the effects of this beholding: 'And we all, with unveiled face, beholding the glory

---

25. Azure, ibid., 224, points out the parallel that exists in both 'the wording and the word order' between 3:16 and Exodus 34:34a in the LXX. Exodus 34:34a reads: ἡνίκα δ ἀν εἰσεπορεύετο Μωυσῆς ἔναντι κυρίου λαλεῖν αὐτῷ περιηρεῖτο τὸ κάλυμμα, while 2 Corinthians 3:16 reads ἡνίκα δὲ ἐὰν ἐπιστρέψῃ πρὸς κύριον, περιαιρεῖται τὸ κάλυμμα. 'Paul compares Moses's removal of his veil when he went "before the Lord" (Exod. 34:34), with God's removal of the veil of unbelief from the mind of any person who turns to the "Lord".'

of the Lord, *are being transformed from one degree of glory to another*. For this comes from the Lord who is Spirit' (3:18, emphasis added). Like Moses, all those who behold the glory of God are transformed in a glory-reflecting way; they become like the image they behold. Paul therefore invites the readers to no longer be enamored by the fading glory of Moses but to rather behold this 'image' (εἰκόνα), whereby the 'Lord who is the Spirit' will transform them *into* this image 'from one degree of glory to another'.[26]

At this point, Paul has not yet disclosed what this 'same image' is, only that in beholding it, one beholds the 'glory of the Lord' and is 'transformed' thereunto 'from one degree of glory to another'. The clarification comes in 4:4: the transformative glory is none other than 'the glory of Christ, who is the image (εἰκὼν) of God.' The climax of this passage is 4:6,[27] where we learn that 'God creates the Christian *by showing a person God's glory on Christ's face*.'[28] The glory that emanates from Jesus' face, in other words, has creative power – in beholding the glory of Jesus, the Spirit of God creates.[29]

This is why Paul connects the dots between conversion and God's creative agency in Genesis 1:3-4: 'For God, who said, "Let light shine out of darkness," has shown in our hearts to give the light of the knowledge of the glory of God in the face of Jesus Christ' (2 Cor 4:6).[30] The same *ex nihilo* creative agency that was at work at the creation of the cosmos, in other words, is at work in the creation of every Christian.[31] God spoke light into darkness and out came a planet teeming with life. God speaks light ('light of the glory of God in the face of Jesus Christ') in

---

26. Azure, ibid., 223, writes, 'Moses, the old covenant messenger, *did not* want the people to see that the old covenant was fading; Paul, on the other hand, the new covenant messenger, *wanted* people to see that the old covenant was not permanent.'

27. 'The verse which sheds the most light on Paul's understanding of glory is 2 Corinthians 4:6. Here, at the end of a long exposition of the theme of δόξα, we discover both the source and the nature of his glory' (Savage, *Power through Weakness*, 111).

28. Peter Balla, '2 Corinthians' in Beale and Carson, *Commentary on the New Testament Use of the Old Testament*, 763-64, emphasis added.

29. See Guthrie, 2 Corinthians, 245-46.

30. 'Most scholars believe Paul draws this reflection as a loose citation from Gen. 1:3' (ibid., 244).

31. 'The Creator who out of darkness brought forth light is the one who has illuminated the heart of the apostle' (Seifrid, *The Second Letter to the Corinthians*, 201).

the dark void of the sinful heart and out comes a new heart teeming with new life.[32]

Despite Paul's apparent appeal to Genesis 1:3-4, however, some scholars have pointed out the thematic similarities with Isaiah.[33] Rather than comparing conversion to God's protological, creation activity (cf. Gen. 1:3-4), some point out that Paul may be appealing to God's eschatological *new creation* promise (cf. Isa. 9:1). According to this reading, the light 'is the long-awaited light of the eschaton, heralding a new creation and commencing the day of salvation.'[34]

However, it is unnecessary to choose between an appeal to protology in Genesis or an appeal to eschatology in Isaiah.[35] In all likelihood, Paul is trying to convey both. 'It may be that what we have in Paul's allusion is a conflation of the Genesis passage and the one from Isaiah,' says Guthrie, 'with the former being read in light of the latter .... If this is the case, then the apostle uses these twin images – God's giving creation's light and the light of re-creation in his new, eschatological age – to speak of the dawning of light in the human heart through the gospel.'[36] Guthrie then summarizes:

> This confession lies at the heart of the gospel. Human beings were created in the image of God (Gen. 1:26), but in the fall the glory attending that image has been lost (Rom. 3:23). Yet, through Christ's obedience to the Father, the curse has been reversed (Rom. 5:12-21), and the glory has been restored through Christ, our 'new Adam' (1 Cor. 15:49 ...). Moreover, God predestined believers to be conformed to the image of the Son (Rom. 8:29 ...). This is 'the same image' into which new covenanters are being transformed, 'from glory to glory' (2 Cor. 3:18).[37]

The context in 2 Corinthians further demonstrates the experience is soteriologically normative; it is not idiosyncratic to Paul and his Corinthian audience. This (re-)creation occurs whenever 'one turns to the

---

32. John Owen's description of this process is penetrating. See Owen, *The Works of John Owen*, 1:77.

33. E.g., Savage, *Power through Weakness*, 111-27.

34. Ibid., 126.

35. See G. K. Beale, *A New Testament Biblical Theology*, 243-44.

36. Guthrie, *2 Corinthians*, 245. See also Harris, *The Second Epistle to the Corinthians*, 333-35; Belleville, *2 Corinthians*, 119.

37. Guthrie, *2 Corinthians*, 246.

Lord' and 'the veil' of unbelief is removed (2 Cor. 3:16) – whenever the 'gospel of the glory of Christ' (2 Cor. 4:4) is proclaimed by 'ambassadors of God' who implore sinners to be 'reconciled to God' (2 Cor. 5:20).[38] The glory of Paul's ministry is therefore superior to the glory of Moses' not only because it is unfading but also because it is effective to do what the glory of Moses' covenant could never accomplish (cf. Gal. 3:15-29; Heb. 8:7-8).[39]

If all this is the case, the quandary of unbelief – introduced above – is doubly baffling. The rejection of Paul's ministry is inexplicable. Savage frames the matter nicely:

> If the glory of Moses prompted the Israelites to shield their eyes because of its unbearable brightness, if the reputation of Moses is now equally luminous in the minds of the Corinthians, how could the allegedly superior glory of Paul be regarded as anything but 'much more' (πολύ περισσότερον) bedazzling? Yet, remarkably, his ministry creates the opposite impression. Many detect no glory at all. It inspires no awe, only pity and revulsion.[40]

To give an account for this seeming inexplicable rejection of the superior glory of Paul's ministry, we return now to Paul's 'veil' metaphor.

Satanic Veil

We have seen that Paul calls attention to Moses' veil as a way of highlighting the intensity of Moses' glory (i.e., it was so bright the sons of Israel could not stand the sight). This he does to point out the supremacy of his own ministry's glory. We have seen also that Paul interprets Moses' action of veiling his face as a preemptive effort to protect Israel from the disillusioning truth of his face's fading glory. Paul does this, again, in contrast to the glory of his own ministry – no veil is required. He invites his readers to compare Moses' fading glory with the unfading glory of his ministry. Paul is not finished with the 'veil'

---

38. See Hoglund, *Called by Triune Grace*, 89-90.

39. It is worth mentioning that the inability of Moses' glory to accomplish what Christ's glory accomplished is not owing to a failure of Moses' covenant per se. Jason DeRouchie points out that the glory of Moses' ministry was never intended to carry the same soteriological creativity that Paul ascribes to Christ's glory here. See Jason S. DeRouchie, 'The Mystery Revealed: A Biblical Case for Christ-Centered Old Testament Interpretation,' *Themelios* 44, no. 2 (2019): 229-30, emphasis added. Footnote 7 in this article is particularly illuminating.

40. Savage, *Power through Weakness*, 111.

metaphor, however. Intent on wringing it of every drop of symbolism, Paul adds layer upon layer of theological reflection. The layer that takes center stage in chapter 4 is *the veil as a satanic obstruction*.

Paul hints at this in 14 when he says that 'their minds were hardened' and in verse 15 when he says that 'to this day whenever Moses is read a veil lies over *their* hearts' (emphasis added). Here Paul begins to shift the metaphor, so that the veil obstructing the view of glory is no longer draped over Moses' face but rather the sons of Israel's hearts. The reason Paul's superior ministry is not celebrated by Paul's opponents is that they could not see Christ's glory therein. Though Christ's glory objectively shown forth in Paul's new covenant ministry, it was not subjectively received and lauded because the natural man's vision is impaired by a satanic veil: 'the god of this world has blinded the minds of the unbelievers, to keep them from seeing the light of the gospel of the glory of Christ' (4:4).[41]

Savage points out that while most commentators give significant attention to the source of this veil ('the god of this world'), very little give attention to the mechanics of its function.[42] After all, it is not as though the raw material of Paul's ministry (which is where Christ's glory shines) is inaccessible to 'the minds of unbelievers'. They hear the same facts of the same message of the same crucified and risen Jesus. In fact, they have the same Scriptures that testify to this same Christological glory (i.e., 'whenever Moses is read a veil lies over their hearts,' which indicates that the glory they are unable to subjectively receive objectively emanates from the writings of Moses). How could they receive the same information and interpret it in such a radically different way?

Savage suggests that the answer has everything to do with what the Corinthians prized 'according to the flesh'. According to the flesh, Jesus lost. When squaring up with the powers that be, Jesus wound up hanging naked and ashamed on a Roman cross. According to Corinthian sensibilities, there is nothing praiseworthy in such a shameful display – they are embarrassed by the display of cruciform self-denial. As such, Satan drapes the veil over the hearts on unbelievers by appealing to their weakness-despising sensibilities.

---

41. See Guthrie, *2 Corinthians*, 239.
42. See Savage, *Power through Weakness*, 154.

In sum, we see that the very same display of Christological glory inspires both worship and revulsion. Once again, we note that the natural man cannot consider the bloody cross beautiful any more than the natural Greek can consider the gospel *wise*, or the natural Jew consider it a *powerful sign*. However, when 'one turns to the Lord, the veil is removed' (3:16), and such a one is thereby able to view Christ's glory aright. Such a vision has an irresistible effect. 'Just as God irresistibly caused the light to flood into the darkness of the first creation,' writes Beale, 'so has he begun to do so with blinded humans in the new creation.'[43] The apparently ugly, foolish, weak gospel is considered beautiful, wise, and powerful only to 'those who are called' (1 Cor. 1:18-25).

Christ's Repellent and Attractive Glory in John 12

Before drawing together the theological implications of our study, we will now corroborate our findings. Do we find this idea of Christ's glory attracting some in faith while simultaneously repelling others in unbelief anywhere else in Scripture (specifically, the New Testament)? Though more could be said, one other passage that seems to corroborate this principle is John 12:36-43.

At the close of the book of signs in the Gospel of John, the evangelist gives an account for the widespread rejection of Jesus' ministry (which eventually culminates with crucifixion). In similar fashion to Paul in our discussion above, John is compelled at this point in his narrative to explain why Jesus has been so resolutely rejected by those who should have welcomed His ministry. If Jesus' own words about Himself are true, why was He not received as the 'light'? How could His contemporaries not have been enlightened? Without some kind of explanation, Jesus looks to have failed at this point in the narrative.

As we saw in chapter 3, the evangelist quotes two passages from Isaiah in this passage (John 12:36-43; cf. Isa. 6:10; 53:1).[44] Speaking of both passages (i.e., the heavenly throne room scene of Isaiah 6 and the suffering servant scene of Isaiah 53), John writes, 'Isaiah said *these things* when he saw his glory and spoke of him' (John 12:41, emphasis

43. Beale, *A New Testament Biblical Theology*, 457.

44. See, Köstenberger, 'John' in Beale and Carson, *Commentary on the New Testament Use of the Old Testament*, 476-83.

added).[45] According to John, the same glory Isaiah describes seeing in the heavenly throne room in Isaiah 6 is manifested in the sufferings of the Messiah in Isaiah 53.[46] 'In the wake of the *two Isaianic quotes* in 12:38 and 12:40,' writes Köstenberger, 'the evangelist concludes that Isaiah saw Jesus's glory.'[47]

The grotesque crucifixion is what divine glory looks like when grace toward sinners is in view.[48] 'The unveiled glory he displayed during his earthly career,' Jonathan King argues,

> was in the form of a slave because this was the form that was most fitting for him to assume as the Messiah in the state of his humiliation. Christ crucified takes the display/revelation of his glory to a whole other level because in this event of the theodrama the form of his humanity on the cross was literally cruciform – the form that was most fitting as Sin-bearer.[49]

Furthermore, this cruciform display of glory seems to be the very thing the Jews reject.[50] In this way, the crucifixion not only displays divine glory, it results from divine glory. God blinds the eyes and hardens the hearts of unbelieving Jews by sending a Messiah whose divine glory they reject as apparent un-glory. Blinded by God with the unwanted glory of Christ, the Jews – fulfilling one Isaianic prophecy (Isa. 6:9-10) – reject Christ

---

45. For more on this topic, see, Ibid., 479-80; Carson, *The Gospel According to John*, 449-50; Ridderbos, *The Gospel According to John*, 445-46; Köstenberger, *John*, 390-93; Harris, *John*, 238. What primarily concerns us at present is the relationship John sees between the glory of Jesus, His crucifixion, and the Jews' rejection.

46. 'Αὐτοῦ' refers to Jesus, as the following περὶ αὐτοῦ makes clear. Apparently Isaiah had a vision of the pre-incarnate glory of Christ (cf. 17:5) – as the one subsisting in God's essence (Phil 2:6)' (Harris, *John*, 238). Similarly, Eusebius of Caesarea writes, 'The prophet then seeing our Savior sitting on his Father's throne in the divine and glorious kingdom, and moved by the Holy Spirit and being about to describe next his coming among humanity and his birth of a Virgin, foretells that his knowledge and praise would be over all the earth,' in Joel C. Elowsky and Thomas C. Oden, eds., *John 11–21*, Ancient Christian Commentary on Scripture: New Testament, 12 vols. (Downers Grove, IL: InterVarsity Press, 2007), 4b:75. Cf., Bruce Henning, 'Jesus as the Rejected Prophet and Exalted Lord: The Rhetorical Effect of Type Shifting in John 12:38-41,' *Journal of the Evangelical Theological Society* 62, no. 2 (2019): 340.

47. Köstenberger, *John*, 391, emphasis added.

48. See King, *The Beauty of the Lord*, 220. Cf. ibid., 222.

49. Ibid.

50. Thus, a parallel seems to be drawn with Jesus' prophetic message and Isaiah's, in that both serve as the judicial hardening instrument God uses. See D. A. Carson, *The Gospel According to John*, 448.

and 'lift him up' (cf. John 12:32), and thereby ironically showcase Christ's glory to a greater (cruciform) extent – fulfilling another Isaianic prophecy (Isa. 52:13–53:12). The same glory that repulsed the Jews enough for them to nail Jesus to wood irresistibly 'draws all men' to Jesus by faith. Only with the eyes of faith, therefore, can one reconcile the seeming contradiction of Christ's beauty and His grotesque death on the cross.[51]

Theological Implications

Thus far, we have established the context of 2 Corinthians 3–4 within the letter as a whole. We then considered 2 Corinthians 3:12–4:6 with special attention to Paul's use of δόξα as a simultaneously compelling and repelling force (i.e., it is rejected by those who see it through the satanic veil of self-glorifying and fleshly values, and is adored by those who are freed from this satanic veil according to the Holy Spirit's illuminating ministry). Subsequently, we saw this very same theological principle of divine glory compelling and repelling in John 12:36-43. We now turn our attention to consider the soteriological and Christological implications in light of our findings. Consider the following implications.

First, our study implies that God's glory includes an aesthetic dimension. Through the Holy Spirit's enlightening ministry, believers see a glory in Christ that is irresistibly compelling. As we saw from chapters 2 and 3, there is something in Christ's glory that is desirable in the estimation of the convert, and he therefore reaches out to apprehend Christ by faith.

Further, apart from the bare concept of desirableness, we may note a theological connection between divine 'glory' and 'beauty', which bears the weight of biblical (Ps. 27:4; Isa. 62:2-3; Zech. 9:16; 2 Pet. 1:17) and historical testimony.[52] In his recent work on the topic, Jonathan King summarizes the relationship between divine beauty and glory this way:

> the beauty of God manifested economically (*pulchritudeo Dei ad extra*) is expressed and perceivable as *a quality of* the glory of God inherent in his work of creation, redemption, and consummation. The display of God's glory is thus always beautiful, always fitting, always entails an aesthetic dimension to it.[53]

---

51. Cf., King, *The Beauty of the Lord*, 209.

52. For example, see Edwards, *Works of Jonathan Edwards Online*, 2:274-75.

53. King, *The Beauty of the Lord*, 51 (emphasis original).

When one is drawn to the beauty of God, one is drawn to His glory through a particular economic manifestation – or 'perceivable quality' – thereof. Because God is simple, and His glory is 'the splendor of brilliance that is inseparably associated with *all of [His] attributes* and his self-revelation in nature and grace',[54] where His glory is revealed, there also is His beauty revealed. Nowhere is this glory revealed more fully than in Christ.[55]

Second, our study implies that Christ shares the same divine glory as the Father and the Spirit, such that the glory He reveals is the glory of the Trinity. This, of course, was the burden of chapter 3, but it bears repeating here. Speaking of John's use of Isaiah 6 and 53, Herman Ridderbos observes that 'the glory of God as the prophet foresaw it in his vision was no other than that which the Son of God had with the Father before the world was and that was to be manifested before the eyes of all in the incarnation of the Word.'[56] Any glory revealed by any distinct person of the Trinity is necessarily constituent to the single divine nature.[57] Thus, when Christ reveals glory, it is not Christ's glory alone but rather the Trinity's glory – the glory of the divine nature the Father, Son, and Spirit share (John 17:5).[58] Michael Allen is instructive on this point:

> The shared glory of the three divine persons befits only God, but this Trinity of love and light does share this inner-Trinitarian visibility. Without bringing creatures to share in this natural knowledge and sight, the loving Lord of eternity does elect that creatures participate in this light and wisdom by grace and according to their creaturely capacity. Our vision of God is not the same as God's own vision, but it is remarkably real nonetheless.[59]

---

54. Bavinck, *Reformed Dogmatics Volume 2*, 252, emphasis added.

55. King, *The Beauty of the Lord*, 150, writes that the 'glory that God formerly had to obscure from Moses's gaze would, in the fullness of time, come to its perfect expression in the glory of God in Christ.'

56. Ridderbos, *The Gospel According to John*, 445.

57. Recall chapter 3, n 21.

58. 'Thus Paul's allusion to the creation of light services his Christological emphasis,' observes Balla ('2 Corinthians,' 764); 'true knowledge of God comes through Jesus Christ, and God himself made it possible for human beings to know him in this way, and this way only.'

59. Michael Allen, *Grounded in Heaven: Recentering Christian Hope and Life on God* (Grand Rapids, MI: Eerdmans, 2018), 83-84.

In the incarnation, therefore, Jesus reveals to us *who God is*. He translates God into *human language and flesh and bones*. Again, Allen is instructive here:

> The attendant condition of the humanity of Christ does not mean that the blessed vision of God in the face of Christ can be reduced to a vision of his humanity. Rather, we see him: the person of the Son of God, 'God of God, Light of Light, Very God of Very God.' Just as the person is subject of all incarnational action, so the person is the object of all beatific vision. We might break this down grammatically. The Son as Son is visible. But the Son as Son is visible by means of his humanity.... [T]he humanity of the Son is the instrument by which the vision of God occurs.[60]

Incredibly, since the Second Person of the Trinity is truly divine – that is, truly God, existing in the same glory as the Father and the Spirit – when He reveals *Himself* to us in His human nature, He is, by His human nature, revealing the glory of the Trinity to us. 'The astounding thing,' Allen goes on to say elsewhere, 'is that the eternal Word by whom all things were created became a creature without ceasing to be that eternal Word, and therefore his very creatureliness constitutes the act of revelation and is the guarantee that revelation is here within creation and accessible to humans.'[61] Astounding indeed.

We are in a position to connect the thesis of this project to the classical-theistic discussions in chapters 2 and 3. Soteriology's aesthetic dimension, wherein saving faith as beholding Christ's revealed glory so that the beholder apprehends by faith the communication of divine beauty, depends entirely on divine immutability. This is because Christ cannot reveal a glory other than the divine nature's immutable glory. The only glory God has is immutable, therefore the only glory Christ can reveal must also be immutable; it cannot in any sense be new.

Having argued positively for our thesis by exploring divine immutability in light of Christology (chapter 3), I propose now to argue the impossibility of the contrary: the rejection of the affirmation advanced here is disastrous. We will limit the implications for such a rejection to two: if the faith-eliciting glory that Christ reveals is not the immutable glory of God's nature and instead results from the incarnation, then

---

60. Ibid., 79.
61. Allen, 'Knowledge of God' in *Christian Dogmatics*, 17.

(a) saving faith places confidence on that which is undependable, and/
or (b) it runs the risk of idolatry. If God changes, and the glory Christ
reveals in the incarnation constitutes such a change, faith elicited by
such a glory would be faith in that which is not dependable. If such were
the case, the God whom Christians worship today is, in a real sense,
different from the God whom saints before the incarnation worshiped.
The former worship a God whose glory includes an actuality that was
mere unknown potentiality to the latter (i.e., the new glory that includes
the incarnation). He is no longer the same God, for He has changed
from one God to another through the process of becoming (from the
God of *glory a* to the God of *glory b*).[62] Some form of process theology[63]
seems unavoidable if Christ's glory, which elicits saving faith from those
who see it, has any new shade added as a result of the incarnation. Such a
glory is necessarily subject to potential change since it itself has resulted
from one.[64]

Even if one avoids process theology with some innovative reformulation (or rejection) of the doctrine of divine simplicity to create space for
accidental attributes in God – with this faith-eliciting glory being one
– saving faith still remains a gamble. If the attribute that makes Christ
the object of saving faith is accidental to God's nature, it is something
God could shake off or morph into something else with no consequence
to His essential self. In such a case, the distinction between His (a)
'ontological' immutability and (b) 'ethical' or 'covenantal' immutability
from His (c) 'relational' mutability offers little comfort. If His 'ethical'
immutability is predicated on His 'ontological' immutability, and His
'ontological' immutability applies only to His essential attributes and *not*

---

62. One may contend that this scenario is describing the same God whose glory changes
over time, just like a husband whose appealing characteristics to his wife change over
time. But even with such a scenario, there is a sense in which the composite husband
thirty years into marriage is a different man than the one who stood at the altar thirty
years prior (he now has x rather than a number of hairs, y rather than b number of
wrinkles, and a z rather than c size waistband).

63. For a helpful overview of process theology, see Stanley J. Grenz and Roger E. Olson,
Twentieth Century Theology: God & the World in a Transitional Age (Downers Grove, IL:
InterVarsity Press, 1992), 130-44.

64. Again, appeals to God's 'ethical' or 'covenantal' immutability at this point are
useless, since all such statements of God's ethical and covenantal commitments in
Scripture are predicated on His ontological commitment, and a development in His glory
is necessarily a development in His ontology.

His accidental ones, creatures who cling to Christ by faith as a result of His accidental glory (i.e., 'relational mutability') find themselves outside of God's necessary ethical constraint.

Another implication of rejecting this thesis is that the alternative is a Christ whose faith-eliciting glory runs the risk of being sub-divine. If the glory for which Christians worship Jesus is not immutable, it cannot be the glory of the divine nature. If Christians do not worship[65] Jesus for His divine nature, for what else are they left to worship Him except His human nature? The *communicatio idiomatum* assures us that our worship of this human Christ is safe from the charge of idolatry only insofar as we can affirm that we worship Him for a glory altogether non-human – indeed, divine. If His worship-eliciting glory begins and ends with His humanity, the incarnation ceases to be any kind of meaningful revelation of God; He has simply allured us to worship the very best of humanity.

Only two options remain if the status of Christ's revealed glory is not the immutable glory of the divine nature: it is either (a) the innovative glory of a new God-man mixture, or else it is (b) the glory of humanity. Both these options are idolatrous because neither can claim God as their true object of – or inspiration for – worship. Relevantly, Bavinck stresses the importance of worshipping Christ for His divinity rather than His humanity. We quote him at length here:

> Christ, accordingly, is most certainly to be worshiped as our mediator, just as God is also venerated and invoked as Creator and so on, but the ground for it lies solely in his deity. He is not God because he is the mediator, but he is the mediator because he is God, with the Father and the Spirit the one and only God, to be praised over all forever. The dignity and the works of the mediator can and may be motives for worship and adoration, just as all sorts of benefits prompt us to worship God. They may also be called 'grounds' for worship insofar as the divine being works and reveals himself in them. But the foundation is the [mediator's] being God alone.[66]

Third, our study implies that unbelief is caused in part by an inability to perceive Christ's glory as beautiful. 'So when the woman saw that the

---

65. Note the equation of 'worship' and the kind of 'saving faith' outlined in the first section of this paper. If saving faith is the glad-hearted apprehension of God for the glory He reveals in Christ, it is worship, that is, the appropriate response of creatures who recognize the worth (or worship-worthiness) of their Creator.

66. Bavinck, *Reformed Dogmatics Volume 3*, 259.

tree was good for food, and that it was a delight to the eyes, and that the tree was to be desired to make one wise, she took the fruit and ate, and she also gave some to her husband who was with her, and he ate' (Gen. 3:6). With this brief moment in the early days of God's creation, sin entered into the world – bringing with it a curse that reverberates to this day. This moment is the tragic catastrophe in the narrative of human history, and in light of the satisfaction Adam and Eve had access to in their unencumbered fellowship with the living God, it should never have happened. The effect of this covenantal act of disobedience is, as we saw in the previous chapter,[67] the enslaving arrival of sin and death (Rom. 5:12-21). The universal spread of sin and death as a direct result of Adam's disobedience implies both federal headship and, relatedly, the covenant of works.[68] Because Adam acted not only as an individual but also as a federal head, all of those under his covenantal headship (i.e., all of humanity) are subject to sin's slavery. Further, as Bavinck points out, the ubiquity of sin and its effects applies not only to the scope of the human race but also to the scope of the individual's capacity: 'As extensive as original sin is in humanity as a whole, so it is also in the individual person. It holds sway over all one's capacities and powers. A person's heart is evil from his or her youth and a source of all sorts of evils (Gen. 6:5; 8:21; Ps. 51:5; Jer. 17:9; Ezek. 36:26; Mark 7:21).'[69]

This does not mean that all of humanity is as evil as it possibly can be at all times, but it does mean that 'the deepest inclination, the innermost disposition, the fundamental directedness of human nature' is 'not turned toward God but away from him'.[70] Berkhof is helpful to caveat that original sin and the total depravity of fallen man that resulted does not imply that man loses 'any of the constitutional faculties necessary to constitute him a responsible moral agent', since 'he still has reason, conscience, and the freedom of choice.' Even so, there is a real inability for the sinner to fulfill his chief end and worship God: 'Man has by nature an irresistible bias for evil. He is not able to apprehend and love spiritual excellence, to seek and do spiritual things, the things

---

67. See discussion on Romans 5 under the heading, 'Redemption Accomplished.'

68. See Fesko, *Death in Adam, Life in Christ*; Fesko, *The Covenant of Works*.

69. Bavinck, *Reformed Dogmatics Volume 3*, 119.

70. Ibid., 120.

of God that pertain to salvation.'[71] This kind of inability to perceive spiritual excellence (or beauty) is of critical import for this project.

Given the state of Adam's sinless enjoyment of God and His creation before the fall, his disobedience invites the kind of incredulity that has driven much of this chapter (i.e., why disbelief?). Why was Eve deceived by the serpent? What about this fruit could have possibly been appealing enough for Eve to dabble with the then-novel act of disobedience? At least one tantalizing feature of the fruit was its aesthetic quality: 'it was a delight to the eyes.'[72] This means that the aesthetic dimension of unbelief for sinners today (the spiritual inability to apprehend divine beauty) corresponds with an aesthetic dimension of the very first sin. This makes sense not only from a historical point of view but also from an anthropological one. Human beings are aesthetically sensitive creatures; as image bearers of God, they are created to worship and reflect divine beauty.[73] That Eve was drawn to aesthetic pleasure in and of itself is neither surprising nor tragic. Rather, the tragedy lies in the fact that Eve was drawn away from aesthetic pleasure in God towards an object of lesser loveliness (i.e., herself).[74]

Therein lies the essence of idolatry: the act of worshiping that which is not God – or, in this instance, the reality of being drawn away from the beauty of God by the tantalizing beauty of not-God. Of course, the rationale behind idol worship is not entirely aesthetic – idols are worshiped for many reasons other than their perceived beauty – but an aesthetic element is nonetheless inescapable.[75] For example, Richard Lints writes,

---

71. Berkhof, *Systematic Theology*, 248.

72. Kenneth A. Mathews summarizes this verse in his commentary of Genesis 1–11: 'The temptation of the fruit is (1) is substance for food, (2) *its appearance*, and (3) its potential for making the woman "wise".' Kenneth A. Matthews, *Genesis 1–11:26*, New American Commentary 1A (Nashville, TN: Broadman & Holman, 1996), 238, emphasis added.

73. This point is argued at length by Richard Lints in his book *Identity and Idolatry: The Image of God and Its Inversion*. He summarizes: 'The image bearer finds purpose in worship, quite obviously not as an object of worship but as the one whose significance and security are defined by the reflection and representation of God.' Richard Lints, *Identity and Idolatry: The Image of God and Its Inversion* (Downers Grove, IL: InterVarsity Press, 2015), 42.

74. Beale explains how the fall is, in a sense, an act of self-worship, G. K. Beale, *We Become What We Worship: A Biblical Theology of Idolatry* (Downers Grove, IL: IVP Academic, 2008), 134. Cf., Lints, *Identity and Idolatry*, 39.

75. It may be asked how this could occur, given God's supreme, definitional beauty. The answer lies in the parasitic nature of idolatry; they appeal to the image bearer because they, in

'The Bible often speaks of this dynamic [of image versus idol] in terms of the connection between the sacred artist and the work of art created. Humans are made by the divine artist as his reflections. The idols were made by the human artists, and in an ironic twist the human artist became a reflection of the idol.'[76] There is good reason that Scripture repeatedly likens idolatry to adultery and sexual immorality.[77] The parallel is made not only because sexual immorality is a form of idolatry, and vice versa (though that is certainly true),[78] and not only because sexual immorality and idolatry resemble one another in their function and effect (though that is also certainly true), but also because both have an intrinsic aesthetic allure. We saw from the context of 2 Corinthians 3–4, for example, that the Corinthians were drawn away from the superior glory of Paul's ministry because they were transfixed on the inferior loveliness of superficial vainglory. There was an attractive quality to the 'super apostles' self-aggrandizement that dazzled them and kept them from appreciating the superior loveliness of Christ in Paul's self-abasement.

From a redemptive-historical point of view, this initial act of idolatry (Gen. 3:6) sets a trajectory for a vicious idolatrous feedback loop for the entire human race. The reason for this feedback loop is owing to a principle that G. K. Beale establishes in his appropriately titled work, *We Become What We Worship*. Beale writes: 'All humans have been created to be reflecting beings, and they will reflect whatever they are ultimately committed to, whether the true God or some other object in the created order. Thus… we resemble what we revere, either for ruin or restoration.'[79] The ruinous effect of this principle can be identified with a certain kind of language. Beale explains:

---

some (albeit, distorted) way, resemble the God they were created to worship. This point has been ably established by Daniel Strange in his work, *Their Rock Is Not Like Our Rock*, 207-08.

76. Lints, *Identity and Idolatry*, 81.

77. E.g., Num. 25:1-5; Hosea 2; 4; James 4:4-5; Rev. 2:12-17.

78. Numbers 25:1-5 illustrates one instance in which the act of idol worship was sexual immorality. That idolatry is a form of adultery is plainly evident when considering the covenantal reality of man with God – adultery is a covenantal transgression against one's spouse, and idolatry is a covenantal transgression against God (that all men, as idolaters in Adam, are *covenant breakers* is a necessary implication of the reality of a creation covenant, which has been winsomely argued by – among others – Gentry and Wellum, *God's Kingdom through God's Covenants*, 69-92).

79. Beale, *We Become What We Worship*, 22.

> Whenever the organs of spiritual perception were seen to be not functioning [in the OT], a certain kind of language was used. We might call this sensory-organ-malfunctioning language. When this language is used in the Old Testament, almost without exception, it refers not just to sinners in general but to only one particular kind of sin – the sin of idol worship![80]

In other words, there is a deadening effect that occurs in the spiritual senses of the idolater. Paul describes this tragic effect of idolatry in Romans 1:18-32.[81] When an idolater exchanges God as the object of worship for 'images resembling mortal man and birds and animals and creeping things',[82] the effects are disastrous: God reveals His wrath from heaven by crystallizing His image bearer's hard-wired nature to 'resemble that which they revere' as He gives the idolater over to his lusts. God lets him worship his own idol. As a result, he becomes futile in his thinking, his heart is darkened,[83] and he becomes a fool. In all this the idolater dishonors his body with his self-destructive devotion to idols (which in turn elicits even more wrath, which manifests itself in even more judgment, etc.).[84] Like a shipwrecked sailor adrift at sea who secures his sure demise by continuing to drink salt water to quench his thirst, the idolater, in doing what he wants (i.e., worshiping idols), is killing himself; he is losing a spiritual taste for that which is his teleological need (i.e., to worship the living God), and is developing a spiritual taste for a poison that can never quench his thirst.

---

80. Ibid., 41.

81. According to Robert Jewett, *Romans: A Commentary* (Minneapolis: Fortress, 2007), 150, 'it is appropriate to consider vv. 18-32 a closely linked argument on the theme of divine wrath, subdivided into two pericopes of roughly equal length with a thematic break at v. 24 with the first of three announcements of divine consignment.'

82. Of the universal application of this verse on all idolaters, Jewett, *Romans*, 162, writes: 'Since every culture displays evidence of suppressing the truth by the adoration of perishable images, demonstrating that the perverse will to "change the glory of the imperishable God" is a universal problem, the gospel elaborated in this letter has an inclusive bearing.'

83. See Jewett, ibid., 159.

84. R. Kent Hughes, *Romans: Righteousness from Heaven* (Wheaton, IL: Crossway, 1991), 57, describes this concept in his commentary as follows, 'The opening phrase of verse 21 tells how perversion to idolatry initially came about…. They [human beings] minimized the vast chasm between the creature and the Creator. This resulted in a progressively degenerating idolatry."

Note, there is never a question of whether or not a person has desire (or 'thirst', to use the above illustration) to worship – specifically, to worship that which is aesthetically pleasing. Such an impulse is inescapable.[85] The crucial question comes down to where that desire terminates. If one attempts to terminate these desires on 'not God', they begin to break down and malfunction. The desperation of the idolater's position can thus be summarized in the following syllogism:

Premise A – an image bearer is created to instinctively worship that which he considers (among other criteria) beautiful.

Premise B – an image bearer's chief end is to worship God,[86] who is alone supremely beautiful.

Premise C – God's judgment of idolatry is to give the offender over to idolatrous acts more and more, to the end that the idolater's perception of God's beauty is blinded.

Conclusion – an image bearer who engages in idolatry is doomed: he cannot cease his idolatry (Premises A and C) and therefore cannot live out his chief end (Premise B).

Because of sin, man's faculties to recognize Jesus' supreme beauty are broken, and their continued exercise to behold and adore objects of lesser loveliness (i.e., idols) only exacerbates and further corrupts those broken faculties. The more he beholds the lesser loveliness of idols, the more he is unable to behold the supreme loveliness of Jesus. It becomes apparent, then, that apart from divine intervention, the idolater's case remains hopeless.

Fourth, our study implies that the regeneration-faith relationship includes a Christological-aesthetic dimension, such that the newly regenerated saint experiences freedom from the satanic veil (regeneration) so as to perceive the irresistible beauty of Christ's glory with the eyes of faith. If the glory-beauty relationship explored above holds true, this statement on 'the glory of God in Christ' is, therefore, a Christological-aesthetic statement. The

---

85. For example, Lints, *Identity and Idolatry*, 80.

86. The truth of the first question and answer of the 1647 Westminster Shorter Catechism will not here be argued for but rather simply taken for granted. Westminster Assembly et al., *The Westminster Shorter Catechism in Modern English* (Phillipsburg, NJ: Presbyterian and Reformed, 1986).

glory that Christ reveals is a window into the *beatitude* of the Trinity. To be drawn by the glory of God in the face of Jesus Christ is to be drawn by the beauty of Jesus Christ.[87] Reflecting on this very dynamic, Augustine writes: 'But "the light shineth in darkness, and the darkness comprehended it not." Now the "darkness" is the foolish minds of men, made blind by vicious desires and unbelief.' This unbelief is the very thing God graciously overcomes with the light of the incarnation: 'And that the Word… might care for these and heal them, "The Word was made flesh, and dwelt among us." For our enlightening is the partaking of the Word, namely, of that life which is the light of men.' Thus the work of Christ is the means by which we come to participate in the Trinity's beatitude, or as Augustine here describes it, our 'contemplation of God': 'And further, the one cleansing of the unrighteous and of the proud is the blood of the Righteous One, and the humbling of God Himself; that we might be cleansed through Him, made as He was what we are by nature, and what we are not by sin, that we might contemplate God, which by nature we are not.'[88]

Here we see the interrelated nature of systematic categories, for even the mention of the word 'drawn' draws the doctrine of effectual calling to the fore. God calls those He predestines unto belief *effectually*. What makes effectual calling effectual on the existential level is, in part, the beauty of Christ. The beautiful Christ is the object of the faith to which God calls the elect.[89] God calls effectually, in other words, with an irresistibly beautiful Christ. 'The Spirit renews the image of God in the believer by revealing the glory of the Son who is the image of the invisible God.'[90] To be clear, this means that regeneration is logically distinct

---

87. Jonathan Hoglund gives significant attention to this activity of the Spirit in *Called by Triune Grace*, 79-122. Cf. Graham A. Cole, *He Who Gives Life: The Doctrine of the Holy Spirit*, Foundations of Evangelical Theology (Wheaton, IL: Crossway, 2007), 262. Cf. King, *The Beauty of the Lord*, 171.

88. Augustine, *On the Trinity*, Book III, 2.4.

89. Matthew Barrett, commenting on the Westminster Confession of faith, points out the Westminster divines' influence from 'the biblical metaphors by stating that the Spirit enlightens the mind to understand (Eph. 1:17-18), takes away the heart of stone and replaces it with a heart of flesh (Ezek. 36:26), renews the will, and effectually draws the sinner to Jesus Christ (John 6:44-45)' (Barrett, *Salvation by Grace*, 34).

90. J. Warren Smith, 'The Fourth-Century Fathers,' in Emery and Levering, *The Oxford Handbook of the Trinity*, 121.

from, and prior to, faith. Regeneration is a work of God,[91] whereas faith is exercised by man. Of course, the two are interrelated, but one is identified as the cause and the other the effect. As Vos puts it, 'The Holy Spirit regenerates the heart; and as the intellect, will, and emotion flow from the heart; this root of life, so they have in principle received at regeneration the capacity to be active believingly, each in its own way.'[92]

I hasten now to recall all the previous caveats made in chapters 1 and 4 about what this does not mean. I am not here reducing the Protestant Reformed conception of the *ordo salutis* merely to aesthetic categories. Nor do I have any desire to *redefine* 'effectual calling'. What I appeal to here is the *fiducia* aspect of genuine saving faith. In true saving faith, brought out by the effectual calling of the Father, the will is fully and joyfully engaged. Saving faith is 'not only a sure knowledge', it is also a 'hearty trust'.[93] 'In the awakened sinner is an impulse,' says Vos, 'a desire, a striving, a hungering and thirsting after God's righteousness. The soul extends itself toward this, moves itself in this direction, so that the whole life is drawn thither.'[94] What the regenerate apprehend with the eyes of faith is a beautiful Christ, who is considered beautiful because of the divine glory He reveals in His justifying person and work. Those who behold Christ with the 'hearty' eyes of faith are most certainly motivated by their need for justification, but they are satiated by the fact that their need for justification is met *by this beautiful* God-man. Thus, the Canons of Dort can describe the experience of effectual calling as a 'most pleasing' and 'marvelous' experience:

> But this certainly does not happen only by outward teaching, by moral persuasion, or by such a way of working that, after God has done his work, it remains in man's power whether or not to be reborn or converted. Rather, it is entirely supernatural work, one that is at the same time most powerful and most pleasing, a marvelous, hidden, and inexpressible work, which is not lesser than or inferior in power to that of creation or of raising the dead, as Scripture ... teaches.[95]

---

91. See Vos, *Reformed Dogmatics*, 641-42.

92. Ibid., 703.

93. Heidelberg Catechism, Q. 21.

94. Vos, *Reformed Dogmatics*, 715.

95. 'The Canons of Dort,' Article 12, as quoted in Barrett, *Salvation by Grace*, 28.

Further, there is a logical connection between this discussion of 'drawing' or 'effectual calling' and regeneration. The reason the effectual call of God is 'most pleasing' and 'marvelous' is that regeneration has rendered the called a new person. What would have been a torturous enslavement for the unregenerate has become sweet satisfaction for the regenerate. This is made clear by the many metaphors the Scriptures use to depict the monergistic work of regeneration. These include the circumcision of the heart (Deut. 30:6; Jer. 31:33; Ezek. 11:19-21; 36:26-27), the new birth (John 3:1-8; 1 John 2:29; 3:9; 4:7; 5:1; 5:18; 1 Pet. 1:3-5), spiritual resurrection (Eph. 2:8-10, Col. 2:11-14), washing or cleansing (Titus 3:4-7), unveiled vision (2 Cor. 3:17-18), and enlightened vision (2 Cor. 4:6; Eph. 1:18).[96] In regeneration, the Spirit fits the regenerate for enjoyment of the conversion experience. Thus faith, for the regenerate, is not a chore but a delight.

Regeneration, as the convert's first subjectively experienced step in the *ordo salutis*, is the Holy Spirit's sovereign activation of the spiritual sight which enables the convert's apprehension of Christ's beauty. Regeneration, then, has a *causal* relationship with faith. Notwithstanding our earlier criticisms of Jonathan Edwards' articulation of justification by faith alone, he explains well the unique aesthetic appreciation for God and His holiness that is acquired in regeneration: 'There is not only a rational belief that God is holy, and that holiness is a good thing; but there is a sense of the loveliness of God's holiness. There is not only a speculative judging that God is gracious, but a sense how amiable God is upon that account; or a sense of the beauty of this divine attribute.'[97]

Jonathan Hoglund has profitably pressed the conversation of effectual calling and regeneration forward in his work *Called by Triune Grace*. According to Hoglund, Reformed theology has helpfully 'sought to avoid the conclusion that God introduces a new substance to the constitution of humanity', and to avoid 'ascribing regeneration to one particular human faculty, as if either a "resurrected" understanding faculty or willing

---

96. For a thorough exposition of these metaphors, see Barrett, *Salvation by Grace*. Barrett also gives a more succinct survey of these metaphors in 'The Scriptural Affirmation of Monergism' in Barrett and Nettles, *Whomever He Wills*.

97. Jonathan Edwards, *Works of Jonathan Edwards Online*, 17:414. Our purposes here are not to elaborate fully on the aesthetic relationship between regeneration, effectual calling, and saving faith but rather to highlight that there is one.

faculty could be abstracted from the whole person.'[98] There is no part of the human that remains unfallen, every part is in need of regeneration (and eventually, glorification). Additionally, Hoglund points out how redemptive-historical accounts of regeneration, advocated by men such as Richard Gaffin[99] and G. K. Beale,[100] have helpfully made use of the New Testament's language of 'spiritual resurrection' to emphasize the inaugurated eschatological aspect of regeneration. And yet, Hoglund maintains that both accounts could benefit from further accentuation. 'We need still an ontology of converting change,' he insists, 'that is, of spiritual resurrection and of the new birth,' an ontology that would give an account of the transition from 'dead' to 'made alive' in Christ that includes 'the cultivation of inclinations in line with Christ'.[101] Hoglund argues that Edwards fits the bill with a contribution of regeneration as a 'communicative' event. Hoglund (following Edwards) thus places the Spirit center stage in regeneration as the completer of divine discourse. The Spirit indwells the regenerate and sweeps him up into divine rhetoric. 'The Spirit testifies to Christ, but the decisive work of the Spirit occurs on the level of disposition. Regeneration is a "communication" of the Spirit's holiness or a participation in the Spirit's nature.'[102] Thus, he can conclude in stark fashion: 'The Spirit does not set off a chain reaction that leads to gracious affections. Rather, when the Spirit is present, gracious affections result. *The Spirit's activity in converting change just is his presence.*'[103] With His presence, the Spirit 'gives new life by an overwhelming impression of the truth, goodness and beauty of God's action in Christ.'[104]

Such a conclusion is, in fact, ancient. Reflecting on the necessity of the Spirit's illuminating ministry, Hilary writes: 'We receive Him [the Spirit], then, that we may know.' The soul's telos, insists Hilary, is the apprehension of God. But the soul cannot exercise its apprehending

---

98. Hoglund, *Called by Triune Grace*, 124.

99. Richard B. Gaffin, *Resurrection and Redemption: A Study in Paul's Soteriology*, 2nd ed. (Phillipsburg, NJ: Presbyterian and Reformed, 1987).

100. Beale, *A New Testament Biblical Theology*.

101. Hoglund, *Called by Triune Grace*, 146-47.

102. Ibid., 166.

103. Ibid., emphasis added.

104. Ibid.

faculties without the enlightening ministry of the Spirit. Just like how 'faculties of the human body, if denied their exercise, will be dormant' (e.g., the eye cannot see without light, the ear cannot hear without sound, the nose cannot smell if there is no scent to smell), 'So, too, the soul of man, unless through faith it have appropriated the gift of the Spirit, will have the innate faculty of apprehending God, but be destitute of the light of knowledge.' Such is the tragic plight of unbelief. But for those who *have* received this gift of the Spirit, 'this gift is with us unto the end of the world, the solace of our waiting, the assurance, by the favours which He bestows, of the hope that shall be ours, the light of our minds, the sum of our souls.'[105]

A powerful attestation to this relationship between effectual calling and regeneration is found in 2 Peter 1:3-4:

> His divine power has granted to us all things that pertain to life and godliness, through the knowledge of him who called us to his own glory and excellence, by which he has granted to us his precious and very great promises, so that through them you may become partakers of the divine nature, having escaped from the corruption that is in the world because of sinful desires.

While the dative structure of verse 3 may be rendered as 'who called us *to* his own glory and excellence',[106] it is more grammatically appropriate to translate it as 'who called us *by* his own glory and grace'.[107] Theologically, it is certainly correct to insist that God calls believers to praise the glory and excellence of Christ, but in this verse Peter is probably citing the 'glory and excellence' of Christ as the instrument for God's calling. Peter assures his readers that they have been made 'partakers of the divine nature' by virtue of being called 'by' God's 'glory and excellence'. Or both (which I find likely). 'Those whom God saves are called by Christ,' says Schreiner, 'and this calling is accomplished through the knowledge

---

105. Hilary, *De Trinitate* 2.35.

106. This is maintained by Gene L. Green, *Jude and 2 Peter* (Grand Rapids, MI: Baker Academic, 2008), 183-84.

107. See Thomas R Schreiner, *1 & 2 Peter and Jude*, Christian Standard Commentary (Nashville, TN: Holman, 2020), 345-46; Robert W. Harvey and Philip H. Towner, *2 Peter & Jude* (Downers Grove, IL: InterVarsity Press, 2009), 35; Peter H. Davids, *The Letters of 2 Peter and Jude* (Grand Rapids, MI: Eerdmans, 2006), 170-71; Richard Bauckham, *Jude, 2 Peter*, Word Biblical Commentary (Waco, TX: Word, 2005), 178-79.

of Christ's divine moral excellence. In other words, when Christ calls people to himself, *they perceive the beauty and loveliness of who he is.*'[108] The interconnectedness between God's divine 'calling,' His 'glory and excellence', and the telos of the called becoming 'partakers of the divine nature' remains a compelling testimony to our central thesis. It seems best to conclude that 'the Spirit's ministry here [in the work of effectual calling and regeneration] is to impress the proper loves or delights that correspond to the excellencies of Christ in the gospel'.[109]

To be clear, this 'impression of the truth, goodness and beauty of God's action in Christ' should not be understood as a synergistic work wherein He offers knowledge and we receive it.[110] The word 'overwhelming' in this quotation is crucial, and it points to the reality that regeneration is a monergistic work of God, accomplished effectually, irrespective of the human beneficiary's involvement. Further, we should note that the Spirit's regenerating work causes far more than mere intellectual recognition of 'the truth, goodness and beauty of God's action in Christ.' The Spirit does not simply come to fulfill the Triune God's speech act with those He indwells, as if His regenerating work can be reduced to the role of a mere educator. He is no less than an educator, but He is most assuredly more.

Man's inability to behold the beauty of the Triune God in the face of Jesus Christ is not overcome by regenerative illumination alone (i.e., illumination *in conversion*, as distinguished from illumination *in sanctification*, which we will explore below) because such an inability is more than mere ignorance or darkness. Rather, such an inability is ultimately attributable to his spiritual death. The sinner does not simply lack knowledge, he is dead. Therefore, the aspects of regeneration whereby the regenerate is illumined by the presence of the Spirit to perceive Christ's beauty rightly is a subset of a far larger miraculous work of spiritual resurrection.

Fifth, our study implies that soteriology and hermeneutics are inextricably connected and that the act of reading Scripture rightly is the act of reading with an aesthetic apprehension of Christ's glory therein. The

---

108. Schreiner, *1 & 2 Peter and Jude*, 346, emphasis added.

109. Ibid., 202.

110. I do not presume to speak for Hoglund on this point, but this is certainly not what *I* mean.

preceding discussions, in addition to having profound implications for Christological aesthetics in soteriology, have profound implications for the relationship between bibliology, soteriology, and hermeneutics. This obviously harkens our attention back to our excurses on hermeneutics in chapter 2. Though the primary emphasis of 2 Corinthians 3:12–4:6 is soteriological, the context concerns pressing hermeneutical issues.[111] In contrasting his own new covenant ministry of life (3:6) with his opponents' old covenant ministry of death (3:7), Paul summarizes their impasse as the difference between spiritual blindness and spiritual sight (3:14-15).[112] There are those who read Moses with a satanic veil over their eyes (4:3-4), obscuring their vision from the glory of the Lord, and those who turn to the Lord (3:16) and therein experience the freedom of the veil from the Holy Spirit (3:17), who brings them into the glorious presence of God by exposing them to the glory of Jesus Christ (3:18; 4:6). The latter see the glory of Jesus' face *when they read Moses*; the former do not.[113]

This means Paul's opponents, who presumably knew the letter of the law front and back (or at the very least revered its accounts of Moses), did not understand its true content. This is because they had not experienced the renewal of regeneration. They could not see the glory of Christ's face, which was truly there in the Scriptures.

Their problem was both *hermeneutical* and *soteriological*. It was hermeneutical in the sense that they could not understand aspects of the Mosaic law that were truly there (i.e., the glory of the face of Jesus Christ that was veiled not by the text itself but by 'the god of this world'). It was soteriological in the sense that the solution to their blindness – the removal of the veil that blinded – was spiritual re-creation. For Paul, there is an absolute antithesis: either readers of Moses read in light of the glory of Christ, and thus read truly and with 'unveiled face', or they read with their minds and hearts draped with a veil that obscures the glory of Christ, and thus read wrongly.

In a real sense, regeneration can be understood as including the initial act of divine illumination (i.e., illumination in *conversion*), which

---

111. See Guthrie, *2 Corinthians*, 224.

112. Seifrid, *The Second Letter to the Corinthians*, 176-178.

113. Ibid., 246.

serves as the prerequisite for all future illumination (i.e., illumination in *sanctification*).[114] Illuminated reading of Scripture is that in which *regenerated* readers, and only regenerated readers, engage.[115] They read in light of the glory of Jesus Christ, which has shone in their hearts soteriologically and now emanates from Scripture as they read.[116] 'The Spirit shines the light of Christ into our hearts and minds,' writes Vanhoozer,

> removing the veil of ignorance (2 Cor 3:12-18) and making us 'children of light' (Eph. 5:8; 1 Thess. 5:5). The whole economy of grace is thus an economy of light inasmuch as it concerns the shining of God's face, in Christ, through the Scriptures and the Spirit, who illumines them, into the hearts of those who themselves become a kingdom of light (cf. Col. 1:13). The economy of light is therefore the gracious way God administers knowledge and understanding from light to light through light.[117]

In his recent work on illumination, *Seeing by the Light: Illumination in Augustine's and Barth's Readings of John*, Ike Miller concludes his volume with a constructive account of illumination.[118] Moving beyond the typical discussions surrounding the 'what' of illumination (i.e., its 'benefits'), Miller describes the 'how' of illumination. Similar to how Hoglund describes the 'how' of effectual calling and regeneration in the above discussion, Miller proposes that the 'means of illumination … is *participation*'.[119] In saying this, he points to the fact that 'illumination'

---

114. Calvin gets at this idea well: '[God] shines forth upon us in the person of his Son by his Gospel, but that would be in vain, since we are blind, unless he were also to illuminate our minds by his Spirit.' John Calvin, *The Second Epistle of Paul to the Apostle to the Corinthians and the Epistles to Timothy, Titus, and Philemon*, trans. T. A. Small (Grand Rapids, MI: Eerdmans, 1997), 57, quoted in Kevin J. Vanhoozer, *Biblical Authority after Babel: Retrieving the Solas in the Spirit of Mere Protestant Christianity* (Grand Rapids, MI: Brazos Press, a division of Baker Publishing Group, 2016), 67.

115. See Scott R. Swain, *Trinity, Revelation, and Reading: A Theological Introduction to the Bible and Its Interpretation* (London: T&T Clark, 2011), 96. Cf., Webster, *The Domain of the Word*, 46.

116. As Hoglund, *Called by Triune Grace*, 90, puts it, 'the revelation of God's glory in the proclaimed gospel is both the content of enlightenment and the instrument by which it is produced.'

117. Vanhoozer, *Biblical Authority after Babel*, 67.

118. Ike Miller, *Seeing by the Light: Illumination in Augustine's and Barth's Readings of John* (Downers Grove, IL: IVP Academic, 2020).

119. Ibid, 187 (emphasis added).

is a broad term. The typical way we use it to describe the Spirit-enabled reading experience is appropriate, but it does not exhaust the term of its significance, which is broad enough to include regeneration itself.

Bringing Hoglund and Miller together then, along with the claims we have made thus far, we might say that in regeneration the Spirit communicates – or sovereignly brings the regenerate into participation with – the glorious *a se* beatitude of the Trinity, mediated through Christ. This He does by presenting Christ to the eyes of the regenerate's heart, and by enabling such hearty vision – which is far more than a mere intellectual act, but also includes the affections – with His renovative presence. This illuminating presence of the Spirit continues to showcase the glory of the Trinity in the face of Jesus Christ with particular application in the reading of Scripture (what we typically mean when we say 'illumination').

In conceptualizing the Spirit's role in facilitating participation with the Trinity's beatitude in this way, we are in good company. In addition to the company we enjoy with Hoglund and Miller, we also enjoy the company of the church fathers. J. Warren Smith notes how Athanasius, 'following the principle that God cannot be known or confessed by sinful humanity unless he reveals himself,' maintains that through the divine Spirit 'the Christian participates in the life of the Triune God and so derives eternal life from God. This participation in the life of God is possible because the Spirit confers the gift of faith by which we may confess Christ in baptism.'[120] Thus, the Spirit is the gift of the Father 'because the Spirit is sent to infuse us with the divine light illuminating the soul and bringing knowledge of God'.[121]

Illuminated reading, in the narrower sense, is the creaturely corollary to divine revelation.[122] There is a delicate symmetry between God speaking and His creatures listening.[123] Illumination enables the

---

120. Smith, 'The Trinity in the Fourth-Century Fathers,' 121.

121. Ibid.

122. See Bavinck, *Reformed Dogmatics Volume* 1.350.

123. E.g., Carter, *Interpreting Scripture with the Great Tradition*, 44-45, writes, 'The miracle of revelation through the writers of Scripture is balanced and complemented by the parallel miracle of the illumination of the readers of the Scripture. Both are works of the Holy Spirit, and neither could occur in a world in which philosophical naturalism was the truth about reality. Neither could be described adequately on the basis of methodological naturalism.'

subjective reception of the objective presentation of divine discourse, and in this way it is the completion of the Triune God's speech-act. In it, the Holy Spirit enlightens the minds of His creatures to see His truth about Christ in Scripture aright.

Importantly, this means illumination is not the circumvention of creaturely activity in reading – as if the reader is entirely passive while spiritual truth is downloaded into him, relieving him of any of his reading responsibilities. Rather, divine illumination activates and sanctifies the reading act, making use of all the reader's efforts. Divine illumination, if rightly understood, incentivizes rigor, not sloth. It would be easy to write illumination off as an irrelevant doctrine in hermeneutics (as some have done) if it carried with it the idea of passivity. By necessity, it would be a conversational non-starter. However, it is 'misguided to appeal to the Holy Spirit as an interpretive shortcut, like some get-out-of-hermeneutical-jail-free card.'[124] 'A theology of illumination,' Webster clarifies, 'avoids both hermeneutical naturalism in which the actings of the mind, unmoved from outside, claim sufficiency for themselves, and hermeneutical immediacy in which seizure by the Spirit breaks off the exercise of intelligence and interpretation becomes rapture.'[125] This is because, as Lydia Schumacher observes (commenting on Augustine's conception of the doctrine), 'illumination bears on the content of thought, not because God imposes thoughts on the human mind but because the intellect, to the extent it has recovered its capacity, comes to know what God already knows in full.'[126] That is to say, in illumination the Holy Spirit does not render powerless His creature's intellectual efforts. He rather activates and sanctifies those efforts. 'Contemplation of the divine Word does not involve the transcendence of the natural acts,' Webster clarifies, 'but their *regeneration and redirection to their proper end* .... The Spirit produces *readers*.'[127] These Spirit-produced readers are not charged to forgo their responsibilities as readers; they are rather equipped to live up to them in a more rounded way than they

---

124. Vanhoozer, *Biblical Authority after Babel*, 105.

125. Webster, *The Domain of the Word*, 61 (emphasis added).

126. Lydia Schumacher, *Divine Illumination: The History and Future of Augustine's Theory of Knowledge*, Challenges in Contemporary Theology (Malden: Wiley-Blackwell, 2011), 63.

127. Webster, *The Domain of the Word*, 27.

would be otherwise.[128] There is no competition between the spiritual illumination and rigorous study. In reality, the truth of illumination should motivate hard interpretive work rather than passivity. It is the assurance that when one puts hermeneutical hand to plow, one labors with Spirit-enlivened power, which guarantees fruit that is far more substantial than mere intellectual assent.[129]

This all has further implications for the Scripture's intended audience. For whom and to whom was the Bible written? What is the Scripture's ideal interpretative community? If what we have said up until this point is true, we must conclude that the answer is the church. We may summarize the argument in the following syllogism:

> *Premise A* – If meaning is contingent upon authorial intent, and
>
> *Premise B* – if the primary author of Scripture is divine, and
>
> *Premise C* – if this divine author's speech-act is veiled to everyone who is not regenerated and illuminated by the Holy Spirit, and
>
> *Premise D* – if *only* those whom the Holy Spirit regenerates and illuminates are able to receive the divine author's speech-act, then
>
> *Conclusion E* – the community of those regenerated and illuminated by the Spirit (i.e., the church) is, alone, an ontologically suitable community for proper interpretation (i.e., interpretation that does justice to the divine as well as human author's intent).

'If we are to engage fittingly in the act of interpretation of Scripture,' writes Webster, 'and to enjoy the fruit by which the labor is rewarded, we must become certain kinds of persons.'[130] This is why Michael Allen and Scott Swain have named the church *the school of Christ*.[131] The Holy Spirit is this school's teacher, and its students are those whom He regenerates and illuminates. Allen and Swain summarize:

> For Christians, reading is an inherently communal enterprise. And reading is a communal enterprise for the same reasons that Christianity

---

128. See Swain, *Trinity, Revelation, and Reading*, 99-100.

129. See Schumacher, *Divine Illumination*, 65.

130. Webster, *The Domain of the Word*, 26.

131. See R. Michael Allen and Scott R. Swain, *Reformed Catholicity: The Promise of Retrieval for Theology and Biblical Interpretation* (Grand Rapids: Baker Academic, 2015), 18 (emphasis original).

is a communal enterprise. God's purpose in the covenant of grace is not simply to reconcile individual persons to himself. When God reconciles individual persons to himself in the covenant of grace, he also binds those persons to other persons, creating a new humanity and an interdependent body (Eph. 2:11-20; 1 Cor. 12:12).[132]

Since right reading (i.e., illuminated reading) is conditioned by soteriology (i.e., regeneration), and since soteriology has an intrinsic corporate shape (i.e., those regenerated are brought into the new covenant community), right reading is a spiritual discipline that cannot be divorced from ecclesial faithfulness.[133] Through the Scriptures God speaks to His Church, and to His Church alone.

On this note, the *corporate* dimension of beholding the glory of God in the face of Jesus Christ cannot be emphasized enough. Indeed, while this discussion may have many implications for the individual's right reading of the text, the primary context of 2 Corinthians 3:12–4:6 is the gathered assembly (e.g., '... whenever Moses is read'). It is not *merely* the individual who sees the glory of God in the face of Jesus Christ when he privately reads, it is also (and, contextually speaking, we might even say *first and foremost*) the case that the *gathered assembly* beholds the glory of God in the face of Jesus Christ together as the Scriptures are read and proclaimed.[134] This has tremendous implications for the importance the corporate dimension of reading. A reader who never reads with the gathered assembly is not receiving the Word as it is intended. The Word of God is for the Church, and should be received and read *with* the Church.

The immediate application for the *individual* in light of the above discussion has everything to do with the reader's posture toward the text in biblical hermeneutics. No regenerated reader approaches the text of Scripture as a neutral observer. This is impossible for the same reason that a square cannot have three sides; the regenerated reader and the text of

---

132. Ibid., 99.

133. The implications this has on the accountability Christian scholarship has to the local church is monumental. While this discussion has largely concerned the universal church, it is clear that the universal church cannot but be manifested through local churches, which renders the Christian scholar's accountability tied intimately to the local church. If this is true, it would by necessity put the work of 'untethered scholars' – who submit to no pastoral oversight and are not faithfully covenanted to a local congregation – into serious jeopardy.

134. I am indebted to Aubrey Sequeira for pointing this out to me in a conversation.

Scripture are not, ontologically, the kinds of subjects that can *neutrally* face one another. When a regenerated reader approaches the Bible, he approaches the inscripturated word of God, through which the Holy Spirit has revealed to him the glory of Jesus Christ so as to transform him into a new creation. Such a reader could only achieve neutral observation through some kind of voluntary amnesia whereby he forgets both his own 'new creation' state and the Scripture's role in transforming him thereunto. Not only is this impossible, it is not even ideal. As Swain puts it,

> the counsel to read the Bible like any other book is ultimately inadequate because it fails to take into account the extraordinary nature of this book. If rationality consists in treating objects in accordance with their natures, then this must go for a rational treatment of the Bible as well. What it *is* must determine how we *approach* it and how we *use* it ... because the Bible is one of the primary means of God's covenantal self-communication in Christ, we must engage the Bible as creatures redeemed and covenanted to God in Christ if we are to engage the Bible truly and profitably.[135]

Conclusion

In this chapter, we have set out to answer the question of unbelief from the existential vantage point of the individual's perception of glory. Taking our cues from Paul's second letter to the Corinthians (3:12–4:6), we first considered chapters 3–4's placement within the letter as a whole. Second Corinthians, we discovered, is written to a people preoccupied with boasting and fleshly standards for glory. The Corinthians were a self-made people who prized boasting and showmanship. Everything about Paul's ministry – from the central message of a crucified Savior to his own weak demeanor – cut against the grain of Corinthian culture. Rather than dialing back and communicating in a way more palatable, Paul cuts even deeper and offends even more. He does this by not only refusing to boast in his strength but indeed boasting in his weakness. They wanted human glory; he gave them human neediness. Paul's overall argument is framed in such a way as to call attention to the antithesis between Corinthian axiology and Christian axiology – the way of upward mobility against the path of descent.[136]

---

135. Swain, *Trinity, Revelation, and Reading*, 4.

136. Special thanks to Ronni Kurtz for a sermon he preached at Emmaus Church in Kansas City, wherein he used this language of Jesus' way as 'the path of descent'.

We then showed that Paul, far from being a despiser of glory, represents a ministry whose glory infinitely surpasses his opponents'. 'The glory of God in the face of Jesus Christ' (2 Cor. 4:6) is not merely comparable to the glory of God in the face of Moses; it is superlative in every conceivable way. This is because the glory in Jesus' face is the glory of the Triune God put on full display – a glory not seen since the creation of the cosmos and a glory capable of (and, indeed, *in the process of*) re-creating the cosmos in the eschaton.

Unbelief results, in part, from a spiritual eyesight problem. Despite the fact that the unbeliever has access to the very same objective information, wherein the glory of Christ emanates, he cannot see it truly. Seeing, he cannot see (Isa. 6:9). This is because his sense perception of true beauty has been broken by sin (or veiled by Satan, or bent inward to terminate on the self). Unable to appreciate the superior glory of Christ, the unbeliever remains infatuated with a glory altogether inferior – the vainglory of self-advancement. Thus, the beauty-loving worshiper has become a grotesque-loving idolater. True glory he regards with disdain; vainglory he regards as honorable.

We then saw the very same principle worked out within a different canonical context. Like 2 Corinthians 3:12–4:6, John 12:36-43 tells the same tragic tale of two opposite reactions to the same display of glory. The divine glory of Jesus (which Isaiah saw in Isaiah 6 and 53) both repulsed some (i.e., the Jews who killed Him) and attracted others (i.e., it was in the display of this cruciform glory that Jesus 'drew all men to himself'). As in the case of 2 Corinthians, the difference-making factor in John is a love for human glory as opposed to divine glory (cf. John 5:44).

'But when one turns to the Lord' and the Spirit of the Lord grants 'freedom', the 'veil is removed' (3:16-17). Through the Spirit's ministry, the blinded unbeliever is able to behold Christ's cruciform glory rightly. The sight of such glory irresistibly draws the unbeliever into adoration and praise. Saving faith therefore becomes the glad-hearted acquiescence to the irresistible beauty of Christ. The aesthetic desires that once terminated on idols now terminate on that for which they were created: the glory of Jesus Christ.

In the apprehension of this kind of Christological glory, we begin to experience the eschaton breaking into the present age through individual conversions. Already then, on the personal and existential level, Isaiah's eschatological prophecy is coming into fruition whenever one turns to the Lord: 'And he shall swallow up on this mountain the covering that is cast over all the peoples, the veil that is spread over all nations. He will swallow up death forever' (Isa. 25:7-8a). But on an even more fundamental level, what the regenerate experiences is an asymmetrical, creaturely *participation* in the Triune God's *a se* beatitude.

CHAPTER SIX

From One Degree of Beauty to Another

[The soul] places herself like a mirror beneath the purity of God, and molds her own beauty at the touch and the sight of the Archetype of all beauty ... such a character will feel as a passionate lover only towards that Beauty which has no source but Itself, which is not such at one particular time or relatively only, which is Beautiful from, and through, and in itself, not such at one moment and in the next ceasing to be such, above all increase and addition, incapable of change and alteration.

GREGORY OF NYSSA[1]

Introduction

We have now arrived at this work's capstone chapter. The goal of this chapter is twofold. First, I intend to summarize the argument developed from chapters 1 through 5. In this summary I place into clear vision the thesis I have developed over the course of five chapters in concise and cogent fashion.

Second, I will begin to scratch the surface of further implications on sanctification and glorification in light of the findings in this thesis. In many ways this work has been a meditation on the role of Christ's beauty in the beginning of the believer's life in Christ. Christological beauty does not begin and end its relevance in regeneration and faith, however. Since our topic concerns the transcendental attribute of the

---

1. Gregory of Nyssa, *On Virginity* xi.356

eternal God, and since theology is theological, its relevance on the whole Christian experience is as ubiquitous as God's relevance.

Summary of Project

In chapter 1, I first raised the broad concern about Protestant systematic-theological neglect on the topic of divine beauty. Granting a couple of notable conceptions, particularly Jonathan King's recent work *The Beauty of the Lord: Theology as Aesthetics*, I proposed this project as a partial remedy to the unfortunate vacuum. Self-consciously building off of King's work – which argues for the importance of treating divine beauty as a locus in systematic theology, rich with pedagogical import – my thesis focuses in on divine beauty's soteriological dimension. This thesis is particularly interested in the role of Christ's beauty in the relationship between regeneration and faith. Again, the thesis I propose is as follows:

> *Beauty is ultimately an attribute of God the Trinity, revealed wherever Triune glory is made manifest, which is preeminently so in the person and work of Christ. When the Holy Spirit regenerates a sinner, He imparts the faculties necessary for such a person to behold the beauty of the Trinity, mediated in Christ. The Spirit imparts these faculties by virtue of His own indwelling presence. In regeneration, the Spirit communicates – or, sovereignly brings the regenerate into participation with – the glorious a se beatitude of the Trinity, mediated through Christ. This He does by presenting Christ to the eyes of the regenerate's heart and by enabling such hearty vision – which is far more than a mere intellectual act, but also includes the affections – with His renovative presence. The* fiducia *component of saving faith therefore has an accompanying aesthetic aspect; it involves the existential recognition of Christ's infinite beauty.*

I then signaled my methodological approach – namely, a full-orbed systematic approach that insists on keeping theology theological. We then saw the historical precedence for sustained meditation on divine beauty by briefly surveying the works of Gregory of Nyssa, Augustine, Anselm of Canterbury, Thomas Aquinas, Martin Luther, John Owen, Jonathan Edwards, Herman Bavinck, Karl Barth, and Hans Urs von Balthasar. Though admittedly selective, such a cross-traditional witness sufficiently legitimates this work's concern. Judged from a variety of traditional perspectives, this project is in good company.

Chapter 1 concluded with the ever-difficult attempt to define beauty. Its difficulty is, of course, owing to the fact that it is an attempt to express the ineffable. This does not render our thesis a non-starter, however, since such is the case for *all our God-talk*. God's infinite incomprehensibility renders all univocal theological language disqualified, even while His accommodated revelation renders theological language real and thus *analogical*. As an attribute of God, beauty is inseparable from other divine attributes and is rightly recognized as the brilliance, the majesty, the splendor of divine truth and goodness. God's Triune beauty *ad extra* is a manifestation of God's Triune beatitude *ad intra*.

Chapter 2 began by upholding the promise made in chapter 1 to keep theology theological. After providing an apologetic for theological metaphysics, I traced the development of classical Trinitarian theism, defending the harmony between Trinitarian theology and the doctrine of divine simplicity with the help of Athanasius, Hilary of Poitiers, and the Cappadocians (Gregory of Nyssa, Gregory of Nazianzus, and Basil of Caesarea).

I connected the dots between the doctrines of divine simplicity, aseity, and creation with chapter 1's discussion of beauty thusly: By virtue of His simplicity, the eternal Triune God is perfectly, immutably, and gratuitously 'of Himself.' As the eternal Father, Son, and Spirit, the Trinity is eternally the plenitude of perfection. He is the *a se* one, and as such He is the eternal and gratuitous source of life and love, and from this overflowing *ad intra* beatitude, He creates. All created life – including all the creaturely dimensions of goodness and truth and beauty – are derivatively participatory in this single Source. What we know to be beautiful, as finite creatures, is beautiful by divine derivation. Indeed, it *is* at all by divine derivation. The source of what the creature recognizes as beautiful is the simple Trinity's eternal beatitude. We might say, in other words, that divine beatitude and divine beauty describe the same reality of the divine nature from different vantage points. Divine beatitude is the divine attribute whereby God delights in Himself, and divine beauty is the divine attribute whereby creatures delight in God's self.

This chapter concluded with a reflection on the biblical, theological, and conceptual cognates of holiness, goodness, glory, and divine beauty. Holiness, as God's Godness, is displayed as glory, which is received either as a dreadful terror or a delightful enjoyment of divine beauty and goodness. What makes the difference for the creature is the presence or absence of God's gracious mediation. To receive God's glory as 'goodness' and 'beauty' is to be graced by God and welcomed into His own ineffable enjoyment.

Chapter 3 presented Christ as the image of the invisible-beautiful God. The Triune beauty discussed broadly in chapters 1 and 2 is brought into focus in the incarnation. Since we have labored to place divine beauty within the context of Triune simplicity, we come into strong agreement with King that 'the display of God's glory is ... always beautiful, always fitting, always entails an aesthetic dimension to it.'[2] Every revelation of God is a revelation of His beauty. If this is true in general, it is necessarily true in the particular revelation of the incarnation – the absolute apex of divine revelation. Here I demonstrated that Christ's revelation of the Triune God is an accommodated, mediated revelation of the Trinity's beauty. I began by considering the incarnation through the lens of divine revelation and then moved into a discussion on the relationship between the incarnation and the Son's immutability.

Here, Chalcedonian Christology came into view, and the related concepts of the *communicatio idiomatum* and the *extra calvinisticum* helped to let the divine mystery of the incarnation speak for itself: *the Son of God, without ceasing to be God, became man, in order to bring God to man, and thereby bring man to God.* In keeping with the theme of resolving tensions, chapter 3 concluded with the apparent contradiction of divine beauty manifested in the horrors of crucifixion. In considering John 12, Isaiah 6, and Isaiah 53 together, I presented the apparent contradiction as the heart of God's divine irony to demonstrate His wisdom by making foolish the wisdom of the wise (1 Cor. 1:18-25). God shows His beauty precisely in the way that offends prideful sensibilities. The cross is a beauty that can only be seen from below. The eyes of faith that reconcile the seeming contradiction of Christ's beauty and His grotesque death on the cross are the eyes of the humbled.

Chapter 4 was something of a sustained caveated excursus. Here I announced my theological allegiance with the Reformed tradition concerning the doctrine of justification by faith alone. This was necessary, since my central thesis may appear to share much resemblance

---

2. King, *The Beauty of the Lord*, 51

with Roman Catholic terminology on the one hand and Edwardsian terminology on the other. Over and against both Rome's conflation of sanctification and justification, with her technical notion of 'faith working through love', and Edwards' revision of *sola fide* with his notion of 'natural fittingness', I affirmed a decidedly Protestant-Reformed soteriology. This I did by developing the doctrinal relationships between the *pactum salutis*, divine election, the *historia salutis*, and the *ordo salutis*, offering a hearty 'amen' to the Reformed tradition regarding all of these topics. Thus, I signaled the intention to contribute my voice to the chorus of Reformed theologians within the Protestant tradition. Harmony, not contention, is what I am after. My contribution of 'regeneration and faith' as 'recognition and apprehension of divine beauty' is not a deviation of the Reformed conception of soteriology but rather an accentuation thereof through the lens of aesthetics.

Chapter 5 is the primary place where I offer this said accentuation. It began with this project's largest section of exegetical work, wherein I examined the Christological and soteriological implications of Paul's use of 'δόξα' in 2 Corinthians 3:12–4:6 and subsequently compared the findings there with John 12:36b-43. Extrapolating from the exegetical work done here, I developed the five following theological implications:

1. God's glory includes an aesthetic dimension.

2. Christ shares the same divine glory as the Father and the Spirit, such that the glory He reveals is the glory of the Trinity.

3. Unbelief is caused by an inability to perceive Christ's glory as beautiful.

4. The regeneration-faith relationship includes a Christological-aesthetic dimension, such that the newly regenerated saint experiences freedom from the satanic veil so as to perceive the irresistible beauty of Christ's glory with the eyes of faith.

5. Soteriology and hermeneutics are inextricably connected, and the act of reading Scripture rightly is the act of reading with an aesthetic apprehension of Christ's glory therein.

To be regenerated so as to see the beauty of the Trinity, mediated by Christ, with the eyes of faith is therefore to be swept up into a kind of asymmetrical participation with the divine life. Again, our thesis is that *When the Holy Spirit regenerates a sinner, He imparts the faculties necessary for such a person to behold the beauty of the Trinity, mediated in Christ .... In regeneration, the Spirit communicates – or, sovereignly brings the regenerate into participation with – the glorious* a se *beatitude of the Trinity, mediated through Christ. The* fiducia *component of saving faith therefore has an accompanying aesthetic aspect; it involves the existential recognition of Christ's infinite beauty.* In the end, chapter 5 sustained and upheld this central thesis.

Beauty and the Christian Life: The Beatific Vision

As I conclude this work, it is worth taking a bit of space to signal the relevance our findings here have on the Christian life, both on this side of Christ's return (sanctification) and on the other (glorification). There is good warrant for linking progressive sanctification and glorification in the same sweep of transformation. Obviously, there is a definite transition wherein death and resurrection signal the actual distinction between progressive sanctification and glorification in the life of the saint. Even those who 'will not all fall asleep' and will be transformed 'in the twinkling of an eye' (1 Cor. 15:51) will not be so transformed in a gentle, unnoticeable way – as if glorification were merely the next small step in a long line of incremental changes. The Christian life *now* and the Christian life *then* are qualitatively different (1 Cor. 13:12; 1 John 3:2).

However, Scripture does seem to hold the two topics conceptually close. Thus, the sanctifying suffering Paul describes as 'light and momentary affliction', he insists, 'is preparing for us an eternal weight of glory beyond all comparison' (2 Cor. 4:17). Going from suffering to sanctification to glorification is the most natural thought progression for Paul. This is why he moves immediately into a discussion about the groaning of our earthly tents (2 Cor. 5:1-3) and the heavenly home we march toward, wherein 'what is mortal' will be 'swallowed up by life' (2 Cor. 5:4). It is no coincidence that the same Spirit whose presence sanctifies us definitively and progressively (1 Cor. 6:11; 1 Pet. 1:2; Heb. 12:14) is named here as the 'guarantee' of glorification (2 Cor 5:5). Notice the continuity between the Spirit's renovative work now and His glorifying work hereafter. 'There is therefore a soteriological trajectory and transformational continuum,' writes Suzanne McDonald, 'between beholding the glory of God by faith now and beholding it by sight in eternity.'[3] Both now and then, the Spirit transforms us into the image of Christ by means of gracious participation with Christ.[4]

Beholding the beauty of Christ is not simply the beginning of the Christian life; it is the whole of it. This is not to flatten the manifold fruits of progressive sanctification to one mere act (i.e., seeing the beauty of Christ) in reductionistic fashion. Michael Allen is right when he says that 'being spiritually minded and viewing the glorious Christ is not to be myopic ... but to view all things in transfigured light. It is no narrow icon but the discipline of having one's whole imagination recast.'[5] Christopher Holmes makes a similar point when he recounts the believer's ongoing experience with God's goodness in the Christian life: 'The more you know, the more strength you acquire to see – and thus to love – God with the eyes of the heart. Purity of heart is coterminous with seeing God in relation to other things, with recognizing that beauty, truth, goodness, and unity are first in God and therefore in other things.'[6] This seems to be the very point Gregory of Nyssa makes when he says, 'Admiration even of the beauty of the heavens, and of the dazzling sunbeams, and, indeed, of any fair phenomenon, will then cease. The beauty noticed there will be but as the hand to lead us to the love of the supernal Beauty whose glory the heavens and the firmament declare, and whose secret the whole creation sings.' He goes on to say that 'the climbing soul, leaving all that she has grasped already as too narrow for her needs, will thus grasp the idea of that magnificence which is exalted far above the heavens.'[7]

Before moving on, it is worth pausing to reflect even further on the importance of the beatific vision on the Christian life. In his recent work, *Grounded in Heaven: Recentering Christian Hope and Life on God*, Michael Allen brings some much-needed balance to recent trends

---

3. Suzanne McDonald, 'Beholding the Glory of God in the Face of Jesus Christ: John Owen and the "Reforming" of the Beatific Vision,' in *The Ashgate Research Companion to John Owen's Theology*, ed. Mark Jones and Kelly M. Kapic (Burlington, VT: Ashgate 2016), 143.

4. See Michael Allen, *Sanctification* (Grand Rapids, MI: Zondervan, 2017), 160-68. Cf., Hans Urs von Balthasar, *The Glory of the Lord*, 1:150.

5. Allen, *Grounded in Heaven*, 98.

6. Christopher R. J. Holmes, *The Lord Is Good: Seeking the God of the Psalter* (Downers Grove, IL: InterVarsity Press, 2018), 47.

7. Gregory of Nyssa, *On Virginity* xi.356.

in Reformed eschatology. Writing as a sympathetic admirer of the Kuyperian Dutch-Reformed tradition as a whole, Allen is concerned that this stream of Reformed theology is in danger of losing sight of an important biblical emphasis in its eschatology. In the laudable effort to extol God's redemptive purposes for creation, has the Kuyperian vision gone too far in its emphasis on heaven's earthiness? Allen argues it has. 'The Kuyperian eschatology,' he says, 'has so emphasized the earthiness of our Christian hope that it has sometimes lost sight of broader biblical priorities and has consequently undercut the catholic tradition's emphasis upon communion with God and the ultimate bliss of the beatific vision.'[8] This overly-earthy eschatological vision Allen refers to as 'eschatological naturalism', which he defines as 'a theological approach that speaks of God instrumentally as a means or instigator of an end but fails to confess substantively that God's identity is our one true end (in whom only any other things are to be enjoyed).'[9]

In this way, Allen intends to avoid two important mistakes. First, he seeks to avoid implying that the 'eschatological naturalism' of the Kuyperian vision is naturalistic across the board, but is rather naturalistic 'only in a targeted manner regarding eschatological confessions'.[10] Second, Allen avoids giving the impression that a proper eschatology has *no room* for a glorified creation; as if true heavenly bliss is to consider the enjoyment of glorified creation a superfluous redundancy. There is a place for enjoyment of God's good gifts, even in heaven, but the beauty of the beatific vision is that all of those gifts will be enjoyed *in God*. Communion with God is therefore not the means to the end, He is rather the end in whom all other enjoyments are enjoyed truly. Hence, the beatific vision of God in Christ is not to ignore creation, but rather to 'view all things in transfigured light'.[11]

Because of how seldom the beatific vision is addressed in Protestant circles,[12] it may seem to some as though it were a doctrine in search

---

8. Allen, *Grounded in Heaven*, 23.

9. Ibid., 39.

10. Ibid., 39.

11. Ibid., 98.

12. For example, you will find a very meager section on the Beatific Vision in Wayne Grudem's *Systematic Theology*, and nothing mentioned in Millard J. Erickson's *Christian Theology*, 3ʳᵈ ed. (Grand Rapids, MI: Baker Academic, 2013), Louis Berkhof's *Systematic*

of biblical rationale. In reality, however, the ubiquity of this 'blessed hope' renders the beatific vision hidden in plain sight. For example, in his pastoral epistles, the apostle Paul often hails the promised hope of Christ's 'appearing'.

He instructs Timothy to 'keep the commandment unstained and free from reproach *until the appearing of our Lord Jesus Christ*' (1 Tim. 6:14). In his second letter to Timothy, Paul's charge to preach the word bears the heavy authoritative force of being 'in the presence of God and of Christ Jesus, who is to judge the living and the dead, and *by his appearing and his kingdom*' (2 Tim. 4:1-2), and he promises a crown of righteousness to 'all who have loved *his appearing*' (2 Tim. 4:8). Even more explicitly, Paul names this appearing 'our blessed hope' in his letter to Titus ('waiting for our blessed hope, *the appearing of the glory of our great God and Savior Jesus Christ*' [Titus 2:13].). To modern ears, there is nothing particularly surprising about this language. Every Christian eschatology looks forward to the appearing of Christ.

But often, modern readers can anticipate this appearing as a means to an end: at the appearing of Christ, we will have glorified bodies and a New Heavens and New Earth to enjoy sinless paradise. However, it is better to view the blessed hope of Christ's appearing not as a means to an end, but as the end itself. Christ's appearing does not merely catapult us into paradise; rather, paradise is paradise *because* there we will behold the glory of God in the face of Jesus Christ, unencumbered by the obscurity of fallen and unglorified nature. The blessed hope is not the appearing of Jesus, which gets us something else (were that the case, that something else would be, in a truer sense, our blessed hope). Rather, the blessed hope *is* the 'appearing of the glory of our great God and Savior Jesus Christ'.

This is clearly evident in two important passages regarding the beatific vision: 1 John 3:2 and 1 Corinthians 13:12. In 1 John 3, the beloved apostle seeks to inspire enduring faithfulness in his audience, in part, by assuring them of their place in the family of God. He writes to a congregation that has been battered by the heartbreaking reality of apostasy. The reality of members with whom they once worshiped and fellowshipped departing not only the church but also the faith

---

Theology, Robert Letham's *Systematic Theology*, or Anthony C. Thiselton's *Systematic Theology* (Grand Rapids, MI: Eerdmans, 2015).

(cf., 1 John 2:18-19) surely must have left them reeling. If such men and women once believed to be true saints have proven themselves to be 'antichrists', what assurance is there for *any* professing believer? With pastoral tenderness, John offers this congregation a framework for identifying true belief. After inviting his audience to look for the various fruits of genuine faith, confident they *will* find ample evidence of the Spirit's ministry in their lives, he exhorts them to 'abide in [Christ], so that when he appears we may have confidence and not shrink from him in shame at his coming' (1 John 2:28). The confidence that arises from this abiding, John says, is appropriate. Like balm applied to an open wound, John marvels at the love of God in adoption: 'See what kind of love the Father has given to us, that we should be called children of God; and so we are' (1 John 3:1a). And it is within the context of encouraging the hearts of his audience that he calls attention to the central eschatological promise included in their inheritance: 'Beloved, we are God's children now, and what we will be has not yet appeared; but we know that when he appears we shall be like him, *because we shall see him as he is*. And everyone who thus hopes in him purifies himself as he is pure' (1 John 3:2-3).

For all the mystery that still shrouds the believer's future glorified state ('...what we will be has not yet appeared...'), John is absolutely confident of one thing: that when Christ appears, 'we shall be like him, *because* we shall see him as he is.' As mentioned before, the mystical nature of this hope can easily elude modern readers,[13] but it should not be missed as the central hope of John. On this verse, and particularly John's description of seeing God 'as he is', Calvin notes, how John

> intimates a new and an ineffable manner of seeing him, which we enjoy not now; for as long as we walk by faith, as Paul teaches us, we are absent from him. And when he appeared to the fathers, it was not in his own essence, but was ever seen under symbols. Hence the majesty of God, now hid, will then only be in itself seen, when the veil of this mortal and corruptible nature shall be removed.[14]

---

13. E.g., precious little is even mentioned on the beatific vision in Robert W. Yarbrough's commentary on this passage in Yarbrough, *1-3 John: Baker Exegetical Commentary on the New Testament* (Grand Rapids, MI: Baker Academic, 2008).

14. John Calvin, *Commentaries on the Catholic Epistles*, trans. John Owen (Edinburgh: UK, Calvin Translation Society, 1855), 206.

According to Calvin, the ignorance of 'what we will be' simply adds to the anticipation of the beatific vision. Such ignorance 'intimates a new and an ineffable *manner* of seeing'. Another feature of this promised hope mentioned in John's epistle that bears immediate relevance on the central thesis of this book is identifiable in the ὅτι (because) of verse 2. John says that 'we shall be like him, *because* we shall see him as he is.' There is a causal relationship between our 'seeing' and our 'being like him'. As Thomas Andrew Bennett notes, the 'theological freight of the text as a whole pushes us to read the second clause as explanatory'.[15] How is it possible for us to be like Him? Answer: *because* we shall see Him as He is. 'The metaphysics of the idea must necessarily elude us,' Bennett goes on to say,

> but the logic is quite familiar to human experience. Bearing witness to great beauty or great ugliness has transformative impact…. John imagines that this principle will apply in toto when we are confronted by the unvarnished beauty of Christ at his arrival. Seeing him 'as he really is' indicates that up until that time, human eyes will not really have apprehended the full beauty and divinity of eternal life and that when they do, the sight will overwhelm and change them.[16]

Which is to say, the beatific vision of Christ will have a similar affect as the faithful sight of those who behold Christ now. When the satanic veil of unbelief is lifted, those liberated by the Spirit behold the glory of God in the face of Jesus Christ and are transformed. And when the veil of fallen and unglorified nature is unveiled at the appearing of Christ, those who behold Him will likewise be ineffably transformed.

The logic of 1 Corinthians 13 works in much the same way as 1 John 3. Like John, Paul is encouraging present obedience motivated by future promises. Unlike 1 John however, Paul is not overly concerned with addressing his audience with a kind of perfect tenderness. If John's audience was burdened with a crippling loss of confidence, marked by fear and timidity, Paul's audience was burdened with the opposite: a misplaced confidence in themselves. With typical Corinthian swagger,

---

15. Thomas Andrew Bennett, *1-3 John: The Two Horizons New Testament Commentary* (Grand Rapids, MI: Eerdmans, 2021), 57.

16. Ibid., 57. Smalley seems to concur with Bennett on this interpretation. See, Stephen S. Smalley, *1, 2, and 3 John: Word Biblical Commentary,* Revised ed. (Grand Rapids, MI: Zondervan Academic, 2006), 139-40.

the Corinthian Church boasted in the impressive manifestations of spiritual gifts in their midst (cf., 1 Cor. 1:7). In chapters 12–14, Paul addresses their hubris and unruly exercise of these gifts. While he does not discourage them from exercising them, and indeed even charges them to 'earnestly desire' them (1 Cor. 14:1), he boldly confronts their disordered priorities. In chapter 13, he elevates the centrality of love as more important (and more *enduring*) than powerful external displays of spiritual gifts ('If I speak in the tongues of men and angels, but have not love, I am a noisy gong or a clanging symbol' [1 Cor. 13:1]).

Were their values rightly ordered according to heavenly realities, the Corinthians would realize that the spiritual gifts of prophecy and knowledge, for example, are temporary means to the enduring gift of love (1 Cor. 13:8-11). Love for Christ – and by extension, all those who are in Christ – is, for Paul, the apex of all our activity. And this love finds its zenith in one single heavenly reality: seeing Christ 'face to face'. 'For now we see in a mirror dimly,' says Paul, 'but then face to face. Now I know in part; then I shall know fully, even as I have been fully known' (1 Cor. 13:12). On this verse, Calvin draws out the comparative element of Paul's logic:

> For we have in the word (in so far as is expedient for us) a naked and open revelation of God, and it has nothing intricate in it, to hold us in suspense, as wicked persons imagine; but how small a proportion does this bear to that vision, which we have in our eye! Hence it is only in a comparative sense, that it is termed obscure.[17]

For Paul, creation itself (which '*declare* the glory of God' according to Psalm 19:1, and whereby God's invisible attributes are 'clearly perceived' according to Romans 1:20) and the special revelation of the Scriptures (who are 'a naked and open revelation of God'), both give us a glimpse of God merely as 'in a mirror dimly'. In saying this, Paul is not implying that general and special revelation are somehow deficient or inaccurate. His comparison does not disparage the revelation of God we have before 'the perfect comes'. Quite the opposite. The logic works thusly: if so great a revelation of God has been given to us now, *how much more* splendid will that vision be wherein we see Him face to face? Such a vision, by comparison, renders the 'naked and open revelation of God' a dimly

---

17. John Calvin, *Commentary on the Epistles of Paul the Apostle to the Corinthians*, trans. John Pringle, vo. 1, (Edinburgh, UK: The Calvin Translation Society, 1848), 431.

lit mirror image of God. And it is in this face-to-face beholding that love endures forever. If such is our future, reasons Paul, should we not prioritize love for God and for the saints above everything else? Ought not our future hope of beatific vision motivate love today? To answer in the negative is to create a massive disjunction between who we are and who we will be. For Paul, then, the loving beatific vision of God is the telos of all our earthly obedience.

Protestant Reformed Christians can therefore appropriately join figures like Gregory of Nyssa and Anselm of Canterbury on their heavenly pilgrimage toward God. On the latter's pursuit of the beatific vision, it is worth mentioning that his *Proslogion* begins and ends with essentially the same prayer. 'Come then, Lord my God,' pleads Anselm in the opening chapter, 'teach my heart where and how to seek You, where and how to find You.'[18] He goes on to say in evocative terms,

> Teach me to seek You, and reveal Yourself to me as I seek, because I can neither seek You if You do not teach me how, nor find You unless You reveal Yourself. Let me seek You in desiring You; let me desire You in seeking You; let me find You in loving You; let me love You in finding You.[19]

By the end of *Proslogion*, the content of his prayer is very much the same, but whereas the opening chapter was a petition, the closing chapter is a thanksgiving: 'For I have discovered a joy that is complete and more than complete. Indeed, when the heart is filled with that joy, the mind is filled with it, the soul is filled with it, the whole man is filled with it, yet joy beyond measure will remain.'[20] Anselm's language here is important because it harmonizes with the heavenly paradox of Gregory's language as well (as we will see below). For Anselm, there is a finality here, but also an ever-expanding excess: 'the heart is filled with that joy,' and yet 'joy beyond measure will remain'. In his commentary on the *Proslogion*, *Anselm's Pursuit of Joy*, Gavin R. Ortlund calls attention to this feature as significant: 'The incompleteness of Anselm's discovery of joy, even here at the end of the book, creates a forward-looking eschatological tilt to the entire project.'[21] He concludes with the striking observation that

---

18. Anselm, *Proslogion*, chap. 1, 84-85.

19. Ibid., 86-87.

20. Ibid., chap. 26, 103.

21. Ortlund, *Anselm's Pursuit of Joy*, 219.

for all the progress Anselm has made in the *Proslogion*, for the decisive exuberance of finding God to be the joy of the human soul, this discovery has not resulted in a relaxation of those impulses that led him to initiate his search for God, but – if anything – has only further aggravated them.... By concluding with an articulation of his love, desire, and hunger for God, Anselm underscores one more time the ultimate thrust of the entire *Proslogion*, which is not only to direct the mind to God as *summum* of all reality, but to direct the soul to God as the *bonum* of all happiness.[22]

This 'further aggravation' is a feature Anselm shares in his articulation of the beatific vision with Gregory of Nyssa. As mentioned before, Gregory's conception of the beatific vision is far more expansive than to merely cover life after death. For Gregory, it is the sum and substance of the whole Christian life. He describes this powerfully in *The Life of Moses*. This work is an extended address to 'Caesarius, man of God,' in which he commends the life of Moses as an example of virtue.[23]

In Book One of this treatise, Gregory offers a historical exposition of Moses' life as recorded in the Pentateuch that modern day biblical scholars would have a difficult time objecting to. But in Book Two, he lays before his reader the riches of pre-modern exegesis with his allegorical and spiritual-theological reading. Moses, for Gregory, is not simply the leader of Israel, he is rather the archetypal philosopher-theologian, striving toward the virtuous life which culminates in the beatific vision. From the life of Moses, according to Gregory, we learn how 'the soul rises higher and will always make its flight yet higher – by its desire of heavenly things.'[24]

In summary fashion, Gregory shows how throughout Moses' life, he experienced greater and greater degrees of glory. From his pursuit of solitude in the desert to his approach to the divine light of the burning bush (unencumbered, having removed his sandals). From his encampment under the cloud to his quenched thirst and filled stomach (drinking from the rock and eating heavenly manna). From his defeat of sinful enemies to his eradication of idolatry. From his communion with God in the tabernacle to his pursuit of God up the mountain.[25]

---

22. Ibid., 221.

23. Gregory of Nyssa, *The Life of Moses*, trans. Abraham J. Malherbe and Everett Ferguson, reprint ed. (New York, NY: HarperCollins, 2006), 131.

24. Ibid., 103.

25. Ibid., 103-04.

Throughout all of this, Gregory points out, Moses was not satisfied. Greater degrees of glory awakened further greater aspirations for more. He thus summarizes the beatific vision in this way:

> Although lifted up through such lofty experiences, he is still unsatisfied in his desire for more. He still thirsts for that with which he constantly filled himself to capacity, and he asks to attain as if he had never partaken, beseeching God to appear to him, not according to his capacity to partake, but according to God's true being. Such an experience seems to me to belong to the soul which loves what is beautiful. Hope always draws the soul from the beauty which is seen to what is beyond, always kindles the desire for the hidden through what is constantly perceived. Therefore, the ardent lover of beauty, although receiving what is always visible as an image of what he desires, yet longs to be filled with the very stamp of the archetype. And the bold request which goes up the mountains of desire asks this: to enjoy the Beauty not in mirrors and reflections, but face-to-face.[26]

For Gregory, this pursuit was nothing less than the telos of the human soul. To pursue the virtuous life was to pursue the beatific vision. This is why, for all his emphasis on consecration and purified living, Gregory can, without a hint of contradiction, emphatically deny that perfection is to 'avoid a wicked life because, like slaves, we servilely fear punishment,' nor is perfection 'to do good because we hope for rewards, as if cashing in on the virtuous life by some businesslike and contractual agreement.' What then is perfection? What is the essence of the virtuous life? According to Gregory, 'falling from God's friendship [is] the *only thing dreadful,* and we consider becoming God's friend the *only thing worthy of honor and desire.*'[27]

To become God's friend is to participate in the beatific vision. This vision is always and forever insatiable. Its insatiability is not owing to the limitations of a fallen or pre-glorified state, but rather to a *finite* state. Because God is infinite, and because His creatures are finite, this constant longing for more intimacy – greater degrees of appreciation for His Beauty – is a feature that will carry over into Heaven. 'This truly is the vision of God: never to be satisfied in the desire to see him. But one must always by looking at what he can see, rekindle his desire to see more.'[28]

---

26. Ibid., 104.

27. Ibid., 132 (emphasis mine).

28. Ibid., 106.

When we are invited to behold the glory (beauty) of the Lord in the face of Jesus Christ, so as to be changed into the image of Christ from one degree of glory to another (2 Cor. 3:18), we are being invited further up and further into participation in the Trinity's eternal, *a se* beatitude. The beauty we see in the face of Christ is the effulgence of the beatitude He enjoys in His divine essence of the Father, with the Spirit. Therefore, the beauty we see in the face of Christ is gratuitous – beckoning us ever more into communion with the Father of Lights. This further communion never dissolves the Creator-creature distinction, but it does ever delight the soul as the everlasting telos of 'the image bearer'. Holmes points out:

> In this life, we do not know God in a direct sense – as does the Son the Father – but through faith, that 'something else' …. The life of Christian discipleship is a matter (in part) of experiencing ever-greater intimacy with the Lord of the life to come. His goodness works in just this way, not only conserving but perfecting us in this life in the glories of the life to come.[29]

Holmes' language of 'perfecting us in this life *in the glories of the life to come*' (emphasis added) is striking and important. What the Spirit does by His participatory rapture, wherein His indwelling presence enables the eyes of our hearts to see the beauty of Christ, is facilitate a kind of space-time portal, sanctifying us progressively with the heavenly glories that await us. These glories, both here and there (or rather, both *now* and *then*), are revealed to us in the person of Christ. Thus, in this sense, there is total continuity between our vision of faith in this life and our sight in the life to come. As John Owen puts it: 'No man shall ever behold the glory of Christ by *sight* hereafter, who doth not in some measure behold it by *faith* here in this world.'[30]

We should emphasize here the Christological nature of the beatific vision. Owen makes a strong point when he describes the beatific vision in this way, 'The enjoyment of Heaven is usually called the *beatific vision*. That is such an intellectual present view, apprehension and sight of God and his Glory, *especially as manifested in Christ*, as will make us *blessed* unto eternity.'[31] Here, Owen charts the course between Calvin, who describes

---

29. Holmes, *The Lord Is Good*, 162.

30. Owen, *Works of John Owen*, 1:288 (emphasis original).

31. John Owen, *Christologia, or, A declaration of the glorious mystery of the person of Christ, God and man with the infinite wisdom, love and power of God in the contrivance and constitution thereof*… (London, 1679; Wing O762), as quoted in Boersma, *Seeing God*, 322, emphasis added.

the beatific vision as a time in which 'Christ's humanity no longer acts as an intermediate bearer of revelation between us and the vision of God',[32] and Bavinck, who objects to the beatific vision on the grounds that it minimizes (or even erases) Christ's epistemological-mediatory role as the revelation of God.[33] J. Todd Billings helpfully frames the issue:

> For Owen, the blessed always behold God's glory through the face of Jesus Christ. Drawing on 2 Corinthians 3:18 and 4:6, Owen, and a strand of the Reformed tradition after him, gives a Christ-centered account of the beatific vision in which Jesus Christ is – precisely – in the middle. Even in the eschaton, we apprehend the Triune God through the face of Jesus Christ.[34]

McDonald agrees with this assessment, taking the centrality of 2 Corinthians 3:18 and 4:6 in Owen's theology even further:

> In Owen's view, the Christological and pneumatological dynamic of the Christian life here and now, and of our eternal salvation, is contained in a nutshell here [in 2 Cor. 3:18, 4:6]. We are to be conformed more and more to Christ the image of God through the work of the Spirit, and one of the chief ways in which we are formed and transformed is by beholding the glory of the Lord, now, partially and by faith; and then at the eschatological consummation by sight as we see face to face and know as we are known.[35]

With respect to his conviction that the beatific vision is a *Christic* vision, Hans Boersma, in his masterpiece *Seeing God: The Beatific Vision in the Christian Tradition*, has shown how Owen is in good company. Notwithstanding idiosyncratic variations among each figure, Boersma demonstrates that the mediation of Christ in the beatific vision is a point shared by most of the tradition's leading lights.[36] Boersma's own reflections on the beatific vision are worth the price of the work as a whole:

---

32. Richard A. Muller, 'Christ in the Eschaton: Calvin and Moltmann on the Duration of the Munus Regium,' *Harvard Theological Review* 74, no. 1 (1981): 48, emphasis added.

33. Herman Bavinck, *Reformed Dogmatics Volume 4: Holy Spirit, Church, and New Creation*, ed. John Bolt, trans. John Vriend (Grand Rapids, MI: Baker Academic, 2008), 722-24. For an analysis on Bavinck's view of the beatific vision, see Boersma, *Seeing God*, 33-40. And for a great comparison and contrast between Calvin and Bavinck, see Billings, *Union with Christ*, 80-86.

34. Billings, *Union with Christ*, 84.

35. McDonald, 'Beholding the Glory of God in the Face of Jesus Christ,' 142-43.

36. Allen seems to agree: 'Reformed theologians (such as Owen and Edwards) have agreed with Gregory of Nyssa that we will not see the divine essence but will see God

> Vision of God is always vision in and through the human Jesus who is identified as the Son of God, in and through whom alone we come to know the Father. The future beatific vision is therefore not a stage beyond the vision of Christ …. Rather, we see God himself – the divine essence – when we indwell the incarnate tabernacle of God through union and communion with Jesus. Sacrament and reality coincide in him. The divine essence does not lie behind or beyond Christ; rather, those who have eyes of faith can see the essence of God in the unity of the person of Christ.[37]

This is something Gregory apparently agrees with Boersma on. 'For, since Christ is understood by Paul as the rock, all hope of good things is believed to be in Christ, in whom we have learned all the treasures of good things to be. He who finds any good finds it in Christ, who contains all good.'[38] The beatific vision that Gregory extols is a vision the beholder enjoys from the place of being firmly fixed in Christ: He is the rock in which Moses hides while receiving the goodness and beauty of God's own beatific presence.

And this Christocentric emphasis on the beatific vision offers us one more opportunity to recall an earlier emphasis of this project, namely participation via union with Christ. In his work, *The Same God Who Works All Things*, Adonis Vidu intimates the relationship between union with Christ and the beatific vision in really striking ways. 'In and through Christ the whole creation … returns to its supernatural source to receive its supernatural end, which is nothing less than communion with the Trinity culminating in the beatific vision. The first act of this return is the incarnation.'[39] To say this much is, as we have seen, rather unremarkable – it is to affirm a Christocentric conception of the beatific vision with much of the Great Tradition. But Vidu goes on to reflect on *how* the incarnation begins to enact creation's 'return to its supernatural end'. The key to this concept is found in the fact in the hypostatic union, Christ took on a true human nature, which experiences the beatific vision. 'On the one hand,' writes Vidu,

---

by means of the theophanic (and specifically Christophanic) disclosure.' *Grounded in Heaven*, 85-86.

37. Boersma, *Seeing God*, 411.

38. Gregory, *The Life of Moses*, 109.

39. Vidu, *The Same God Who Works All Things*, 158.

Christ has the vision of God from conception, while on the other hand throughout his earthly life he discovers (as man) the manifold ways in which God may be participated in and experienced, particularly through the experience of loss and want characterized by the human condition.[40]

In other words, from one perspective Christ was not lacking in His beatific vision, such that He needed to receive it in the flesh (He is, after all, *omniscient* in His divine nature). On the other hand, He increases 'in the beatific vision throughout' His life, in such a way that is 'proportionate and instrumental to an increase in Christ's own human capaciousness for God.'[41] This was not for His sake, but for ours.[42] The beatific vision we experience, in other words, is a vision Christ recapitulated for us perfectly throughout His earthly ministry and beyond. It is the beatific vision of Christ's perfect human nature that the believer is united to by the Spirit! *This* is the divine love that the believer is swept up into when he is united to Christ (Rom. 5:5), and the love he ever-increasingly grows into, culminating in the beatific vision. We quote Vidu here at length:

> Not only is the love a consequent of the Spirit's personal presence (thus an ontological priority of uncreated over created grace), but this love is specifically Christ's love of the Father. The Spirit who indwells the believer is, then, precisely the Spirit that has first been formed by Christ's humanity.... It is not the believer's own love that enables the Spirit to indwell him. Rather, it is the love by which Christ loves the Father, and the Father loves Christ, that is poured into our hearts. Love is not our contribution to the gift of grace. Rather, love is itself a gift that is prepared for us by Christ.[43]

In other words, in the incarnation, the Son began experiencing beatific love for the Father as a man. This experience was not meeting a deficiency He had before the incarnation; it is rather a fitting missional correspondence of a processional reality: the Son was recapitulating the beatific vision of human destiny. When God's love is poured into the hearts of believers through the Holy Spirit (Rom 5:5), they are, in a very real way, being brought into the beatific vision that Christ experiences

---

40. Ibid., 273.

41. Ibid., 273.

42. 'In this way Christ recapitulates human destiny, leading to his glorified post-resurrection human nature.' Ibid., 273.

43. Ibid., 318.

in His human nature. Thus, Gregory is absolutely right: 'He who finds any good finds it in Christ, who contains all good.'[44]

Conclusion

The beauty of the divine, revealed in Christ, is a notion rife with potential for further academic contemplation. This is fitting, since such contemplation is nothing short of the everlasting telos of man. The Christian life begins with soteriological vision of Christ. The putrid idolatry that once held the affections of the regenerate captive suddenly lose their luster in the brilliance of Christ's beautiful light. That which was previously veiled by Satan is unveiled by the Spirit, and the light that shines from Christ on the once-darkened soul has creative power (2 Cor. 4:4-6). The eyes of faith that behold Christ as the Savior and justifier of sin thereby consider Him *lovely*. Thus, the Christian life begins with the Spirit of Christ regenerating – imparting the spiritual sense faculties to see *by virtue of His very own presence* – and thereby opening the eyes of faith, which behold the beauty of the Trinity in the face of Jesus Christ.

Awakened by his need for a Savior, the regenerate is justified when he looks to Christ with the eyes of faith – Christ is the satiation of this need. But the eyes of faith do not cease beholding the beauty of God in the face of Jesus Christ at that point. Never bored, never disappointed, ever-desirous for more, the regenerate beholds the beauty of Christ continuously forever. Further up, further in, forever is the delight of his soul.[45] What begins as *sight by faith* now continues as *sight by glorified vision* in heaven. Herein the image bearer enjoys his telos: he is a begraced participant in the Trinity's eternal, *a se* beatitude, and he is such a participant by virtue of being *in Christ*. The excellencies of the beauty he beholds in the face of Jesus Christ will never be exhausted, not because the glorified soul will somehow be short of time to exhaust them but because they are by definition *inexhaustible*.

---

44. Gregory, *The Life of Moses*, 109.

45. This is, of course, Lewis' phrase, which is perhaps nowhere described so well as when Jewel the Unicorn stands on the edge of Aslan's country, beholding new glimpses of *true* Narnia: 'He stamped his right fore-hoof on the ground and neighed and then cried: "I have come home at last! This is my real country! I belong here. This is the land I have been looking for all my life, though I never knew it till now. The reason why we loved the old Narnia is that it sometimes looked a little like this. Bree-hee-hee! Come further up, come further in!"' (Lewis, *The Last Battle*, 106).

Bibliography

Alexander, T. Desmond, and Brian S. Rosner, eds. *New Dictionary of Biblical Theology*. Downers Grove, IL: InterVarsity Press, 2000.

Allen, Michael. *Grounded in Heaven: Recentering Christian Hope and Life on God*. Grand Rapids, MI: Eerdmans, 2018.

———. *Sanctification*. Grand Rapids, MI: Zondervan, 2017.

Allen, Michael, and Scott R. Swain, eds. *Christian Dogmatics: Reformed Theology for the Church Catholic*. Grand Rapids, MI: Baker Academic, 2016.

Allen, R. Michael, ed. *Theological Commentary: Evangelical Perspectives*. New York: T&T Clark, 2011.

Allen, R. Michael, and Scott R. Swain. *Reformed Catholicity: The Promise of Retrieval for Theology and Biblical Interpretation*. Grand Rapids, MI: Baker Academic, 2015.

Allison, Gregg R. *Roman Catholic Theology and Practice: An Evangelical Assessment*. Wheaton, IL: Crossway, 2014.

Ames, William. *The Marrow of Theology*. Translated by John Dykstra Eusden. Grand Rapids, MI: Baker Books, 1968.

Anatolios, Khaled. *Retrieving Nicaea: The Development and Meaning of Trinitarian Doctrine*. Grand Rapids, MI: Baker Academic, 2018.

Anselm of Canterbury. *The Major Works*. Edited by Brian Davies and G. R. Evans. New York: Oxford University Press, 1998.

Aquinas, Thomas. *Summa Theologiae*. Translated by The Fathers of the English Dominican Province. Westminster: Christian Classics, 1983.

Ayres, Lewis. *Nicaea and Its Legacy: An Approach to Fourth-Century Trinitarian Theology*. Reprinted. Oxford: Oxford University Press, 2009.

Azure, Christopher P. 'A New Humanity in the Risen Christ: Paul's Use of ΚΑΙΝΗ ΚΤΙΣΙΣ in 2 Corinthians 5:17 as a Metaphor from New Foundations.' PhD diss., Midwestern Baptist Theological Seminary, 2017.

Balthasar, Hans Urs von. *The Glory of the Lord: A Theological Aesthetics*. Edited by Joseph Fessio and John Kenneth Riches. Translated by Erasmo Leiva-Merikakis. 2nd ed. Vol. 1: *Seeing the Form*. San Francisco, CA: Ignatius Press, 2009.

Banks, Robert. *Reconciliation and Hope: New Testament Essays on Atonement and Eschatology Presented to L. L. Morris on His 60th Birthday*. Grand Rapids, MI: Eerdmans, 1974.

Barr, James. *The Concept of Biblical Theology: An Old Testament Perspective*. Minneapolis: Fortress, 1999.

———. *The Semantics of Biblical Language*. Eugene, OR: Wipf & Stock, 2004.

Barrett, Jordan P. *Divine Simplicity: A Biblical and Trinitarian Account*. Minneapolis: Fortress, 2017.

Barrett, Matthew. *Canon, Covenant and Christology: Rethinking Jesus and the Scriptures of Israel*. Downers Grove, IL: IVP Academic, 2020.

———. *Salvation by Grace: The Case for Effectual Calling and Regeneration*. Phillipsburg, NJ: P&R Publishing, 2013.

———. *Simply Trinity: The Unmanipulated Father, Son, and Spirit*. Grand Rapids, MI: Baker, 2021.

———, ed. *The Doctrine on Which the Church Stands or Falls: Justification in Biblical, Theological, Historical, and Pastoral Perspective*. Wheaton, IL: Crossway, 2019.

Barrett, Matthew, and Tom J. Nettles, eds. *Whomever He Wills: A Surprising Display of Sovereign Mercy*. Cape Coral, FL: Founders, 2012.

Barth, Karl. *Church Dogmatics, Vol. II/1: The Doctrine of God*. Edited by G. W. Bromiley and T. F. Torrance. Translated by T. H. L. Parker,

W. B. Johnston, Harold Knight, and J. L. M. Haire. Edinburgh: T&T Clark, 1957.

Bartholomew, Craig G., ed. *A Manifesto for Theological Interpretation.* Grand Rapids, MI: Baker Academic, 2016.

Bates, Matthew W. *The Birth of the Trinity: Jesus, God, and Spirit in New Testament and Early Christian Interpretations of the Old Testament.* New York: Oxford University Press, 2016.

Bauckham, Richard. *Word Biblical Commentary: Jude, 2 Peter.* Waco, TX: Word, 2005.

Bavinck, Herman. *Essays on Religion, Science, and Society.* Edited by John Bolt. Translated by Harry Boonstra and Gerrit Sheeres. Grand Rapids, MI: Baker Academic, 2013.

———. *Reformed Dogmatics Vol. 1: Prolegomena.* Edited by John Bolt. Translated by John Vriend. Grand Rapids, MI: Baker Academic, 2003.

———. *Reformed Dogmatics Vol. 2: God and Creation.* Edited by John Bolt. Translated by John Vriend. Grand Rapids, MI: Baker Academic, 2003.

———. *Reformed Dogmatics Vol. 3: Sin and Salvation in Christ.* Edited by John Bolt. Translated by John Vriend. Grand Rapids, MI: Baker Academic, 2003.

———. *Reformed Dogmatics Vol. 4: Holy Spirit, Church, and New Creation.* Edited by John Bolt. Translated by John Vriend. Grand Rapids, MI: Baker Academic, 2008.

———. *Reformed Ethics.* Edited by John Bolt. Vol. 1: Created, Fallen, and Converted Humanity. Grand Rapids, MI: Baker Academic, 2019.

Beale, G. K. *A New Testament Biblical Theology: The Unfolding of the Old Testament in the New.* Grand Rapids, MI: Baker Academic, 2011.

———, ed. *The Right Doctrine from the Wrong Texts? Essays on the Use of the Old Testament in the New.* Grand Rapids, Mich: Baker Books, 1994.

———. *We Become What We Worship: A Biblical Theology of Idolatry.* Downers Grove, Ill: IVP Academic, 2008.

Beale, G. K., and D. A. Carson, eds. *Commentary on the New Testament Use of the Old Testament*. Grand Rapids, Mich. : Nottingham, England: Baker Academic; Apollos, 2007.

Beardsley, Monroe C. *Aesthetics from Classical Greece to the Present: A Short History*. Tuscaloosa, AL: University of Alabama Press, 1998.

Beeke, Joel R., and Paul M. Smalley. *Reformed Systematic Theology*. Vol. 1: *Revelation and God*. Wheaton, IL: Crossway, 2019.

Belleville, Linda L. *2 Corinthians*. Downers Grove, IL: IVP Academic, 1996.

Bello, Rafael Nogueira. *Sinless Flesh: A Critique of Karl Barth's Fallen Christ*. Bellingham, WA: Lexham, 2020.

Bennett, Thomas Andrew. *1-3 John: The Two Horizons New Testament Commentary*. Grand Rapids, MI: Eerdmans, 2021.

Berkhof, Louis. *Systematic Theology*. Edinburgh: Banner of Truth, 1998.

Betz, John R. 'After Heidegger and Marion: The Task of Christian Metaphysics Today.' *Modern Theology* 34, no. 4 (2015): 565-97.

———. 'Theology Without Metaphysics? A Reply to Kevin Hector.' *Modern Theology* 31, no. 3 (2015): 488-500.

Billings, J. Todd. *Calvin, Participation, and the Gift: The Activity of Believers in Union with Christ*. New York: Oxford University Press, 2007.

———. *Union with Christ: Reframing Theology and Ministry for the Church*. Grand Rapids, MI: Baker Academic, 2011.

———. 'United to God through Christ: Calvin on the Question of Deification,' *Harvard Theological Review* 98, no. 3 (July 2005); 315-34.

Billings, J. Todd, and I. John Hesselink, eds. *Calvin's Theology and Its Reception: Disputes, Developments, and New Possibilities*. Louisville: Westminster John Knox, 2012.

Bird, Michael F., and Scott Harrower, eds. *Trinity Without Hierarchy: Reclaiming Nicene Orthodoxy in Evangelical Theology*. Grand Rapids, MI: Kregel, 2019.

Bock, Darrell L., and Robert L. Webb, eds. *Key Events in the Life of the Historical Jesus: A Collaborative Exploration of Context and Coherence.* Grand Rapids, MI: Eerdmans, 2010.

Boersma, Hans. *Heavenly Participation: The Weaving of a Sacramental Tapestry.* Grand Rapids, MI: Eerdmans, 2011.

_____. *Scripture as Real Presence: Sacramental Exegesis in the Early Church.* Grand Rapids, MI: Baker Academic, 2017.

_____. *Seeing God: The Beatific Vision in Christian Tradition.* Grand Rapids, MI: Eerdmans, 2018.

Boff, Leonardo. *Trinity and Society.* Eugene, OR: Wipf & Stock, 2005.

Bowald, Mark Alan. *Rendering the Word in Theological Hermeneutics: Mapping Divine and Human Agency.* Bellingham, WA: Lexham, 2015.

Brown, David. *The Divine Trinity.* London: Duckworth, 1985.

Bruce, F.F. *1 and 2 Corinthians.* Grand Rapids, MI: Eerdmans, 1992.

Bultmann, Rudolf, Roy A. Harrisville, and Rudolf Karl Bultmann. *The Second Letter to the Corinthians.* Minneapolis: Augsburg, 1985.

Bychkov, O. V., and James Fodor, eds. *Theological Aesthetics After von Balthasar.* Burlington, VT: Ashgate, 2008.

Calvin, John. *Institutes of the Christian Religion.* Translated by Henry Beveridge. Peabody, MA: Hendrickson Publishers, 2008.

_____. *Commentaries on the Catholic Epistles.* Translated by John Owen. Edinburgh: UK, Calvin Translation Society, 1855.

_____. *The Second Epistle of Paul to the Apostle to the Corinthians and the Epistles to Timothy, Titus, and Philemon.* Translated by T. A. Small. Grand Rapids, MI: Eerdmans, 1997.

Cameron, Nigel M. de S., ed. *The Power and Weakness of God.* Edinburgh: Rutherford House, 1990.

Candler, Peter M., and Cunningham, Conor. eds., *Belief and Metaphysics.* London, UK: SCM Press, 2007.

Cara, Robert J. *Cracking the Foundation of the New Perspective on Paul: Covenantal Nomism versus Reformed Covenantal Theology.* Ross-Shire: Christian Focus, 2017.

Carnes, Natalie. *Beauty: A Theological Engagement with Gregory of Nyssa.* Eugene, OR: Cascade, 2014.

Carson, D. A., ed. *The Enduring Authority of the Christian Scriptures.* Grand Rapids, MI: Eerdmans, 2016.

———. *The Gospel According to John.* Grand Rapids, MI: Eerdmans, 1991.

Carson, D. A., and Douglas J. Moo. *An Introduction to the New Testament.* 2nd ed. Grand Rapids, MI: Zondervan, 2005.

Carson, D. A., Peter Thomas O'Brien, and Mark A. Seifrid, eds. *Justification and Variegated Nomism.* 2 vols. Grand Rapids, MI: Baker Academic, 2001, 2003.

Carter, Craig A. *Contemplating God with the Great Tradition: Recovering Trinitarian Classical Theism.* Grand Rapids, MI: Baker Academic, 2021.

———. *Interpreting Scripture with the Great Tradition: Recovering the Genius of Premodern Exegesis.* Grand Rapids, MI: Baker Academic, 2018.

Charnock, Stephen. *The Complete Works of Stephen Charnock, B.D. Vol. 1.* Reprinted. Edinburgh, UK: Banner of Truth, 2010.

Childs, Brevard S. *Biblical Theology of the Old and New Testaments: Theological Reflection on the Christian Bible.* Minneapolis: Fortress, 1993.

———. *Myth and Reality in the Old Testament.* Eugene, OR: Wipf & Stock, 1962.

———. *Old Testament Theology in a Canonical Context.* 2nd ed. Philadelphia: Fortress, 1994.

Chong, Vicente. *A Theological Aesthetics of Liberation: God, Art, and the Social Outcasts.* Eugene, OR: Pickwick, 2019.

Clark, John C., and Marcus Peter Johnson. *The Incarnation of God: The Mystery of the Gospel as the Foundation of Evangelical Theology.* Wheaton, IL: Crossway, 2015.

Cole, Graham A. *God the Peacemaker: How Atonement Brings Shalom.* Downers Grove, IL: InterVarsity Press, 2009.

———. *He Who Gives Life: The Doctrine of the Holy Spirit.* Foundations of Evangelical Theology. Wheaton, IL: Crossway, 2007.

———. *The God Who Became Human: A Biblical Theology of Incarnation.* New studies in Biblical Theology 30. Downers Grove, IL: InterVarsity Press, 2013.

Cooper, Jordan. *In Defense of the True, the Good, and the Beautiful: On the Loss of Transcendence and the Decline of the West.* Ithaca, NY: Just and Sinner, 2021.

Cortez, Marc. *Christological Anthropology in Historical Perspective: Ancient and Contemporary Approaches to Theological Anthropology.* Grand Rapids, MI: Zondervan, 2016.

Covolo, Robert S. 'Herman Bavinck's Theological Aesthetic: A Synchronic and Diachronic Analysis.' *The Bavinck Review* 2 (2011): 43-58.

Crim, K., and V.P. Furnish, eds. *Interpreter's Dictionary of the Bible, Supplementary Volume.* New York: Abingdon, 1976.

Crisp, Oliver. *Jonathan Edwards among the Theologians.* Grand Rapids, MI: Eerdmans, 2015.

———. *Jonathan Edwards on God and Creation.* New York: Oxford University Press, 2012.

Crisp, Oliver, and Fred Sanders, eds. *Advancing Trinitarian Theology: Explorations in Constructive Dogmatics.* Grand Rapids, MI: Zondervan, 2014.

Crowe, Brandon D. *The Last Adam: A Theology of the Obedient Life of Jesus in the Gospels.* Grand Rapids, MI: Baker Academic, 2017.

Davids, Peter H. *The Letters of 2 Peter and Jude.* Grand Rapids, MI: Eerdmans, 2006.

Dawson, Michael. *Jesus Ascended: The Meaning of Christ's Continuing Incarnation.* London: T&T Clark, 2004.

Delattre, Roland André. *Beauty and Sensibility in the Thought of Jonathan Edwards: An Essay in Aesthetics and Theological Ethics.* Eugene, OR: Wipf and Stock, 2006.

DeRouchie, Jason S. 'The Mystery Revealed: A Biblical Case for Christ-Centered Old Testament Interpretation.' *Themelios* 44, no. 2 (2019): 226-248.

Dolezal, James E. *All That Is in God: Evangelical Theology and the Challenge of Classical Christian Theism.* Grand Rapids, MI: Reformation Heritage, 2017.

———. *God Without Parts: Divine Simplicity and the Metaphysics of God's Absoluteness.* Eugene, OR: Pickwick, 2011.

Doolan, Gregory T. *Aquinas on the Divine Ideas as Exemplar Causes.* Washington, D.C.: The Catholic University of America Press, 2008.

Dorner, Isaac A. *Divine Immutability: A Critical Reconsideration.* Translated by Robert R. Williams and Claude Welch. Minneapolis: Fortress, 1994.

Duby, Steven J. 'Divine Immutability, Divine Action and the God-World Relation.' *International Journal of Systematic Theology* 19, no. 2 (2017): 144-162.

———. *God in Himself: Scripture, Metaphysics, and the Task of Christian Theology.* Downers Grove, IL: IVP Academic, 2019.

Eco, Umberto. *The Aesthetics of Thomas Aquinas.* Translated by Hugh Bredin. Cambridge, MA: Harvard University Press, 1988.

Edinburgh Conference in Christian Dogmatics, and Nigel M. de S Cameron, eds. *The Power and Weakness of God: Impassibility and Orthodoxy.* Edinburgh: Rutherford House Books, 1990.

Edwards, Jonathan. *Works of Jonathan Edwards Online.* 73 vols. Edited by Paul Ramsey. Jonathan Edwards Center at Yale University, 2008.

Eglinton, James. 'Vox Theologiae: Boldness and Humility in Public Theological Speech.' *International Journal of Public Theology* 9 (2015): 5-28.

Ehrman, Bart D. *Misquoting Jesus: The Story Behind Who Changed the Bible and Why.* New York: Harper Collins, 2007.

Elowsky, Joel C., and Thomas C. Oden, eds. *John 11–21.* Ancient Christian Commentary on Scripture: New Testament IVb. Downers Grove, IL: InterVarsity Press, 2007.

Emery, Gilles, and Matthew Levering, eds. *The Oxford Handbook of the Trinity.* Oxford Handbooks. New York: Oxford University Press, 2011.

Erickson, Millard J. *Christian Theology,* 3rd Ed. Grand Rapids, MI: Baker Academic, 2013.

Fabro, Cornelio. *Participation et causalité selon s. Thomas d'Aquin.* Louvain, IT: Publications Universitaires, 1961.

Farley, Edward. *Faith and Beauty: A Theological Aesthetic.* Burlington, VT: Ashgate, 2001.

Farmer, Craig S., Timothy George, and Scott M. Manetsch, eds. *John 1-12.* Reformation Commentary on Scripture: New Testament IV. Downers Grove, IL: IVP Academic, 2014.

Feenstra, R. J., and Cornelius Plantinga. *Trinity, Incarnation and Atonement: Philosophical and Theological Essays.* Notre Dame, IN: University of Notre Dame Press, 1984.

Feinberg, John S. *No One Like Him: The Doctrine of God.* Wheaton, IL: Crossway, 2001.

Ferguson, Sinclair B. *The Holy Spirit.* Contours of Christian Theology. Downers Grove, IL: InterVarsity Press, 1996.

Feser, Edward. *Five Proofs of the Existence of God.* San Francisco, CA: Ignatius Press, 2017.

———. *The Last Superstition: A Refutation of the New Atheism.* South Bend, IN: St. Augustine's Press, 2008.

Fesko, J. V. *Death in Adam, Life in Christ: The Doctrine of Imputation.* Ross-Shire: Christian Focus, 2016.

———. *Reforming Apologetics: Retrieving the Classical Reformed Approach to Defending the Faith.* Grand Rapids, MI: Baker Academic, 2019.

———. *The Covenant of Works: The Origins, Development, and Reception of the Doctrine.* New York: Oxford University Press, 2020.

———. *The Trinity and the Covenant of Redemption.* Ross-Shire: Christian Focus, 2016.

Forte, Bruno. *The Portal of Beauty: Towards a Theology of Aesthetics.* Translated by David Glenday and Paul McPartlan. Grand Rapids, MI: Eerdmans, 2008.

Frame, John M. *A History of Western Philosophy and Theology*. Phillipsburg, NJ: P&R Publishing, 2015.

―――. 'Scholasticism for Evangelicals: Thoughts on All That Is In God by James Dolezal.' *Frame-Poythress*. November 25, 2017. Accessed August 26, 2020. https://frame-poythress.org/scholasticism-for-evangelicals-thoughts-on-all-that-is-in-god-by-james-dolezal/.

Gaffin, Richard B. *Resurrection and Redemption: A Study in Paul's Soteriology*. 2nd ed. Phillipsburg, NJ: Presbyterian and Reformed, 1987.

García-Rivera, Alex. *The Community of the Beautiful: A Theological Aesthetics*. Collegeville, MN: Liturgical Press, 1999.

Garner, David B. *Sons in the Son: The Riches and Reach of Adoption in Christ*. Phillipsburg, NJ: P&R Publishing, 2016.

Gathercole, Simon J. *Defending Substitution: An Essay on Atonement in Paul*. Grand Rapids, MI: Baker Academic, 2015.

Gentry, Peter John, and Stephen J. Wellum. *God's Kingdom through God's Covenants: A Concise Biblical Theology*. Wheaton, IL: Crossway, 2015.

―――. *Kingdom Through Covenant: A Biblical-Theological Understanding of the Covenant*. 2nd ed. Wheaton, IL: Crossway, 2018.

Gerson, Lloyd P. *Platonism and Naturalism: The Possibility of Philosophy*. Ithica, NY: Cornell University Press, 2020.

Gignilliat, Mark S. *A Brief History of Old Testament Criticism: From Benedict Spinoza to Brevard Childs*. Grand Rapids, MI: Zondervan, 2012.

Green, Garrett. *Imagining Theology: Encounters with God in Scripture, Interpretation, and Aesthetics*. Grand Rapids, MI: Baker Academic, 2020.

Green, Gene L. *Jude and 2 Peter*. Grand Rapids, MI: Baker Academic, 2008.

Gregory. *Homilies on the Song of Songs*. Translated by Richard A Norris. Atlanta, GA: Society of Biblical Literature, 2012.

Gregory. *The Life of Moses*. Translated by Abraham J. Malherbe and Everett Ferguson. Reprinted ed. New York, NY: HarperCollins, 2006.

Grenz, Stanley J, and Roger E Olson. *20th Century Theology: God and the World in a Transitional Age*. Downers Grove, IL: InterVarsity Press, 1997.

Grudem, Wayne A. *Systematic Theology: An Introduction to Biblical Doctrine*. Grand Rapids, MI: Zondervan, 1994.

Gunton, Colin E. *The Promise of Trinitarian Theology*. 2nd ed. New York: T&T Clark, 2003.

Guthrie, George H. *2 Corinthians*. Grand Rapids, MI: Baker Academic, 2015.

Haines, David. *Natural Theology: A Biblical and Historical Introduction and Defense*. Landrum, SC: The Davenant Press.

Hardy, Edward Rochie, ed. *Christology of the Later Fathers*. Louisville, KY: Westminster John Knox, 2006.

Harris, Murray J. *John*. Exegetical Guide to the Greek New Testament. Nashville, TN: B&H Academic, 2015.

———. *The Second Epistle to the Corinthians: A Commentary on the Greek Text*. Grand Rapids, MI: Eerdmans, 2013.

Harrison, Carol. *Beauty and Revelation in the Thought of Saint Augustine*. New York: Oxford University Press, 1992.

Hart, David Bentley. *The Beauty of the Infinite: The Aesthetics of Christian Truth*. Grand Rapids, MI: Eerdmans, 2005.

———. *The Experience of God: Being, Consciousness, Bliss*. New Haven, CT: Yale University Press, 2013.

Hart, John-Mark. 'Triune Beauty and the Ugly Cross: Towards a Theological Aesthetic.' *Tyndale Bulletin* 66, no. 2 (2015): 293-312.

Harvey, Robert W., and Philip H. Towner. *2 Peter & Jude*. Downers Grove, IL: InterVarsity Press, 2009.

Hasel, Gerhard F. *Old Testament Theology: Basic Issues in the Current Debate*. 4th ed. Grand Rapids, MI: Eerdmans, 1991.

Hector, Kevin. *Theology without Metaphysics: God, Language, and the Spirit of Recognition.* New York: Cambridge University Press, 2011.

Henning, Bruce. 'Jesus as the Rejected Prophet and Exalted Lord: The Rhetorical Effect of Type Shifting in John 12:38-41.' *Journal of the Evangelical Theological Society* 62, no. 2 (2019): 329-40.

Henry, Carl F.H. *God, Revelation, and Authority.* 3 vols. Waco, TX: Word, 1979.

Hick, John. *The Many-Faced Argument: Recent Studies on the Ontological Argument for the Existence of God.* Eugene, OR: Wipf & Stock, 2009.

von Hildebrand, Dietrich. *Beauty in the Light of the Redemption.* Steubenville, OH: Hildebrand Project, 2019.

Hinlicky, Paul R. *Divine Simplicity: Christ the Crisis of Metaphysics.* Grand Rapids, MI: Baker Academic, 2016.

Hoglund, Jonathan. *Called by Triune Grace: Divine Rhetoric and the Effectual Call.* Downers Grove, IL: IVP Academic, 2016.

Holmes, Christopher R. J. *The Lord Is Good: Seeking the God of the Psalter.* Downers Grove, IL: InterVarsity Press, 2018.

Horton, Michael Scott. *Justification.* 2 vols Grand Rapids, MI: Zondervan, 2018.

———. *Lord and Servant: A Covenant Christology.* Louisville: Westminster John Knox, 2005.

House, Paul R. *Old Testament Theology.* Downers Grove, IL: IVP Academic, 2018.

Hughes, R. Kent. *Romans: Righteousness from Heaven.* Wheaton, IL: Crossway, 1991.

Hume, David. *Essays: Moral and Political.* London: George Routledge and Sons, 1894.

Irenaeus. *Proof of the Apostolic Preaching.* Translated by Joseph P. Smith. New York: Paulist Press, 1990.

Jeffery, Steve, Michael Ovey, and Andrew Sach. *Pierced for Our Transgressions: Rediscovering the Glory of Penal Substitution.* Wheaton, IL: Crossway, 2007.

Jenkins, Gary W., Kirby, W.J. Torrance and Comerford, Kathleen M. eds., *From Rome to Zurich, between Ignatius and Vermigli: Essays in Honor of John Patrick Donnelly, SJ.* Leiden, NL: Brill Publishers, 2017.

Jenson, Matt. *Theology in the Democracy of the Dead: A Dialogue with the Living Tradition.* Grand Rapids, MI: Baker Academic, 2019.

Jenson, Robert W. *Systematic Theology.* New York: Oxford University Press, 2001.

Jewett, Robert. *Romans: A Commentary.* Minneapolis: Fortress, 2007.

Johnson, Jeffrey D. *The Failure of Natural Theology: A Critical Appraisal of the Philosophical Theology of Thomas Aquinas.* Conway, AR: Free Grace Press, 2021.

Jones, Mark, and Kelly M Kapic, eds. *The Ashgate Research Companion to John Owen's Theology.* Burlington, VT: Ashgate, 2016.

Junius, Franciscus. *A Treatise on True Theology: With the Life of Franciscus Junius.* Translated by David C. Noe. Grand Rapids, MI: Reformation Heritage, 2014.

Kaiser, Walter C. *The Uses of the Old Testament in the New.* Eugene, OR: Wipf & Stock, 2001.

Kaiser, Walter C., and Moisés Silva. *Introduction to Biblical Hermeneutics: The Search for Meaning.* Rev. and expanded ed. Grand Rapids, MI: Zondervan, 2007.

Kapic, Kelly M., and Bruce L. McCormack, eds. *Mapping Modern Theology: A Thematic and Historical Introduction.* Grand Rapids, MI: Baker Academic, 2012.

Kincade, James. 'Karl Barth and Philosophy.' *The Journal of Religion* 40, no. 3 (1960): 161-69.

King, Jonathan. *The Beauty of the Lord: Theology as Aesthetics.* Bellingham, WA: Lexham, 2018.

Köstenberger, Andreas J. *John.* Grand Rapids, MI: Baker Academic, 2004.

Köstenberger, Andreas J, L. Scott Kellum, and Charles L Quarles. *The Cradle, the Cross, and the Crown: An Introduction to the New Testament.* Nashville, TN: B&H Academic, 2016.

Köstenberger, Andreas J., and Richard Duane Patterson. *Invitation to Biblical Interpretation: Exploring the Hermeneutical Triad of History, Literature, and Theology*. Grand Rapids, MI: Kregel, 2011.

Kreeft, Peter. *Socrates' Children: The 100 Greatest Philosophers*. Volume II: Medieval Philosophers. South Bend, IN: St. Augustine's Press, 2015.

Kruger, Michael J. *The Question of Canon: Challenging the Status Quo in the New Testament Debate*. Downers Grove, IL: InterVarsity Press, 2013.

La Cugna, Catherine Mowry. *God for Us: The Trinity and Christian Life*. Reprinted. New York: Harper Collins, 2006.

Lee, Dorothy. *Transfiguration*. London: Continuum, 2004.

Lee, Sang Hyun, ed. *The Princeton Companion to Jonathan Edwards*. Princeton, NJ: Princeton University Press, 2020.

Legaspi, Michael C. *The Death of Scripture and the Rise of Biblical Studies*. New York: Oxford University Press, 2010.

Leithart, Peter J. *Traces of the Trinity: Signs of God in Creation and Human Experience*. Grand Rapids, MI: Brazos, 2015.

Letham, Robert. *Systematic Theology*. Wheaton, IL: Crossway, 2019.

————. *The Holy Trinity: In Scripture, History, Theology, and Worship*. Revised and Expanded. Phillipsburg, NJ: P&R Publishing, 2019.

————. *Union with Christ: In Scripture, History, and Theology*. Phillipsburg, NJ: P&R Publishing, 2011.

Levering, Matthew. *Engaging the Doctrine of Creation: Cosmos, Creatures, and the Wise and Good Creator*. Grand Rapids, MI: Baker Academic, 2017.

————. *The Achievement of Hans Urs von Balthasar: An Introduction to His Trilogy*. Washington, D.C.: Catholic University of America Press, 2019.

Lewis, C. S. *Surprised by Joy: The Shape of My Early Life*. Orlando: Harvest, 1958.

Lewis, C. S. *The Abolition of Man*. San Francisco: HarperCollins, 2001.

————. *The Last Battle*. Revised. New York: HarperCollins, 1994.

————. *The Voyage of the Dawn Treader*. Revised ed. New York: HarperCollins, 1994.

Lints, Richard. *Identity and Idolatry: The Image of God and Its Inversion*. Downers Grove, IL: InterVarsity Press, 2015.

Longenecker, Richard N. *Biblical Exegesis in the Apostolic Period*. 2nd ed. Grand Rapids, MI: Eerdmans, 1999.

Louie, Kin Yip. *Beauty of the Triune God: The Theological Aesthetics of Jonathan Edwards*. Eugene, OR: Pickwick, 2013.

Mattes, Mark C. *Martin Luther's Theology of Beauty: A Reappraisal*. Grand Rapids, MI: Baker Academic, 2017.

Matthews, Kenneth A. *Genesis 1–11:26*. The New American Commentary 1A. Nashville, TN: Broadman & Holman, 1996.

McCall, Thomas H. *Against God and Nature: The Doctrine of Sin*. Wheaton, IL: Crossway, 2019.

McClymond, Michael James, and Gerald R. McDermott. *The Theology of Jonathan Edwards*. New York, NY: Oxford University Press, 2012.

McGinnis, Andrew M. *The Son of God Beyond the Flesh: A Historical and Theological Study of the Extra Calvinisticum*. New York: T&T Clark, 2014.

Miller, Ike. *Seeing by the Light: Illumination in Augustine's and Barth's Readings of John*. Downers Grove, IL: IVP Academic, 2020.

Moltmann, Jürgen. *History and the Triune God: Contributions to Trinitarian Theology*. Translated by John Bowden. New York: Crossroad, 1992.

————. *The Crucified God*. Minneapolis: Fortress, 2015.

————. *The Trinity and the Kingdom: The Doctrine of God*. Minneapolis: Fortress, 1993.

Moreland, J. P., and William Lane Craig. *Philosophical Foundations for a Christian Worldview*. Downers Grove, IL: IVP Academic.

Morello, Sabastian. *The World as God's Icon: Creator and Creation in the Platonic Thought of Thomas Aquinas*. Brooklyn, NY: Anglico Press, 2020.

Motyer, J. Alec. *The Prophecy of Isaiah: An Introduction and Commentary*. Downers Grove, IL: IVP Academic, 1993.

Muller, Richard A. 'Christ in the Eschaton: Calvin and Moltmann on the Duration of the Munus Regium.' *Harvard Theological Review* 74, no. 1 (1981): 31-59.

Murray, John. *Redemption Accomplished and Applied*. Grand Rapids, MI: Eerdmans, 2015.

Nash, Ronald H. *The Concept of God*. Grand Rapids, MI: Zondervan, 1983.

Niehaus, Jeffrey Jay. *Ancient Near Eastern Themes in Biblical Theology*. Grand Rapids, MI: Kregel, 2008.

O'Collins, Gerald. *The Beauty of Jesus Christ: Filling Out a Scheme of St. Augustine*. New York: Oxford University Press, 2020.

Ollenburger, Ben C., ed. *Old Testament Theology: Flowering and Future*. Winona Lake, IN: Eisenbrauns, 2004.

Olson, Roger E., and Christopher A. Hall. *The Trinity*. Grand Rapids, MI: Eerdmans, 2002.

Oppy, Graham, ed. *Ontological Arguments*. New York: Cambridge University Press, 2018.

Orr, Peter. *The Risen and Ascended Christ*. New Studies in Biblical Theology 47. Downers Grove, IL: InterVarsity Press, 2018.

Ortlund, Gavin. *Anslem's Pursuit of Joy: A Commentary on the Proslogion*. Washington, D.C.: The Catholic University of America Press, 2020.

———. *Theological Retrieval for Evangelicals: Why We Need Our Past to Have a Future*. Wheaton, IL: Crossway, 2019.

———. *Why God Makes Sense in a World That Doesn't: The Beauty of Christian Theism*. Grand Rapids, MI: Baker Academic, 2021.

Owen, John. *Biblical Theology*. Morgan, PA: Soli Deo Gloria Publications, 2012.

————. *The Works of John Owen*. Edited by William H. Goold. 16 vols. Edinburgh: Banner of Truth, 2000.

Pannenberg, Wolfhart. *Systematic Theology*. Translated by G. W. Bromiley. 3 vols. Grand Rapids, MI: Eerdmans, 1991.

Pauw, Amy Plantinga. *'The Supreme Harmony of All': The Trinitarian Theology of Jonathan Edwards*. Grand Rapids, MI: Eerdmans, 2002.

Perrin, Nicholas, and Richard B. Hays, eds. *Jesus, Paul, and the People of God: A Theological Dialogue with N. T. Wright*. Downers Grove, IL: IVP Academic, 2011.

Placher, William. *A History of Christian Theology: An Introduction*. Philadelphia: Westminster, 1983.

Poythress, Vern S. *Logic: A God-Centered Approach to the Foundation of Western Thought*. Wheaton, IL: Crossway, 2013.

Radde-Gallwitz, Andrew. *Basil of Caesarea, Gregory of Nyssa, and the Transformation of Divine Simplicity*. New York: Oxford University Press, 2009.

Rahner, Karl. *The Trinity*. 3rd ed. Tunbridge Wells, Kent: Burns & Oates, 1986.

Ramos, Alice M., ed. *Beauty and the Good: Recovering the Classical Tradition from Plato to Duns Scotus*. Washington, D.C.: The Catholic University Press, 2020.

Ramsey, Michael. *The Glory of God and the Transfiguration of Christ*. Oregon: Wipf & Stock, 2009.

Reeves, Michael. *Delighting in the Trinity: An Introduction to the Christian Faith*. Downers Grove, IL: IVP Academic, 2012.

Ridderbos, Herman N. *The Gospel According to John: A Theological Commentary*. Translated by John Vriend. Grand Rapids, MI.: Eerdmans, 1997.

Rookmaaker, H. R. *Modern Art and the Death of a Culture*. Reprinted. Wheaton, IL: Crossway, 1994.

Rosner, Brian S. *Paul and the Law: Keeping the Commandments of God*. Downers Grove, IL: InterVarsity Press, 2013.

Routledge, Robin. *Old Testament Theology: A Thematic Approach.* Downers Grove, IL: IVP Academic, 2012.

Sailhamer, John H. *Introduction to Old Testament Theology: A Canonical Approach.* Grand Rapids, MI: Zondervan, 1995.

Sammon, Brendan Thomas. *The God Who Is Beauty: Beauty As a Divine Name in Thomas Aquinas and Dionysius the Areopagite.* Eugene, OR: Pickwick, 2013.

Sammon, Brendan Thomas. *Called to Attraction: An Introduction to the Theology of Beauty.* Eugene, OR: Cascade, 2017.

Sanders, Fred. *The Triune God.* New Studies in Dogmatics. Grand Rapids, MI: Zondervan, 2016.

Sanders, Fred, and Scott R. Swain, eds. *Retrieving Eternal Generation.* Grand Rapids, MI: Zondervan, 2017.

Savage, Timothy B. *Power through Weakness: Paul's Understanding of the Christian Ministry in 2 Corinthians.* New York: Cambridge University Press, 1996.

Schreiner, Patrick. *The Ascension of Christ: Recovering a Neglected Doctrine.* Bellingham, WA: Lexham, 2020.

Schreiner, Thomas R. *1 & 2 Peter and Jude.* Christian Standard Commentary. Nashville, TN: Holman, 2020.

Schreiner, Thomas R. *New Testament Theology: Magnifying God in Christ.* Grand Rapids, MI: Baker Academic, 2008.

Schumacher, Lydia. *Divine Illumination: The History and Future of Augustine's Theory of Knowledge.* Challenges in Contemporary Theology. Malden, MA: Wiley-Blackwell, 2011.

Scruton, Roger. *Beauty.* New York: Oxford University Press, 2009.

Seifrid, Mark A. *Christ, Our Righteousness: Paul's Theology of Justification.* Downers Grove, IL: InterVarsity Press, 2000.

———. *The Second Letter to the Corinthians.* Grand Rapids, MI: Eerdmans, 2014.

Sherry, Patrick. *Spirit and Beauty.* 2nd ed. London: SCM Press, 2002.

Silva, Thiago Machado. 'Scripture as Revelation in Herman Bavinck's Theology.' *Puritan Reformed Journal* 10, no. 1 (2018): 154-71.

Smalley, Stephen S. *1, 2, and 3 John: Word Biblical Commentary*, Revised, Edition. Grand Rapids, MI: Zondervan Academic, 2020.

Steward, Gary. 'Jonathan Edwards's Reception and Alteration of Sola Fide.' Paper presented at the Annual Meeting of Evangelical Theological Society, Denver, CO, 2017.

Stonehouse, Ned Bernard, and Paul Woolley, eds. *The Infallible Word: A Symposium by the Members of the Faculty of Westminster Theological Seminary*. 2nd ed. Phillipsburg, NJ: Presbyterian and Reformed, 1967.

Stout, Harry S., ed. *The Jonathan Edwards Encyclopedia*. Grand Rapids, MI: Eerdmans, 2017.

Strange, Daniel. *Their Rock Is Not Like Our Rock: A Theology of Religions*. Grand Rapids, MI: Zondervan, 2014.

Strobel, Kyle C. *Jonathan Edwards's Theology: A Reinterpretation*. Edinburgh: T&T Clark, 2014.

Studebaker, Steven M., and Robert W. Caldwell III. *The Trinitarian Theology of Jonathan Edwards: Text, Context, and Application*. Burlington, VT: Ashgate, 2012.

Swain, Scott R. *Trinity, Revelation, and Reading: A Theological Introduction to the Bible and Its Interpretation*. London : T&T Clark, 2011.

Taylor, Charles. *A Secular Age*. Reprint. Cambridge, MA: Harvard University Press, 2018.

Taylor, W. David O. *The Theater of God's Glory: Calvin, Creation, and the Liturgical Arts*. Grand Rapids, MI: Eerdmans, 2017.

Thiessen, Gesa Elsbeth, ed. *Theological Aesthetics: A Reader*. Grand Rapids, MI: Eerdmans, 2005.

Thiselton, Anthony C. *Systematic Theology*. Grand Rapids, MI: Eerdmans. 2015.

Torrance, T. F. *Incarnation: The Person and Life of Christ*. Edited by Robert T. Walker. Downers Grove, IL: IVP Academic, 2015.

_____. *The Christian Doctrine of God: One Being Three Persons*. New York: T&T Clark, 2001.

Turretin, Francis. *Institutes of Elenctic Theology, 3 vols*. Edited by James T. Dennison. Translated by George Musgrave Giger. Philippsburg, NJ: P&R Publishing, 1997.

Tyson, Paul. *Returning to Reality: Christian Platonism for Our Times*. Eugene, OR: Cascade Books, 2014.

Van Til, Cornelius. *A Christian Theory of Knowledge*. Phillipsburg, NJ: Presbyterian and Reformed Publishing Co., 1969.

_____. *An Introduction to Systematic Theology: Prolegomena and the Doctrines of Revelation, Scripture, and God*. Edited by William Edgar. 2nd ed. Phillipsburg, NJ: P&R Publishing, 2007.

_____. *Common Grace and the Gospel*. Edited by K. Scott Oliphint. 2nd ed. Phillipsburg, NJ: P&R Publishing, 2015.

_____. *The Defense of the Faith*. 3rd ed. Phillipsburg, NJ: Presbyterian and Reformed, 1967.

Vanhoozer, Kevin J. *Biblical Authority after Babel: Retrieving the Solas in the Spirit of Mere Protestant Christianity*. Grand Rapids, MI: Brazos, 2016.

_____. *Is There a Meaning in This Text? The Bible, the Reader, and the Morality of Literary Knowledge*. Landmarks in Christian Scholarship. Grand Rapids, MI: Zondervan, 2009.

Vanhoozer, Kevin J., Craig G. Bartholomew, Daniel J. Treier, and N. T. Wright, eds. *Dictionary for Theological Interpretation of the Bible*. Grand Rapids, MI: Baker Academic, 2005.

Venema, Cornelis P. *The Gospel of Free Acceptance in Christ: An Assessment of the Reformation and New Perspectives on Paul*. Edinburgh: Banner of Truth, 2006.

Viladesau, Richard. *Theological Aesthetics: God in Imagination, Beauty, and Art*. New York: Oxford University Press, 2013.

Von Hildebrand, Dietrich. *Aesthetics: Volume I*. Edited by John F Crosby. Translated by Brian McNeil. Steubenville, OH: Hildebrand Project, 2016.

Vos, Geerhardus. *Redemptive History and Biblical Interpretation: The Shorter Writings of Geerhardus Vos*. Edited by Richard B Gaffin Jr. Phillipsburg, NJ: Presbyterian and Reformed, 1980.

Vos, Geerhardus J. *Reformed Dogmatics (Single Volume Edition): A System of Christian Theology*. Edited by Richard B. Gaffin. Bellingham, WA: Lexham, 2020.

Ware, Bruce A. 'An Evangelical Reformulation of the Doctrine of the Immutability of God.' *Journal of the Evangelical Theological Society* 29, no. 4 (1986): 431-46.

————. *Father, Son, and Holy Spirit: Relationships, Roles, and Relevance.* Wheaton, IL: Crossway, 2005.

————, ed. *Perspectives on the Doctrine of God: Four Views*. Nashville, TN: B&H Academic, 2008.

————. *The Man Christ Jesus: Theological Reflections on the Humanity of Christ*. Wheaton, IL: Crossway, 2013.

Ware, Bruce A., and John Starke. *One God in Three Persons: Unity of Essence, Distinction of Persons, Implications for Life*. Wheaton, IL: Crossway, 2015.

Waters, Guy Prentiss. *Justification and the New Perspectives on Paul: A Review and Response*. Phillipsburg, NJ: P&R Publishing, 2004.

Webster, John. *God without Measure: Working Papers in Christian Theology*. Vol. I: *God and the Works of God*. New York: T&T Clark, 2018.

————. *The Domain of the Word: Scripture and Theological Reason*. New York: T&T Clark, 2014.

Weinandy, Thomas G. *Does God Change? The Word's Becoming in the Incarnation*. Still River, MA: St. Bede's Publications, 1985.

Wellum, Stephen J. *God the Son Incarnate: The Doctrine of Christ*. Foundations of Evangelical Theology. Wheaton, IL: Crossway, 2016.

Westminster Assembly, Douglas F. Kelly, Philip B. Rollinson, and Frederick T. Marsh. *The Westminster Shorter Catechism in Modern English*. Phillipsburg, NJ: Presbyterian and Reformed, 1986.

Willis, E. David. *Calvin's Catholic Christology: The Function of the So-Called Extra Calvinisticum in Calvin's Theology.* Leiden: Brill, 1966.

Wolterstorff, Nicholas. *Art in Action: Toward a Christian Aesthetic.* Grand Rapids, MI: Eerdmans, 1980.

Wright, N. T. *Justification: God's Plan & Paul's Vision.* Downers Grove, IL: IVP Academic, 2016.

—————. *The New Testament and the People of God.* Minneapolis: Fortress, 1992.

Yarbrough, Robert, W. *1-3 John: Baker Exegetical Commentary on the New Testament.* Grand Rapids, MI: Baker Academic, 2008.

Zahnd, Brian. *Beauty Will Save the World: Rediscovering the Allure and Mystery of Christianity.* Lake Mary, MO: Charisma House, 2012.

—————. *Sinners in the Hands of a Loving God: The Scandalous Truth of the Very Good News.* Colorado Springs, CO: WaterBrook, 2017.

Zizioulas, John D. *Being as Communion: Studies in Personhood and the Church.* Crestwood, NY: St. Vladimir's Seminary Press, 1985.

Subject Index

Scripture Index

ISBN: 978-1-5271-0913-1

No Shadow of Turning
Divine Immutability and the Economy of Redemption

Ronni Kurtz

While divine immutability enjoyed a broad affirmation through much of theological antiquity, it has fallen on harder times in modernity. Seen as a holdover from overly philosophical theology, divine immutability has often been characterized as rendering God static and incapable of having meaningful relationships with his creation. This book aims to counter this claim in hopes of demonstrating that divine immutability does not handicap soteriology but is a necessary and vital component of God's economy of redemption.

If you're looking for a primer not just on immutability but also on the Christian doctrine of God, biblical hermeneutics, the Great Tradition, and the systematic nature of theology, this is it.

Matthew Emerson
Dean of Theology, Arts and Humanities, Floyd K Clark Chair of Christian Leadership, Professor of Religion, Oklahoma Baptist University, Shawnee, Oklahoma

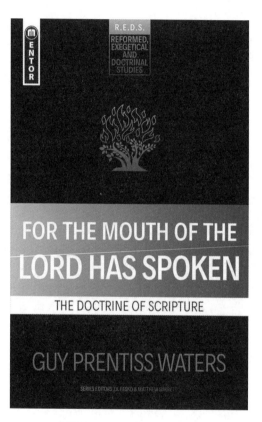

R.E.D.S.
REFORMED,
EXEGETICAL
AND
DOCTRINAL
STUDIES

FOR THE MOUTH OF THE LORD HAS SPOKEN

THE DOCTRINE OF SCRIPTURE

GUY PRENTISS WATERS

SERIES EDITORS J.V. FESKO & MATTHEW BARRETT

ISBN: 978-1-5271-0607-9

For the Mouth of the Lord Has Spoken

The Doctrine of Scripture

Guy Prentiss Waters

There is no book better than the Bible. It is God's own word. He breathed it into existence. He does wonderful things in and by it. But there is hardly a book more assailed, mocked, and assaulted than the Bible. New Testament Professor Guy Prentiss Waters delves into the doctrine of Scripture. Addressing the revelation, inspiration, inerrancy, sufficiency and perspicuity of the Bible, he also engages with what some other prominent theologians had to say on the subject.

What can be more important than understanding the Book that God gave us? Dr. Guy Waters thoroughly, carefully, and winsomely sets before us the riches of the doctrine of Scripture. He alerts us to faulty thinking of the past and the present and also commends to us a faithful and orthodox view of the Bible, the very words of God, which are life itself.

Stephen J. Nichols
President, Reformation Bible College, CAO Ligonier Ministries,
Sanford, Florida

Christian Focus Publications

Our mission statement —

STAYING FAITHFUL
In dependence upon God we seek to impact the world
through literature faithful to His infallible Word, the Bible.
Our aim is to ensure that the Lord Jesus Christ is presented as
the only hope to obtain forgiveness of sin, live a useful life and
look forward to heaven with Him.

Our books are published in four imprints:

CHRISTIAN
FOCUS

Popular works including
biographies, commentaries, basic
doctrine and Christian living.

CHRISTIAN
HERITAGE

Books representing some of the
best material from the rich heritage
of the church.

MENTOR

Books written at a level suitable
for Bible College and seminary
students, pastors, and other serious
readers. The imprint includes
commentaries, doctrinal studies,
examination of current issues and
church history.

CF4•K

Children's books for quality Bible
teaching and for all age groups: Sunday
school curriculum, puzzle and activity
books; personal and family devotional
titles, biographies and inspirational
stories — because you are never too
young to know Jesus!

Christian Focus Publications Ltd,
Geanies House, Fearn, Ross-shire,
IV20 1TW, Scotland, United Kingdom.
www.christianfocus.com